The Prophet and Power

Critical Currents in Latin American Perspective
Ronald H. Chilcote, Series Editor

*Democracy: Government of the People or
Government of the Politicians?*
José Nun

Cardoso's Brazil: A Land for Sale
James Petras and Henry Veltmeyer

*People's Power: Cuba's Experience with Representative Government,
Updated Edition*
Peter Roman

The Prophet and Power

Jean-Bertrand Aristide, the International Community, and Haiti

Alex Dupuy

ROWMAN & LITTLEFIELD PUBLISHERS, INC.
Lanham • Boulder • New York • Toronto • Plymouth, UK

ROWMAN & LITTLEFIELD PUBLISHERS, INC.

Published in the United States of America
by Rowman & Littlefield Publishers, Inc.
A wholly owned subsidiary of The Rowman & Littlefield Publishing Group, Inc.
4501 Forbes Boulevard, Suite 200, Lanham, Maryland 20706
www.rowmanlittlefield.com

Estover Road, Plymouth PL6 7PY, United Kingdom

British Library Cataloguing in Publication Information Available

Library of Congress Cataloging-in-Publication Data

Dupuy, Alex.
  The prophet and power : Jean-Bertrand Aristide, the international community, and Haiti,
/ Alex Dupuy.
      p. cm. — (Critical currents in Latin American perspective)
  Includes bibliographical references and index.
  ISBN-13: 978-0-7425-3830-6 (cloth : alk. paper)
  ISBN-10: 0-7425-3830-3 (cloth : alk. paper)
  ISBN-13: 978-0-7425-3831-3 (pbk. : alk. paper)
  ISBN-10: 0-7425-3831-1 (pbk. : alk. paper)
  1. Haiti—Politics and government—1986– 2. Aristide, Jean-Bertrand.
  3. Democratization—Haiti—History. 4. Social change—Haiti—History. I. Title.
  F1928.2.D87 2007
  972.9407'3—dc22

                              2006023838

Printed in the United States of America

∞™ The paper used in this publication meets the minimum requirements of American
National Standard for Information Sciences—Permanence of Paper for Printed Library
Materials, ANSI/NISO Z39.48-1992.

To Franck

Contents

Foreword

Alex Dupuy has already written two thorough, well-researched, and highly appreciated books on the political economy and social history of Haiti from 1700 to 1995: *Haiti in the World Economy: Class, Race, and Underdevelopment in Haiti since 1700* (1989) and *Haiti in the New World Order: The Limits of the Democratic Revolution* (1997). Some of his most recent articles have also dealt partially with the Aristide phenomenon. Today he is offering the most comprehensive scholarly and objective study on the leadership of Aristide at the national and international level.

Alex is an organic scholar. He was born and studied in Haiti and in the United States and was raised in a family that has two ancestors—General Bazelais, chief of staff of Dessalines, and Officer Dupuy, secretary of Dessalines—among the signatories of the 1804 Act of Independence of Haiti. As such, he is motivated by a quest and a mission: the quest, to know and understand for himself the intricacies and troublesome political instability and endemic underdevelopment of the country after two hundred years of independence; and the mission, to extend that knowledge and understanding to others for a necessary change. He feels that an important historical event occurred in the 1980s when a peaceful popular movement, aided by the instrumental role played by a small unknown priest with a doctrine of liberation theology, overthrew the lengthy and calamitous dictatorship of the Duvaliers, as well as the "Duvalierism without the Duvaliers" supported by the local bourgeoisie and industrialized nations, notably the United States. Why has Aristide, who was elected president in 1990 and 1999, been dominating Haitian politics, even now, despite being in exile since 2004?

This is the challenge that this book takes up and answers successfully. *The Prophet and Power: Jean-Bertrand Aristide, the International Community, and Haiti* is not a biography of Aristide. Its main goal is to show, first, that Aristide's leadership was not spontaneous but came out of a popular movement that took years to gain the strength to overthrow the Duvalierist plague and, second, that this leadership was bound to confront the imperialist globalization of the core countries, that is, the demand of the popular movement for a maximalist democracy versus the core countries' insistence on a minimalist democracy. Maximalist or redistributive democracy is a democratic order based on economic and political rights, without which "the exercise of other rights would be limited for most citizens," whereas minimalist democracy is "a democratic order based on a minimally regulated market system and limited to civil and political rights." My purpose here is merely to highlight some fascinating aspects that seem so specific to a country where surrealism is a fact of life in such a way that the impossible is rampant and the possible scarce. These aspects that, among others, attracted the undivided attention of the author are Aristide's adoption of liberation theology, his hybrid political behavior, and the "Aristide backlash" or the backlash of political rights that he was instrumental in institutionalizing.

The importance of Aristide's liberation theology in overthrowing the Duvalierist regime is very well known. How did Aristide use it to take over the leadership of the popular movement? Mainly through the politicization of religious faith: the Christian faith, with its teaching of miracles, divine intervention, and the infallibility of the word of the messiah or prophet, and the Vodou faith, with its "power of the point," which, when given by a *hougan* (Vodou priest), allows the receiver to disappear and be invulnerable to bullets. The fusion of some elements of the two cults is not unusual in Haiti. The masses who state that Aristide was a prophet or a messiah, as he claimed, firmly believed he was protected by a divine force, a *loa*, against all perils. In demonstration after demonstration, the crowd never failed to shout, "Don't you touch the prophet, or you will be burned!" Burning here could be a reference to the literal—a tire set on fire around the neck of an enemy (such as père Lebrun)—or to the metaphysical hellfire.

Dupuy emphasizes the hybrid behavior or language of Aristide. It is not that different from the "myth-splitting" of Claude Levi-Strauss (twins are considered good deities and venerated in some countries, bad deities and killed in other places). This hybridity is highly cultivated by Aristide in his concept that he and the people are *marassa* (twins), and that he and René Préval in particular are marassa. In Haitian Vodou, marassa are twins endowed with supernatural power and thus are exceptional, almost infallible, human beings and great potential leaders. They must avoid being jealous of each other and acting against each other, but it is evident that the shrewder one will be able to manipulate the other or even exploit the latter's weaknesses or fears. Aristide was evidently the shrewder. According to Raoul Peck in *Monsieur le Ministre . . . Jusqu'au bout de la patience*, Préval, whose bodyguards were unconditional supporters of Aristide, was a fearful president who once said, "At the rate things are going, one day, I would not be surprised to see myself lying in a pool of my own blood." Besides, while the Haitian people as a marassa remained poor, Aristide grew rich.

No less significant is the splitting of Aristide into two different presidents. From 1990 to September 1991, he devoted his concept of liberation theology and marassa to strengthen and unite the various base ecclesiastic communities, and he helped them become a powerful popular movement clamoring for its political, economic, and social rights that had been ignored or denied for centuries. His commitment before and during the first period of his rule (February–September 1991) earned him the respect and admiration of millions of poor people who saw him as a role model. Unfortunately, the second period (1994–2004) revealed a second Aristide, who used the same tools of the first period to centralize the power of the popular movement under his absolute power. It was a costly mistake that he paid for dearly. Important supporters who left him or were dropped joined the ranks of the opposition, and his leadership started to unravel.

The term *Aristide backlash* means that he fought at the risk of his life for the political, economic, and social rights of the poor against several dictators and then, when he became one, those same rights came back to haunt him. Being in the unbearable situation where he would have to obliterate the result of so many years of sacrifice and death, his attempts to crush freedom of expression, freedom of the press, freedom of assembly, and freedom of dissent were weak and inefficient. In chapter 5, dealing with the "low-intensity war" against Aristide, Dupuy analyzes with precision and in great detail the demise of Aristide's second presidency at the hands of the bourgeoisie and a sector of the middle class prompted by the United States, France, and Canada. In short, Aristide was forced out of power and sent into exile for the second time.

In the chaos that still exists, the only bright spot is the survival of some of the rights the popular movement fought for. While the Washington Consensus, which, according to Dupuy, "basically seeks to weaken the interventionist powers of the state and open the Third World economies to the markets and capital of the advanced or core capitalist countries," is hanging in the wind, the masses are continuing their struggle for real freedom and equitable economic conditions. It is a struggle that deserves the world's encouragement and unconditional fraternal support.

Franck Laraque
Professor Emeritus
City College of New York

Preface

In 1997, I published *Haiti in the New World Order: The Limits of the Democratic Revolution*. That book analyzed the struggles that led to the overthrow of the thirty-year hereditary Duvalier dictatorship in 1986, blocked the attempts by the Haitian Army to reestablish a permanent dictatorship, and led to the victory of liberation theologian Father Jean-Bertrand Aristide in the presidential election of 1990. The argument of the book was cast in light of the debate on the post–Cold War "New World Order," what it meant for the foreign policy of the United States in particular, and the limits it placed on left-of-center governments in the Third World or peripheral capitalist countries to pursue progressive, state-interventionist, and redistributive policies that challenged the free-trade, free-market doctrines of the core capitalist countries. It was in that context that I analyzed Aristide's program of government and first seven months in office before he was overthrown by the military in a coup d'état in September 1991; the three years he spent in exile in the United States; and his eventual return to Haiti by a United States–led UN multinational force in October 1994 to complete the remaining eighteen months in his five-year term.

In analyzing Aristide's interrupted first term in office, I revealed two contradictory tendencies in his political practice. On the one hand, his embrace of liberation theology, and especially its "option for the poor" doctrine, led him to articulate, like no one else could have, the aspirations of the majority of Haitians for a more just, more equal, and more empowering democratic society. On the other hand, those same theological views of politics led him to see himself as a prophetic, charismatic leader who had a direct, symbiotic relationship with the "prophetic" people and who could interpret their needs, interests, and aspirations without mediating organizations such as political parties with clearly defined rules of governance and accountability between leaders and their constituents. I interpreted this second tendency as fundamentally antidemocratic and authoritarian, and much of *Haiti in the New World Order* was meant to show how the unfolding of these two contradictory tendencies in Aristide's political practice during the first seven months of his presidency confused his supporters and played into the hands of his enemies to justify their coup d'état of September 1991.

By the time Aristide returned from exile in 1994 to complete the remaining year and a half of his first term, I also came to the conclusion that he had definitively broken with his commitment to the radical and egalitarian policies he had previously advocated and which had earned him the unconditional adoration of the poor majority.

The Prophet and Power: Jean-Bertrand Aristide, the International Community, and Haiti is in many ways a continuation of *Haiti in the New World Order*. However, besides covering Aristide's entire political career as president, it differs from *Haiti in the New World Order* in other ways. First, it recasts the argument about Haiti's position in the international division of labor of the capitalist world system and the struggles for democracy that unfolded since the 1980s in light of the debates on globalization and the "new imperialism." Second, it reconsiders Aristide's politics and political practice in both his first and second terms by focusing on the relations, dynamics, and conflicts of power between him and the principal domestic and international actors. And, third, it analyzes the post-Aristide era, the main objectives of the interim government of Prime Minister Gérard Latortue from 2004 to 2006, and the significance of René Préval's victory in the elections of February 2006 for the transition to democracy in Haiti.

In *The Prophet and Power*, I try to explain two paradoxes. First, a popular democratic movement swept Aristide to power in February 1991 as the purported champion of the impoverished majority and their demand for a more just, more equal, and more participatory democratic society, or what I call a *maximalist democracy*. Aristide's overthrow by the military seven months into his first term solidified his image as defender of the interests of the majority against the tiny but wealthy Haitian ruling class and its foreign backers fearful of any change in the status quo. The passive and active resistance of a majority of the population against the military junta that toppled Aristide compelled the United States to lead a UN multinational intervention force to remove the junta and restore Aristide to power in October 1994. Aristide left office in February 1996 still commanding great popular support, even though, as I mentioned above, it had become clear to me that he had by then abandoned his commitment to the radical and egalitarian policies he once advocated.

Reelected for a second and final term as president in December 2000 and assuming office in February 2001, Aristide's objective this time was to consolidate his and his party's power and preserve the prebendary and clientelistic characteristics of the state he had vowed to dismantle in 1991. To maintain power, Aristide relied on armed gangs, the police, and authoritarian practices to suppress his opponents, all the while cultivating a self-serving image as defender of the poor. That strategy did not work, though, as his government became increasingly discredited and his popularity waned. While *Haiti in the New World Order* depicted the dual tendencies of Aristide's political practice during his first term, one of the main contributions of *The Prophet and Power* is to show, through the use of the concept of hybridity and an analysis of the relations and dynamics of power between fractions of the dominant classes, how the authoritarian tendency became predominant in the 2000–04 period, undermined his legitimacy, discredited his government and his Lavalas party, and played a major role in his second overthrow. Consequently, unlike in 1991, the majority of the population did not rally to save Aristide from being forced out in 2004 or clamor for his return afterward. This does not mean, however, that the majority of the population welcomed the illegitimate interim Latortue government. Instead, the majority pressed for new elections to restore legitimacy to government—in which Aristide could not participate. The majority of Haitians, then, had moved beyond Aristide.

The Prophet and Power also seeks to explain another paradox. In the period 1990–94, Aristide enjoyed the support of important sectors of the progressive, left-of-center, middle-class intelligentsia, most of whom became members of the coalition known as the National Front for Democracy and Change (FNCD). The FNCD had been the spearhead of the opposition to the neo-Duvalierist forces who tried unsuccessfully to reimpose a military dictatorship during the five years that followed the overthrow of Jean-Claude Duvalier in 1986. Lacking a political party of his own, Aristide ran for the presidency in 1990 under the banner of the FNCD. A rift developed between the FNCD and Aristide after he became president, but when the military overthrew him in September 1991, the FNCD opposed the military junta and fought for Aristide's return in 1994.

By 1996, however, the rupture between the FNCD and Aristide became permanent. But it was not only former allies within the FNCD who broke with Aristide and his Lavalas movement. The core cadres of the Lavalas movement who had formed the Lavalas Political Organization (OPL in French) within the Lavalas Political Platform coalition and who dominated parliament in 1995 also parted ways with Aristide and renamed their party the Organization of the People in Struggle (still OPL in French). Aristide then formed his own Lavalas Family (FL) party and henceforth became OPL's bitter rival. But the FNCD and the OPL did not just become Aristide's and FL's opponents who sought to challenge him democratically. Rather, in 2000 they would join with neo-Duvalierists, who were their bitter enemies in 1986–94, and other centrist and right-of-center parties to form the Democratic Convergence coalition fostered by the International Republican Institute and supported by the most zealous and right-wing elements of the Republican Party and the George W. Bush administration to oppose and undermine Aristide's second presidency. Later still, they would rally behind the former members of the Haitian Army and its paramilitary death squads to force Aristide out of power in 2004, and they would embrace the unconstitutional and illegitimate interim government of Prime Minister Latortue, whose primary objective was to crush what remained of the Lavalas party and Aristide's armed supporters.

Forming alliances with one's former enemies is the sine qua non of politics. But rather than taking that as a given, I thought it necessary and useful to offer a sociological explanation for their behavior rooted in the social relations and structures of Haiti in the context of the global politics of the core powers, the United States in particular, and the exigencies of the "Washington Consensus."

In short, then, I wrote *The Prophet and Power* to offer a comprehensive and systematic analysis of what could be called the Aristidean interlude in the struggle for democracy in Haiti, and the possibilities open to the majority to extend that project by and for themselves rather than surrendering their collective agency to false prophets.

The Prophet and Power draws from *Haiti in the New World Order* and other publications. The section "The Duvalier Dictatorship and Black Nationalism" and parts of "The Hereditary Dictatorship and the New 'Pact of Domination' with the Bourgeoisie" in chapter 2 are taken from *Haiti in the World Economy: Class, Race, and Underdevelopment since 1700* (Boulder, CO: Westview Press, 1989), 155–85. Chapter 3 is a revised version of chapters 3 and 4 (pp. 47–92), and chapter 4 is a revised version of chapters 5 and 6 (pp. 93–135), of *Haiti in the New World Order* (Boulder, CO: Westview Press/HarperCollins, 1997). Lastly, the section "The February 2006 Election and the Future of Haiti without Aristide" in chapter 7 is a revised version of "Haiti Election 2006: A Pyrrhic Victory for René Préval?" *Latin American Perspectives* 33, no. 3 (May 2006), and is reprinted with permission. Unless otherwise indicated, all translations from the French or Haitian Creole are my own.

I am indebted to many people who contributed in different ways to my writing *The Prophet and Power*. First, I am dedicating this book to Franck

Laraque as a token of my admiration and gratitude for his encouragement and all that I have learned from him over the years about Haiti, Haitian politics, and political principles. I also want to thank him and Gina Ulysse for their valuable comments and suggestions on the chapters of this book. I have also benefited immensely from the panels that Robert Fatton, Carolle Charles, Henry "Chip" Carey, Robert (Bob) Maguire, and I have organized at past annual meetings of the Latin American Studies Association, the Caribbean Studies Association, and the Haitian Studies Association. My ongoing discussions with Robert, Bob, and Leslie Desmangles have also been invaluable to me.

I also wish to thank LeGrace Benson, Wanda Dupuy, and Leslie Desmangles for their assistance with the book cover. LeGrace generously provided and allowed me the use of two photographs she had taken of street wall murals in Haiti. Leslie helped me choose the two photographs from among the twenty LeGrace sent me. From these original photographs, Wanda created a composite image for the book cover.

Last, but not least, I want to thank Susan McEachern and Sarah Wood at Rowman & Littlefield Publishers for their assistance.

Chapter One

Globalization, the "New World Order Imperialism," and Haiti

On February 28, 2004, James Foley, the U.S. ambassador to Haiti, offered President Jean-Bertrand Aristide a stark choice: either leave Haiti or be killed by former members of the defunct Haitian Army who had launched an armed uprising against his government and were threatening to attack Port-au-Prince. Aristide decided on the first option and left the next day aboard a private plane contracted by U.S. government officials. This was the second time Aristide was removed from office before the end of his presidential term. The first time was in September 1991 when the Haitian military toppled him seven months after he assumed office as Haiti's first truly democratically elected president. Returned to office by President Bill Clinton in October 1994 after a three-year exile in the United States, Aristide ceded power to René Préval, his democratically elected successor, in February 1996. Re-elected in December 2000 and inaugurated in February 2001, Aristide's second five-year term ended prematurely exactly three years later.

In 1991, Aristide, then a radical liberation theologian priest, came to office as one of the most popular charismatic leaders Haiti and the Caribbean had ever known. As the purported champion of the impoverished majority, his mandate was to reverse nearly two hundred years of despotic government, repression, exploitation, and injustice by the country's tiny wealthy economic and political ruling classes and to create a more just, egalitarian, and democratic society. Aristide's overthrow early in his first administration, combined with the contradictions of his policies and politics, ensured that that agenda would not be implemented, but the population fiercely resisted the imposition of a permanent dictatorship by the military junta and fought for his reinstatement as the legitimate president of Haiti.

After his three years in exile, Aristide returned, backed by a U.S.-led multinational force authorized by the United Nations to complete the remaining

1

eighteen months of his first term. During his exile and by the time of his re-election in 2000, however, Aristide had undergone a major transformation. He had left the priesthood and no longer advocated liberation theology or railed against capitalism or imperialism. Although he still purported to defend the interests of the poor, his real aim was to monopolize political power and use the latter to promote his interests and those of the middle-class func-tionaries and elected leaders of his Fanmi Lavalas (Lavalas Family) party, down to the clientelistic network of neighborhood gangs he had formed among the poor in the urban ghettos, especially in Port-au-Prince. When he left in February 2004, Aristide had become a discredited, corrupted, and in-creasingly authoritarian president who had betrayed the trust and aspirations of the poor majority. Except for armed gangs and some supporters who re-mained loyal to him, the population as a whole offered no resistance to the rebels from the disbanded Haitian Army that forced him from office and did not clamor for his reinstatement as they had in 1991.

This book is about the rise and unmaking of this enigmatic Caribbean leader. But the book is more than an analysis of Aristide's controversial po-litical career. Though focused on the rise and fall of Aristide from power, the book is first and foremost a study of the crisis of democratization in a poor, underdeveloped peripheral society with a long history of prebendary rule by dictators and a tiny ruling class dependent on economic ties with and politi-cal support from various capitalist classes and governments in the advanced or core capitalist countries. The book, in short, is a study in the exercise of power, understood to be a relational phenomenon that "expresses at one and the same time the intentions and purposes of agencies and institutions and the relative balance of resources they can deploy with respect to each other" (Held 1995, 170).

More specifically, the book is a study of the relations among and the rel-ative power of social classes, governments, and institutions in the context of the hierarchy of the capitalist world system. It is a study of the structures and relations of power between Haiti and the core countries and the institutions and resources they control, the relations and conflicts between dominant and subordinate classes, and the social forces struggling for and against social change in Haiti. It is in this context that the book will analyze the signifi-cance of Aristide's rise to power and why his overthrow will not resolve the crisis of democratization that his election and reelection generated. Thus, inasmuch as this book is a study of the different sites, relations, agencies, and practices of power, it is also an attempt to assess the limits of democra-tization in a small, underdeveloped, poor, dependent, and polarized society like Haiti in the contemporary era of globalization and what is called the "new imperialism."

GLOBALIZATION AND THE
"NEW WORLD ORDER IMPERIALISM"

It is now commonplace in public discourse for people to use the words *globalization* and *New World Order* when talking about the seemingly epochal changes that have taken place since the end of the Cold War and the collapse of the Soviet Union in 1989. The meanings of these two terms obviously differ according to the perspective of the person using them. My purpose here is not to analyze their various interpretations, but to outline what *I* mean by these terms and what I see as their implications for the period under consideration in Haiti, namely, 1990 to 2006, or the rise and fall of Jean-Bertrand Aristide from political power and the struggles to shape Haitian politics in the post-Aristide era. I contend that although *globalization* and *New World Order* refer to two very different phenomena in the contemporary era and should not be used interchangeably, their convergence since 1990 has had serious implications for politics and policy making in peripheral or underdeveloped countries such as Haiti.

On the one hand, the term *globalization* originated in the early 1970s and refers to a process of integration of all parts of the world in the international division of labor of the capitalist world system, a concomitant weakening of the power of peripheral states, and the strengthening of the power of transnational corporations and global institutions controlled by the core states. On the other hand, the "New World Order" refers to the unchallenged dominance of capitalism since the dissolution of the Soviet Union and the collapse of the socialist bloc in 1989, and the unchallenged status of the United States as the only global superpower. These facts are the basis for the emergence of what has been referred to as the "new imperialism."

The terms *New World Order* and *new imperialism* refer to a change in the geopolitical configuration and balance of power in the world and hence to a new era of dominance by a single superpower. If, as Immanuel Wallerstein argues, by *hegemony* we mean not omnipotence but the ability of a great power to "impose its rule and its wishes (at the very least by effective veto power) in the economic, political, military, diplomatic, and even cultural arenas" (1985, 38), then clearly the United States can no longer be considered hegemonic in the post–Cold War era. The United States became hegemonic at the end of World War II and remained so until 1973. Its transnational corporations (TNCs) operated without much challenge during that period. Beginning in 1973, however, Western European and Japanese TNCs began to challenge the hegemony of the U.S. ones, and by the mid-1980s they had gained control over production and distribution networks once dominated by U.S. TNCs; Japanese investments abroad began to rival U.S. investments in extent and in scope (Arrighi 1991, 148–49). Thus, 1973 could be said to have marked the beginning of the processes we associate with the contemporary era of globalization.

Nonetheless, if it is not hegemonic in the strict sense described above, the United States remains the single most powerful and competitive economy in the world, and it enjoys today an absolute military superiority. The United States is the only superpower capable of projecting its military power globally, and this fact allows it to remind its major European, Japanese, and East and South Asian competitors that they must still rely on the United States to ensure stability and the continued flow of vital resources, without which their economies could be imperiled. As David Harvey argues, control over the Middle East and its vast oil deposits is the key to the United States' strategic global dominance. U.S. interest and involvement in the region grew steadily since World War II, and it became the primary power broker after the British withdrew militarily from the region in the late 1960s. But since 1980, and particularly since the Gulf War of 1990 and the current war against Iraq, the projection of its military to create and maintain client states in the region has become the hallmark of U.S. power. The United States, moreover, would like to extend its control not only over Middle East oil supplies but into the Caspian Basin and Latin America (especially Venezuela) as well. As Harvey concludes, controlling the global supply of oil would allow the United States to control the global economy for the next fifty years and, with it, check the challenges to its global dominance posed by Europe, Japan, and the other East and South Asian countries, including China, that compete with the United States in the realms of production, trade and finance (Harvey 2003, 20–25).

The United States, however, is not only seeking to control the world's oil supplies to maintain its global dominance. Well before, but particularly since, the end of the Cold War, the objective of U.S. foreign policy has been to create what the famous National Security Council strategic document of the Cold War known as NSC-68 referred to as "a world environment in which the American system can survive and flourish" (Layne and Schwartz 1993, 5). A consensus emerged among the foreign policy intelligentsia that the world in the post–Cold War era is becoming more dangerous and unstable because it is now more fragmented and torn by regional power politics and national, ethnic, and religious conflicts. Thus, to provide stability and maintain world order, the United States, as the only global superpower, must act to prevent the world from reverting to its pre-1939 characteristics. The United States, in other words, must become an interventionist, imperialist state to preserve the world order that serves its interests (Dupuy 1997, 3–4).

Niall Ferguson summarizes that perspective best. Those who dislike U.S. hegemony, he argues, should understand that "rather than a multipolar world of competing great powers, a world with no hegemon at all may be the real alternative to U.S. primacy." Furthermore, such "apolarity could turn out to mean an anarchic new Dark Age: an era of waning empires and religious fanaticism; of endemic plunder and pillage in the world's foreign regions; of economic stagnation and civilization's retreat into a few fortified enclaves" (Ferguson 2004, 34). Such a chaotic, unstable, and ungovernable world, others argue, would be ripe for terrorists, nationalists, and drug traffickers to take advantage of advances in worldwide communication and transportation to "engage in low-intensity conflicts that can be detrimental to the interests of the United States and its friends" (Coll 1992, 49).

As Michael Ignatieff points out, it is not enough for the United States to be the most powerful or the most hated imperial power. Being an empire means

enforcing such order as there is in the world and doing so in the American interest. It means laying down the rules America wants (on everything from markets to weapons of mass destruction) while exempting itself from other rules (the Kyoto Protocol on climate change and the International Criminal Court) that go against its interest. (Ignatieff 2003)

Samuel Huntington summarized the overall character of the new U.S. imperialism thusly: for a while now, he argues, the United States has been attempting, or perceived to be attempting, more or less unilaterally to

pressure other countries to adopt American values and practices regarding human rights and democracy; prevent other countries from acquiring military capabilities that could counter American conventional superiority; enforce American law extraterritorially in other societies; grade countries according to their adherence to American standards on human rights, drugs, terrorism, nuclear proliferation, missile proliferation, and now religious freedom; apply sanctions against countries that do not meet American standards on these issues; promote American corporate interests under the slogans of free trade and open markets; shape World Bank and International Monetary Fund policies to serve those same corporate interests; intervene in local conflicts in which it has relatively little direct interest; bludgeon other countries to adopt economic policies and social policies that benefit American economic interests; promote American arms sales abroad while attempting to prevent comparable sales by other countries; force out one UN secretary-general and dictate the appointment of his successor; expand NATO . . . ; undertake military action against Iraq . . . ; and categorize certain countries as "rogue states," excluding them from global institutions because they refuse to kowtow to American wishes. (Huntington 1999, 48)

Even more concisely than Huntington, Zbigniew Brzezinski, former national security advisor to President Jimmy Carter, points out that what makes the United States the "only comprehensible global superpower" is its supremacy in the four decisive domains of global power: Its global military power is unmatched; its economy remains the "main locomotive of global growth, even if challenged in some aspects by Japan and Germany"; it retains its lead in cutting-edge technology; and "despite some crassness, it enjoys [a cultural] appeal that is unrivaled, especially among the world's youth" (Brzezinski 1997, 24).

It is in the context of U.S. global dominance and power projection in the post–Cold War era, then, that we can best understand the convergence of this "New World Order imperialism" and the processes that are associated with globalization. If, on the one hand, *New World Order imperialism* means the dominance and projection of U.S. power globally to advance the country's particular economic, political, and cultural interests, then *globalization*, on the other hand, implies the increasing competition among the advanced or core capitalist economies, a handful of semiperipheral countries (the so-called Newly Industrialized Countries or NICs), and a transnational elite whose capital is now freer to penetrate every corner of the world. Indeed, so intense is this competition that some members of the foreign policy intelligentsia like Huntington warn that it is not in the interests of the United States to act like a "lonely sheriff" and pursue a unilateralist strategy predicated on the use of U.S. military power to remake the world after its own image, as the neoconservatives within the current Bush administration would have it. Instead, Huntington argues, the United States ought to use its position as the only superpower to "elicit cooperation from other countries [especially Europe] to deal with global issues in ways that satisfy American interests" (Huntington 1999, 48).

The "new imperialism," then, refers to the dominance, but not hegemony *strictus sensus*, of a single superpower and intense competition among transnational elites that are no longer constrained in their global operation by the East–West rivalry of the Cold War and whose capital is now freer to penetrate every corner of the world. As Michael Storper has shown, globalization is a complex process of intersecting territorialized and organizational dynamics that involves in some cases the repositioning of some territorially specific assets or firms into globalized positions of dominance. In other cases, it involves the devaluation of territory-specific assets or products subsequent to the penetration of local markets by imported substitutes resulting from changes in the taste and consumption patterns of middle classes. Globalization also means territorial integration of production and organization to achieve economies of scale, leading to the deterritorialization, market penetration, and devaluation of localized firms or services. And, in still other cases, it leads to the reinvention of territorialized assets due to product differentiation or changes in production standards resulting from territorial integration (Storper 1997, 35).

Globalization, in short, involves the movement of capital, commodities, information, and labor across state boundaries. The reconfiguration of the international division of labor associated with the globalization process means that the production, consumption, investment, financing, and trade of goods and services are now dispersed throughout the developed and underdeveloped parts of the world economy. In this sense, then, globalization is synonymous with capitalism itself. Since its emergence in the sixteenth century, capitalism has exhibited the characteristics depicted above. As Karl Marx and Friedrich Engels wrote in 1848:

> The need of a constantly expanding world market for its products chases the bourgeoisie all over the surface of the globe. It must nestle everywhere, settle everywhere, establish connexions everywhere.
>
> The bourgeoisie has through its exploitation of the world-market given a cosmopolitan character to production and consumption in every country. . . . All old-established national industries have been destroyed or are daily being destroyed. They are dislodged by new industries, whose introduction becomes a life and death question for all civilised nations, by industries that no longer work up indigenous raw materials, but raw materials drawn from the remotest zones; industries whose products are consumed, not only at home, but in every quarter of the globe. In place of old wants, satisfied by the productions of the country, we find new wants, requiring for their satisfaction the products of distant lands and climes. In place of the old local and national seclusion and self-sufficiency, we have intercourse in every direction, universal inter-dependence of nations. (Marx and Engels 1978, 476)

Thus, *globalization* is simply another term for the expansion and reconfiguration of production, trade, communication, investment, and capital accumulation within and between nation-states and regions of the capitalist world system. Moreover, rather than *eliminating* the historical division of the world system into core, semiperipheral, and peripheral states, globalization *exacerbates* this division. Capital, trade, investments, and technology continue to remain highly concentrated among the core economies of Europe, North America, and Japan. The enhanced mobility of capital is not accompanied by a massive spread of investment, employment, and development in the peripheral countries. Their economies continue to be subordinated to and dependent on those of the core; and the world economy as a whole is becoming *more* hierarchical, *more* polarized, and *more* unequal (Dupuy 2001, 94–95).

With the integration of all countries of the world into the capitalist world economy, the competition among the core capitalist states to divide the world economy into distinct zones over which they exercise greater or lesser influence has intensified. Three such regional blocs exist, namely the European Economic Community, North America, and East Asia, but within the context of the global dominance of the United States, as previously argued. Within this "triad" structure (Stallings 1995, 352–53), nation-states or regions become integrated in the world economy through trade, investment, and production relations in proportion to their position in the international division of labor in general and within their triad in particular. Thus, in contrast to the core economies, which trade and invest mostly among themselves and secondarily with the rest of the world, Latin America and the Caribbean trade mostly with the United States, the Asian NICs trade mostly among themselves and with Japan, and Sub-Saharan Africa trades mostly with the European Union (Stallings 1995, 354).

In general, despite the expansion and intensity of the flows of money-capital, technology, information, goods, services, and production processes, the hierarchical structure of the world economy and its division of labor has not changed dramatically. Neither have the mechanisms of unequal exchange between core and peripheral countries to reverse the flow of part of the total profit or surplus from the periphery to the core, thereby continuing and even increasing the disparities between the core and peripheral zones in the world economy.[1] As Immanuel Wallerstein has argued, the hierarchical structure of the productive processes in the world economy has led to an increased polarization between core and peripheral zones in terms of income levels, standards of living, and the spatial accumulation and concentration of capital (1996, 30). The concentration of capital in core zones that resulted from the historical processes of unequal exchange provided further justification for the core states to create strong state machineries to ensure that peripheral states remained relatively weaker and unable to develop their capacity to challenge the power of core states. With stronger states at their disposal, core powers could and did pressure peripheral countries to "accept, even promote, greater specialization in their jurisdiction in tasks lower down the hierarchy of commodity chains, [and] utilizing lower paid work-forces," thereby creating the "so-called historical levels of wages which have become so dramatically divergent in different zones of the world-system" (Wallerstein 1996, 32).

The position of countries in the international division of labor today is still determined by whether they produce high-value commodities and services based on highly skilled and informational labor, high-volume commodities with low labor costs, or raw materials based on natural endowments, or whether their labor is devalued, redundant, and marginalized (Castells 1996, 1:145–47). Indeed, as Manuel Castells and others argue, the competitiveness of an economy in the international division of labor is highly dependent on the capacity of national governments to manage not only their trade with other countries, but to provide tax write-offs and subsidies for human resources training, technological innovation and development, government markets, research and development, and exports (Castells 1996, 1:105; Petras 2000, 191).

National governments continue to play a major role in increasing the strength and competitiveness of their economies, especially those of the core and the small number of "newly industrialized" countries. There is strong evidence that the economically most successful countries since World War II have been those where the state played a larger role in enhancing the national economy's global competitiveness, as with the achievement of self-sufficiency in British, French, German, and Spanish commercial aviation through the production and sale of Airbus aircraft, or Western European competitiveness in several advanced sectors such as consumer electronics, telecommunications, aerospace, pharmaceuticals, and nuclear energy (Evans 1997, 68–69; Castells 1996, 1:105–6).

As James Petras further argues, the state, especially in the core countries, has played a vital role in creating the dynamics we now call globalization. The global spread of multinational corporations and finance capital would not have been possible without the intervention of the core states. The expansion of the market in the former Soviet Union, Eastern Europe, China, and Vietnam, for example, could not have happened without the crucial role of the imperialist states, especially the United States. Most of the major trade agreements and trading blocs were devised and enacted by core states. And the state provided huge tax windfalls and subsidies to, and lowered labor costs for, private capital. As Petras aptly puts it, the "scale and scope of nation-state activity has grown to such a point that one needs to refer to it as the New Statism rather than the free market. Globalism is in the first instance a product of the New Statism and continues to be accompanied and sustained by direct state intervention" (2000, 207).

But this is nothing new. As Wallerstein has shown, the capitalist world system is characterized by a separation between the economic and the political arena, which consists of putatively sovereign states with autonomous decision-making powers within their respective jurisdictions backed up by the use of force to sustain them (Wallerstein 1996, 31). This separation allows state rulers to contain and control the struggle for power, the conflicts among classes, the organization and relations of production, and the movement of goods, capital, and labor-power within their respective jurisdictional boundaries (48–49). The significance of this point is that state rulers do not act only to promote the interest of their state vis-à-vis others in the interstate system of the capitalist world system but to organize, control, and facilitate the accumulation of capital within their own state as well. States control the movements of goods (e.g., trade tariffs, "anti-dumping" laws), money-capital (e.g, restricting foreign investments in certain sectors), and labor-power (immigration and emigration policies) across their borders. They regulate the social relations of production between capital and labor. They legislate modes of labor control. They redistribute taxes to capitalists more than to other classes or groups. They absorb or subsidize the costs of infrastructure development (energy, transportation, communication, information) and of "strategic" industries. And they use the power of the state, including its armed power, to advance the interests of their capitalists vis-à-vis those of other states in the interstate system of the world economy (47–60 and *passim*).

By contrast, the strength of the state in the Third World or peripheral countries, and its ability to withstand external pressures and determine policy, depends largely on the internal characteristics of the nation-state and its relation with the core country that exercises the greatest influence on it. As Barbara Stallings has shown, core powers in the "triad" influence the policies of the peripheral countries in their respective spheres through mechanisms such as preferential bilateral trade agreements; by incorporating countries that offer favorable terms to core country multinational corporations in the trade and production networks of the core; through direct foreign investments (DFI); and through conditional bilateral government loans and aid, and multilateral loans from the international financial institutions (IFIs) such as the World Bank and the International Monetary Fund (IMF) (Dupuy 2001, 103).

In general, Stallings argues, the role of the state in the economy and the types of policies adopted by peripheral countries reflect the model of capitalism practiced in the core countries on which they are most dependent ideologically, politically, financially, and for their markets. Thus, one finds that even though the triad advocates export-led growth for the peripheral countries as a whole, the state plays a greater role in the economic policies of the Asian countries incorporated in the Japanese zone (e.g., by subsidizing credit, assisting with marketing strategies, and obtaining access to technology) than the Latin American and Caribbean countries who adopt U.S.-influenced policies such as reducing impediments to trade and investments, devaluing currencies, and tax and other institutional reforms. The role of the state is by far weakest in Sub-Saharan Africa. This is largely due not only to the prebendary characteristics of those states but also to the inability of their bloated yet weak bureaucracies to collect information or devise and implement strategies of any sort, including the structural adjustment policies recommended by the IMF (Stallings 1995, 354–72).

It is at this juncture that one can best understand the convergence between the dynamics of globalization and the ideological propositions clustered under the Washington Consensus. Coined by John Williamson in 1989, the "Washington Consensus" reflected the ideology and political objectives of the state actors and policy makers of the Reagan administration that were expressed in the set of "liberalizing policy reforms" of the Washington-based institutions—the World Bank, the IMF, and the Inter-American Development Bank—initially devised for the countries of Latin America (Williamson 1990; Dupuy 2005b, 48).

The formulation of these policy reforms corresponded with the collapse of the Soviet system and the discrediting of central planning and state-centered development models of the 1950s to the 1970s in the Third World (Naim 2000, 509). The Consensus discouraged state planning and import substitution development strategies and instead pushed "market-friendly" economic policies that emphasized an outward orientation and moved away from state controls of prices and interest rates toward "getting the prices right" (Easterly 2001, 135). The advocates of the Washington Consensus exploited the huge debts accumulated by Third World countries—largely at the urgings of the World Bank—to demand that they restructure their economies, open them more to the operation of the market, and facilitate the takeover of their assets by foreign capital (Dupuy 2005b, 43).

Despite the widespread adoption of the Consensus policies in Third World peripheral countries during the 1980s and 1990s, however, most of them have performed poorly and have not experienced the sustained level of growth that was expected, thereby dealing "a blow to the optimism surrounding the 'Washington Consensus' prior to the experience of the last two decades" (Easterly 2001, 138). This is a grim forecast, especially in light of the fact that 99 percent of the more than one billion workers who will join the labor force over the next twenty-five years will come from the underdeveloped or peripheral countries. No doubt, the existence of such a vast reserve pool of cheaper labor is (and has always been) advantageous to core capital, which can outsource parts of the advanced, highly skilled, computerized labor processes to the Asian NICs, India, and Mexico but at much lower costs than—and at the expense of—workers in the core countries (Tabb 2001, 24).

If not development, then, the polarization between the core countries of the North and the peripheral countries of the South amounts to what some analysts like William Robinson refer to as a world war between the "global rich and powerful minority against the global poor, dispossessed and outcast majority" (1996, 14). If we confine ourselves to the post–World War II period, two directly opposite trends can be observed in the world economy: a growing equality in incomes and living standards among the advanced or core capitalist countries of Western Europe, North America, and Japan on the one hand, and a growing inequality in incomes and living standards between these advanced countries and the underdeveloped countries of Africa, Asia, and Latin America on the other. According to the United Nations Development Program (UNDP), even though the share of the world's population living in extreme poverty declined from 29 percent to 23 percent in 1999 due to population growth, that still left 2.8 billion people living on less than $2 a day, and 1.2 billion of them barely surviving on less than $1 a day and below the international poverty line defined as an "income or expenditure level below which a minimum, nutritionally adequate diet plus essential non-food requirements are not affordable" (UNDP 1996, 222; 2002, 17–20). Of the seventy-three countries who compile data on income inequality, forty-eight of them have experienced widening inequalities since 1950, sixteen have experienced no change, and only four, representing just 4 percent of the world's population, have registered a decline in inequality (UNDP 2002, 17–20). Consequently, 790 million people are undernourished, 1 billion have no access to safe drinking water, 2.4 billion lack adequate sanitation, 1 billion lack adequate shelter, 2 billion have no electricity, 1 billion adults are illiterate, and more than 880 million lack access to basic health services (UNDP 1998, 49; 1999, 22; 2000, 30).

The level of inequality may be looked at another way: 1 percent of the richest people in the world received as much combined income (in 2000) as did 57 percent of the world's poorest; the income of the richest 10 percent of the U.S. population is equal to that of 43 percent of the world's poorest, which is to say that 25 million Americans had as much income as nearly 2 billion people worldwide. Globally, the income of the richest 5 percent of people in the world is 114 times that of the poorest 5 percent (UNDP 2002, 19). According to the World Bank, the world's high-income countries—some thirty-three countries plus Hong Kong—have 14.9 percent of the world's population but 78.4 percent of the global product (World Bank 2001, 275).

According to the household surveys conducted in 1990, 2000, and 2002 by the Economic Commission on Latin America and the Caribbean (ECLAC) and its projections of extreme poverty levels as of 2004, 96 million people, or 18.6 percent of the total regional population, are extremely poor, while 222 million (including those 96 million), or 42.9 percent of the region's population, are considered poor (ECLAC 2005, 25). If we consider the case of the Caribbean in particular, nearly half of the countries have 20 percent or more of their population living in poverty. They include Anguilla (21%), Belize (33.5%), British Virgin Islands (22%), Cuba (20%), Dominica (39%), Dominican Republic (44.9%), Grenada (32.1%), Guyana (43.2%), Haiti (75%), Saint Kitts and Nevis (30.5% and 32%, respectively), Saint Vincent and the Grenadines (37.5%), Saint Lucia (25%), and Trinidad and Tobago (21.2%) (ECLAC 2005, 33).

Poverty, and its experience, varies by gender and race.[2] In Latin America and the Caribbean, women have higher rates of poverty, higher rates of unemployment, suffer greater wage discrimination, have less income of their own, are more economically dependent, have less access to and use or control over resources, are more politically disempowered, and are more subject to violence than men. There is, however, an important difference between Latin America and the Caribbean in terms of the relationship between race or ethnicity and poverty. In Latin America, indigenous peoples and peoples of African descent to a large extent are poorer; are more discriminated against; are paid less for comparable work; have higher rates of unemployment; have less access to resources, education, and health care; are less culturally recognized; and are less empowered than other groups. In the Caribbean, by contrast, peoples of African descent are in the majority, though in many countries such as Belize, Dominica, Guyana, Saint Vincent and the Grenadines, and Trinidad and Tobago, there are sizeable portions of other ethnic/racial groups. Consequently, and as a result of the structural changes that took place after independence in most of the countries of the Caribbean, peoples of African— or in some countries like Guyana and Trinidad and Tobago, of Indian descent—are less excluded socially, politically, economically, and culturally and hence are more proportionally represented in the socially, economically, and politically privileged classes than in Latin America (ECLAC 2005, 44–49).

DEMOCRACY AND SOCIAL JUSTICE

If the Washington Consensus discussed above reflects the economic policies of the "New World Order imperialism" of the United States in the contemporary era of globalization, the promotion of democracy serves as its political counterpart. The promotion of democracy, however, especially in underdeveloped, poor, and weak peripheral states, is undermined by the shift in the locus and power of decision making to IFIs and economically powerful private local and international actors (Robinson 1996, 18). Governments everywhere are compelled to surrender the formulation of development, fiscal, and monetary policy to international regulatory institutions such as the World Bank, the IMF, and the U.S. Agency for International Development (USAID) and to embrace their free-market, structural-adjustment, and privatization formulas. Through these reforms, the state is being transformed into what the World Bank calls a "market-friendly state" (World Bank 1991), or what others call less benignly a leaner, meaner state reduced to performing those essential functions necessary for the unregulated operation and accumulation of private and transnational capital, or simply, "accumulation by dispossession" (Harvey 2003, 145–52).

Thus, as peripheral states with long legacies of dictatorship have been undergoing a steady process of democratization, their ability to formulate social policies to meet the basic needs of their citizens and the greater demand for public goods is being eroded by the processes of globalization and their subordination to the imperatives of transnational corporations and financial institutions backed by the power of the core states, the United States in particular. The international financial institutions have not only eroded the peripheral states' capacity to formulate and implement their own economic policies but, equally as important, have defined the limits of democracy. Basically the latter is reduced to the holding of periodic competitive elections subject to international supervision, and adherence to the market principles and free-trade policies established by the IFIs, who penalize uncooperative governments by withholding or discontinuing aid (Wickham 1998, 23).

It is in this double sense that I argue that the current historical conjuncture is characterized by the tendency to reduce politics to a mere problem of technical efficiency and top-down policy implementation. For if by *politics* we mean the right and the ability of a people to determine the agenda of their government, then both this right and this ability are being severely undermined by the subordination of the peripheral states to the dictates of international regulatory institutions and powerful private actors who are not subject to democratic control and accountability. Thus, the formal trappings of sovereignty and democracy notwithstanding, the restructuring of the state into a market-friendly or neoliberal state means the de facto marginalization of the popular sectors from the political process, the election of weak governments with very limited political agendas negotiated among and between the domestic and international elites, and the transfer of ultimate veto power over the state to those elites. William Robinson aptly refers to this exclusionary political system as a "low-intensity democracy . . . aimed not only at mitigating the social and political tensions produced by elite-based and undemocratic status quo, but also at suppressing popular and mass aspirations for more thoroughgoing democratization of social life" (1996, 6).

It is in the context described above that the phenomenon of Aristide and the struggles for democracy that emerged in Haiti in the 1980s can be best understood. Before I discuss the forces struggling for democracy in Haiti, however, it may be useful to situate them in the context of the ongoing debate on the meaning of democracy and the conflicts they have generated. I take as my point of departure the Universal Declaration of Human Rights adopted by the United Nations in 1948, which defined a set of rights to which it said all human beings were entitled regardless of distinctions "of any kind, such as race, colour, sex, language, religion, political or other opinion, national or social origin, property, birth or other status" (Art. 2).[3] For my purposes here, the rights delineated in the thirty articles of the Declaration may be grouped under three categories: civil and political, economic, and cultural.

Civil and political rights are considered to be the "right to life, liberty and security of the person" (Art. 3); the right not to be tortured or subjected to cruel, inhuman, or degrading treatment (Art. 5); the right to equal protection under the law and against any discrimination (Art. 7); the right to be free from arbitrary arrest, detention, or exile and to have a fair hearing by an independent and impartial tribunal for charges brought against an individual, including the presumption of innocence until proven guilty according to law in a public trial (Arts. 9, 10, and 11); the right to free movement within one's country and to leave and return to one's country (Art. 13); the right to have a nationality and to change nationality; the right to own property without fear of arbitrary dispossession; the right to freedom of thought, conscience, religion, and peaceful assembly and association; and the right to take part in the government of one's country either directly or through freely chosen representatives by means of periodic and free elections (Arts. 15–21).

Economic rights include the right to work and to choose one's place of employment; the right to just and fair working conditions, to equal pay for equal work, to just and fair remuneration ensuring an existence "worthy of human dignity, and supplemented, if necessary, by other means of social protection," and to protection against unemployment; the right to join and form trade unions to protect one's interests; the right to rest and leisure and reasonable limitations of work and paid holidays; the right to a "standard of living adequate for the health and well-being of [oneself and one's family], including food, clothing, housing and medical care and necessary social services, and the right to security in the event of unemployment, sickness, disability, widowhood, old age or other lack of livelihood in circumstances beyond [one's] control"; and the right to a free education, at least "in the elementary and fundamental stages," and technical, professional, and higher education accessible to all on the basis of merit (Arts. 23–26).

Cultural rights include the right to participate freely and fully in the cultural life of the community, to enjoy the arts, to share in the benefits and advancements of science, and to have "protection of the moral and material interests resulting from any scientific, literary or artistic production" that one creates (Art. 27).

Since 1948, a number of international covenants, conventions, and protocols have been adopted to enhance and reinforce these sets of rights. Among the most important, for my purposes, are the International Covenant on Economic, Social, and Cultural Rights (1966, came into force in 1976) and the

Convention on the Elimination of All Forms of Discrimination against Women (1979, entry into force 1981) and its Amendment (1995, not yet in force). The significance of these conventions is not that all the countries that have ratified them have observed them in practice, but that they legitimize the continuing struggles for greater equality and social justice by those who are marginalized, oppressed, and exploited on the basis of their class, race, ethnicity, or gender.

Again for my purposes here, I will focus primarily on the relationship between civil, political, and economic rights. My basic premise is that all the rights stipulated in the Declaration are interrelated, interdependent, and equally important to human dignity and that no one order of rights, especially the first order of civil and political rights, can be secured unless all other rights, especially economic, are addressed and protected as well. Let me also make it clear that, *pace* John Roemer, for citizens of a country to be able to practice their rights, or to be in a position to have the opportunity for self-realization, such a society must provide a level of material welfare that guarantees a minimum and healthy standard of living to all citizens (Roemer 1994, 11–13).

More concretely, this proposition means that no one can enjoy any right, such as civil and political rights, unless that individual also has the essentials for a healthy and active life. It is the responsibility of the state to provide that individual with the basic material welfare that alone can prevent him or her from falling into a state of abject deprivation and need. Otherwise, self-agency is unsustainable and the individual becomes vulnerable to exploitation, dependence, and coercion. Put differently, insofar as unequal relations of power and distribution of wealth, income, and resources generate asymmetries of life-chances, or the chances for individuals to participate fully and share in the socially generated economic, political, and cultural goods and opportunities of their society, then such individuals can be said to be in a situation of *nautonomy*. Under nautonomic conditions

> a common structure of political action is not possible, and democracy becomes a privileged domain operating in favor of those with significant resources. In such circumstances, people can be formally free and equal, but they will not enjoy rights which shape and facilitate a common structure of political action and safeguard their capacities. (Held 1995, 171–72)

Now, saying that securing economic or welfare rights—such as the ones stipulated in the Universal Declaration—is equally as important as guaranteeing civil and political rights immediately brings up the question of resources and the ability of a poor and underdeveloped country like Haiti to deliver them. That is, difficult as it may be under current circumstances, one can envision the possibility of a democratic government in Haiti that guarantees and protects civil and political rights, as is the case in most of the independent English-speaking Caribbean countries that formed the Caribbean Community (CARICOM). But it is far more difficult to argue that it could also provide for the welfare of its population in terms of a minimum and healthy standard of living, social security, and education, much less the other rights included in the Universal Declaration (enhanced by subsequent conventions and protocols) that are necessary for the possibility of self-realization and the absence of nautonomic situations for the majority of the population. The fact that the attempts to establish a democratic government in Haiti since 1990 have not succeeded in securing any of those rights for all its citizens does not rule out the possibility that it could at some point in the future achieve at least civil and political rights without making much progress toward securing economic rights.

I will argue, however, that a democracy that prioritizes civil and political over economic rights will deny most citizens the ability to access and exercise even the former, because it will not alter the conditions of nautonomy for the majority and will make such a democracy a privilege domain for the wealthy and powerful classes. As Immanuel Wallerstein put it, democracy

is about equality. . . . Without equality in all arenas of social life, there is no possible equality in any arena of social life, only the mirage of it. Liberty does not exist where equality is absent, since the powerful will always tend to prevail in an inegalitarian system. (2003, 166)

The struggle for democracy that unfolded in the late 1980s in Haiti has from the beginning revolved around defining what type of democracy would be created and whose interests it would serve. Three broad social forces could be identified and were arrayed against one another. The first was the neo-Duvalierist forces who opposed the democratic movement and sought to perpetuate the Duvalierist dictatorships that came to power in 1957 and 1971 and ended with the ouster and exile of Jean-Claude Duvalier in February 1986. For the first five years after his departure, the neo-Duvalierists attempted to suppress the growing democratic movement and reimpose a permanent military dictatorship, but to no avail. Unable to prevent the electoral victory of Aristide in 1990, they succeeded in overthrowing his government in September 1991, forcing Aristide into exile and imposing a brutal military dictatorship that targeted his supporters for repression. The junta stayed in power until a UN-approved multinational intervention led by the United States removed it from power and restored Aristide to the presidency in October 1994. Lacking an institutional basis of power after Aristide disbanded the Haitian Armed Forces in 1995, former members of the army nonetheless played a crucial role in forcing Aristide out of power for a second time in February 2004.

While some sectors of the defunct military and ruling class continue to call for a full reinstatement of the Haitian Army and are fundamentally opposed to democracy, others joined the political process to contest the new national and presidential elections that were held on February 7, 2006, because they understood that in the current conjuncture the core powers and the international organizations and institutions they control find it more difficult to justify (unlike during the Cold War) support for governments that come to power by means other than "free and fair" democratic elections. For that reason, the international community's support for the interim government led by Prime Minister Gérard Latortue that was installed after Aristide's overthrow was conditioned on organizing and holding new comprehensive elections and transferring power to a legitimate government.

Thus, the second social force that emerged in the post-Duvalier era comprised those who equated democracy with a laissez-faire capitalist economy and embraced the perspective of the Washington Consensus. They sought to limit democracy as much as possible to the guarantee of civil and political rights so as not to disturb the extant system of unequal distribution of wealth, income, and resources and to maintain Haiti's position in the international division of labor as a supplier of cheap labor, both domestically and in other parts of the hemisphere through labor migration. I will call this a *minimalist democracy*. By that, I mean a democratic order based on a minimally regulated market system and limited to civil and political rights, which usually are taken to mean the holding of free elections, the right of individuals and political parties to organize freely and to run for office, a free press, and the free expression of ideas, beliefs, and political agendas without government interference. In fact, these were the minimum criteria the international and donor community set for a government that emerged from these processes to be considered democratic and legitimate. This version of democracy is compatible with an "individualist liberal political agenda," as Wallerstein suggests (2003, 150), because it allows citizens to protect and pursue their individual or organized self-interests by pressing their claims against their elected government. But, as previously mentioned, capitalism creates a separation between the political and economic spheres, thereby making possible a significant transfer of power from the state to the owners of private property and the market. Ellen Meiksins Wood takes that argument further by positing that the economic sphere becomes invulnerable to democratic power:

> Protecting that invulnerability has even become an essential criterion of democracy. This definition allows us to invoke democracy *against* the empowerment of people in the economic sphere. It even makes it possible to invoke democracy in defense of a *curtailment* of democratic rights in other parts of "civil so-

ciety" or even in the political domain, if that is what is needed to protect property and the market against democratic power (1995, 235, emphasis in original).

That argument may be looked at yet another way. Insofar as capitalism privileges the owners of private property and investors of capital, the state cannot but act to ensure the profitability and prosperity of those interests because its own stability and viability depends on the process of capital accumulation. This is especially so in a "democratic" society where the legitimacy of and electoral support for the government depends on the performance of the economy and the private sector to satisfy the demands of consumers. Thus, governments must pursue "a political agenda that is at least favourable to, that is, biased towards, the development of the system of private enterprise and corporate power." Because of these constraints, it would be difficult for elected officials "to carry out the wishes of an electorate committed to reducing the adverse effects on democracy and political equality of corporate capitalism" (Held 1995, 247). In other words, democracy must disempower the people if it is to serve the interests of capital.

Yet, as Wallerstein contends, the struggle for equality has not acquiesced to this structural imperative, but instead has led to an increase in popular demand for democratization that has meant an "unceasingly upward curve in the level of redistribution [of income, resources, and welfare provisions], spreading not only upward within countries, but also outward to more and more countries and therefore upward within the world-system as a whole" (2003, 157). No doubt, conservatives everywhere oppose this kind of democratization and have struggled to limit and reverse as much as possible the demands for redistribution. And it is in that sense that we must understand the "neoliberal offensive of the 1980s and the globalization rhetoric of the 1990s [as efforts] to stem the increase" (ibid.).

The popular movement that emerged in the 1980s in Haiti was an expression of that global struggle for equality and insisted on a democracy that empowered the people rather than the propertied classes and the foreign investors, and hence led to a more just and egalitarian society. Thus, in contrast to the supporters of the liberal version of democracy in Haiti outlined above, the popular movement sought to create what I will call a *maximalist* or *redistributive democracy*. The proponents of this version of democracy understood that without securing economic or redistributive rights, the exercise of all other rights would be limited for most citizens because the profound inequalities in wealth, income, and resources in Haiti would maintain them in conditions of nautonomy. Thus, those who equated democracy with securing civil, political, *and* economic rights also understood that this could be achieved only through a restructuring of the extant society and its function in the international division of labor. It is precisely in the context of this increasing demand for a more redistributive and egalitarian democratization and the reaction to it in Haiti and by the core powers, especially the United States, that we must situate and understand the phenomenon of Aristide.

In the chapters that follow, I will argue that the crisis of democratization and of governance in Haiti since 1987 stemmed primarily from the unresolved struggles around the two alternative visions of democracy sketched out above and whose interests they would serve. Let me add quickly, however, that the divisions between the proponents of minimalist democracy on the one hand and maximalist democracy on the other do not correspond neatly to the class divisions of Haitian society nor to the opponents and supporters of Aristide and his Lavalas movement (or, after 1996, his Fanmi Lavalas party). Instead I will argue the following: Although it is true that to the extent they supported democracy at all, the dominant classes (and the core country governments and IFIs) and most of the middle-class political parties sought to limit it to its minimalist version, it does not follow that Aristide and his Lavalas party were the only proponents of the more radical maximalist democracy. Instead, an important distinction needs to be made between (1) the popular movement for democracy and Aristide as the leader of that movement against the dictatorships between 1987 and 1991 and (2) Aristide after he and the cadres of his Lavalas movement (in 1991) and Fanmi Lavalas party came to power (2000–04).

While the contradictions that led Aristide to break with the objectives of the popular democratic movement that brought him to power were always present, there is no doubt that, at least in the 1987–91 period, he captured and articulated like no one else could have the aspirations of the vast majority of Haitians for a just and egalitarian maximalist democracy as I have described it. However, Aristide's theocratic views of politics, combined with his and his cadres' class interests, as well as the constraints of the domestic and world-systemic structures of power (both political and economic), led him to break with the agenda of the mass movement to pursue the same clientelistic and prebendary practices as his predecessors and conform to the interests of the dominant classes, the foreign investors, and the core powers and their financial institutions. But, having broken with the traditional "pact of domination" (defined in chapter 2) between the political class and the dominant economic class to ally himself (in the early period) with a radical and radicalizing mass movement, Aristide, much more so than his cadres, came to be seen as the symbol or signifier of that radicalism even after he abandoned it when in power (both in 1991 and 1994–95, and most clearly in 2000–04). Thus, no matter how much he tried to accommodate the dominant classes and the core powers, both in his first and second terms, they never trusted or accepted him as one of their own and instead sought—successfully—to destroy him. This rejection and enmity, I will argue, though in part the result of Aristide's contradictory behavior and the fears and distrust of the dominant classes and the core powers, pushed Aristide toward an increasingly authoritarian political practice that ultimately sealed his demise.

Aristide's questionable commitment to democracy (minimalist or maximalist) notwithstanding, his rise to power served as a catalyst for the impoverished masses to enter the political arena as never before and to demand not only that they be recognized as equal citizens but also that the state respond to their needs and interests. Aristide failed to live up to the expectations of the mass movement that brought him to power and in many ways set it back during his two terms in office. But, although weakened and even paralyzed during Aristide's second term by the polarization between Aristide and his foreign-backed opposition, the struggle for democracy resurfaced, albeit timidly, during the two years of the Latortue government and culminated in the electoral victory of René Préval on February 7, 2006.

The essential mission of the interim government of Prime Minister Latortue that replaced Aristide in March 2004 was to pacify the country and prepare new elections. To achieve that goal, Latortue and his government cracked down not only on Aristide's armed supporters, known as *chimères* (in French) or *chimès* (in Creole), but also on the populations of the slums, especially of Port-au-Prince, that were considered Aristide strongholds. Latortue also persecuted the key leaders or activists of Lavalas in an effort to weaken the party or cause it to splinter before the elections. That strategy succeeded, but it discredited the interim government for its human rights violations in the process and paved the way for Préval's victory on February 7.

Préval's reelection represents a major victory for the popular democratic sector because he was seen as the only candidate in a field of thirty-three presidential aspirants to represent the interests of the poor majority. The presidential election, then, was a major defeat for those Haitian elite- and foreign-backed forces that coalesced to oppose and overthrow Aristide in 2004. Those forces had hoped that, with Aristide gone, one of their own could win the presidency. Allowed to exercise their franchise, a majority of the people spoiled the plans of the dominant classes once again.

But the February 2006 elections also spelled the end of the Aristidean debacle. Despite his past links to Aristide and the Lavalas movement, Préval distanced himself from both and ran under the banner of his LESPWA (Hope) Platform and not that of the Lavalas Family party. No doubt he owed his victory to the support of the poor majority who once backed and fought for Aristide. But by voting for him, the people signaled that they wanted to break with the politics of false prophets. They chose Préval because, of all the candidates who ran, the majority of voters believed he best represented their interests. But Préval also received the support of some sectors of the middle class and the bourgeoisie and is eager to form a new pact with the dominant classes and attract foreign aid and investments. How he will balance these contradictory interests during the next five years will be the major challenge of his administration. But it is also clear that the image and objectives he is presenting so far signal a fundamental break with the Aristidean past.

Given Haiti's shattered economy, its weak position in the international division of labor, and the constraints the imperatives, or rules, of the world market and its enforcers will impose on the new Préval government, the best that the popular democratic movement can hope for during the next five years would be to create the conditions for a stable and functioning minimalist democracy. Such an accomplishment could in turn allow for the continued struggle to enlarge the democratic space so that the people can become self-actualizing agents and democracy will cease to be the privileged domain of the wealthy and powerful few.

NOTES

1. Wallerstein defines *unequal exchange* as occurring when any differential in a market, resulting either from the scarcity of a complex production process or created by force, leads to the flow of commodities between zones "in such a way that the area with the less 'scarce' item 'sold' its items to the other area at a price that incarnated more real input (cost) than an equally priced item moving in the opposite direction." This process of unequal exchange leads to "a transfer of part of the total profit (or surplus) being produced from one zone to another. Such a relationship is that of coreness-peripherality. By extension we call the losing zone a 'periphery' and the gaining zone a 'core.' The names in fact reflect the geographical structure of economic flows" (Wallerstein 1996, 31–32).

2. Poverty also varies by age. In Latin America as a whole, children are at higher risks of poverty and have higher rates of extreme poverty than any other group (ECLAC 2005, 45–47).

3. It must be pointed out that the language of the Declaration is gendered and not gender-neutral as I present it here. Throughout the document, men are taken as the signifier and referents of the rights delineated in the thirty articles.

Chapter Two

Before Aristide: Class Power, State Power, and the Duvalier Dictatorships, 1957–1990

CLASS POWER AND STATE POWER IN PERIPHERAL SOCIETIES

As mentioned in the first chapter, a democracy that does not challenge the existing class structure of Haitian society will guarantee that the powerful and the privileged continue to prevail while maintaining the impoverished majority in nautonomic conditions. The state is the institution in society vested with "the authority to make binding decisions for people and organizations juridically located in a particular territory and to implement these decisions using, if necessary, force." But the state is simultaneously an instrument and a "pact of domination" whose character is determined by the "interrelations between the various parts of the state apparatus, on the one hand, and the most powerful classes or class fractions, on the other" (Rueschemeyer and Evans 1985, 47). As we saw, those who control the state regulate the conflicts between classes, the organization and relations of production, and the movement of goods, capital, and labor within their respective jurisdictional boundaries for the purpose of the accumulation of capital within their respective nation-state and between states in the capitalist world system.

But if, in the core capitalist countries, state rulers have historically and generally acted on behalf, if not necessarily or always at the behest, of the capitalist classes vis-à-vis the working classes to make the endless accumulation of capital possible (Wallerstein 1996, 48–49), the fact remains that the interests of state rulers and capitalists do not always converge. They sometimes pursue contrasting and conflicting logics, and they do not always express the "pact of domination" between themselves and the economically dominant classes similarly, whether domestically or internationally. This is so because of the separation between the economic and political arenas discussed previously. Capitalists are primarily interested in pursuing profit wherever they can, and in the accumulation of more and more capital. They do so by operating in continuous space and time, shifting their investments, relocating their firms, and merging or going out of business. By contrast, statesmen and politicians are primarily interested in the exercise of power and in the power of their state vis-à-vis that of others. They are for the most part confined within fixed territorial boundaries (except, of course, when they engage in territorial conquest), are constrained politically and militarily within their state or by the actions of other states, and are in one way or another responsible to other social actors—be they classes, elite or kinship groups, the citizenry, or other social groups (Harvey 2003, 27).

The separation of the economic and political arenas of power, then, means that state actors can sometimes act autonomously from and even in conflict with economically dominant classes. This is especially so in the peripheral economies, due largely to their different modes of incorporation into the capitalist world system, the weakness of their economies, the use of state power as a means of social advancement by state actors, and the different "pacts of domination" between state actors, domestic economically dominant classes, and international capitalist interests and their financial and regulatory institutions. It is here that I find Clive Thomas's propositions on the postcolonial state useful, especially since he formulated them in light of the experiences of the colonial and postcolonial Caribbean slave economies.

Thomas's argument may be summarized as follows. Starting from the premise that the state is always constructed in the context of specific class and power relations within society, he argues that the colonial state in the Caribbean reflected the power not only of the colonial administration but of the colonial planter class as well. Whereas the colonial administration responded first and foremost to the interests of the colonial power, the colonial planter class derived its power directly from its control over the productive structures of the colony, that is, the plantation system. The colonial state represented and defended the interests of the colonial planters vis-à-vis the subordinate classes within the colony, but those were not always compatible with the interests of the metropolitan ruling classes (or those sectors with direct interests in the colonies, such as the mercantile bourgeoisie) and in fact often conflicted with them. Thus, insofar as state power did not always reflect or correspond to the class power of the planters, there was what Thomas refers to as a "clear nonequivalence of state power and the power of the ruling classes, a nonequivalence that also points to the potential separation between the exercise of state power and the interests of the ruling classes" (1984, 68).

Thomas gives another reason why the state in peripheral, postcolonial societies acquires autonomy from the economically dominant classes. The underdeveloped and heterogeneous structures of production in peripheral societies make it impossible for any single indigenous class to become the economically dominant class. In such conditions, the limited scope of production and of private capital accumulation also restricts the material basis for the expansion of the state itself. Consequently, Thomas concludes, in order for the state to serve "the overall interests of the ruling class in these circumstances, [it] must promote the growth of commodity relations, yet it is constrained from doing so by the dominant structures of these social formations and the interests that cluster around them" (1984, 70).

CLASS POWER AND STATE POWER IN HAITI

Contrary to Thomas, I will argue that, in the case of Haiti, rather than serving the "overall interests" of the postcolonial Haitian ruling class, the state created by the emerging political classes during the revolutionary period and after independence entered into direct competition and conflict with the economic ruling class to appropriate part of the economic surplus. Rather than acting to promote the growth of commodity relations, that is, to develop the productive forces of the economy in order to expand the scope of production and of private capital accumulation, the state did the exact opposite: It stifled such expansion by competing with the private sector to accumulate wealth. Thus, rather than serving as an instrument for the development of commodity production and of the economy, and hence of both the economic ruling class and the working classes as a whole, the state became a primary site for the promotion of the interests of a fraction of the dominant classes that would use the state as a source of private enrichment. These practices are at the root of the "prebendary" state system in Haiti.

A new dominant but fractionalized class emerged during the revolution and after Haiti became independent in 1804. That fractionalized class consisted, on the one hand, of the class of predominantly mulatto property owners who originated from the *affranchis* class of "freemen" in Saint-Domingue and, on the other hand, the new black bourgeoisie formed during the regimes of Toussaint Louverture in 1801–03 and Jean-Jacques Dessalines in 1804–06. That fraction of the dominant class was created by using the instruments of state power and corruption to plunder the public treasury and redistribute properties taken from the former French planters and from mulatto property owners (under Dessalines). These practices gave rise to the prebendary state by institutionalizing corruption, establishing the nonequivalence of state power and the power of the ruling classes, and separating state power from the interests of the economic ruling class in general while creating a mutual interdependence between them.[1] The dominant class, then, comprised a private-sector commercial bourgeoisie and a state bourgeoisie.

The urban-based commercial bourgeoisie that developed during the nineteenth century served as the principal link between Haiti and the world economy through its control of the import and export businesses. By the mid-twentieth century, that class, along with the state bourgeoisie, consisted of between 1 and 2 percent of the population and included mulattoes, blacks, and European and Levantine expatriate businessmen, primarily from Syria and Lebanon, who settled permanently in Haiti in the late 1800s and early 1900s and intermarried with Haitians. Disaggregated in terms of the sectors they controlled, about 30 percent were in import/export businesses, 25 percent were in industry, 30 percent were large landowners and rich speculators, and 15 percent were high public functionaries, administrators, high-ranking military officers, and other professionals such as lawyers and physicians (Voltaire 1982, 8).

A middle class consisting of about 4 percent of the population was made up of medium and small property owners, retail merchants, shop owners, school and university teachers, and professionals in both the private sector and the administrative cadres of the civil administration, state agencies, and public enterprises, as well as the officer corps of the military. Education increasingly became an important means of passage into the middle class and the lower stratum of the bourgeoisie even though the clientelistic system associated with the prebendary state remained the primary means of entry into state civil service employment and the military.

An urban working class concentrated mostly in the capital city of Port-au-Prince and representing about 30 percent of the active population had also been formed. The majority of workers were employed in the service sector (private, public, informal), and a smaller proportion worked in the industrial sector (private, public, informal; mining/extractive, import-substitution, export manufacturing, construction) in mostly small and medium-size enterprises. The vast majority of the population, however, remained rural and involved in agriculture, whether as landless wage laborers or small, medium-size, or large landowners (Moral 1961, 64; Pierre-Charles 1967, 143; Schmidt 1971, 179; Doubout and Joly 1976, 218–19; Nicholls 1979, 189).

The significance of this class formation was threefold. The first significance was that the Haitian dominant class remained divided and weak. Despite early attempts to do so, the dominant class was unable to maintain the plantation system established by the French during the colonial period and transform the majority of the former slaves into a landless proletariat on the plantations. Since it could not create a proletariat, the dominant class could not develop large-scale industries, and for the most part it turned to commerce and to the importation and exportation of commodities as its primary basis of wealth accumulation. The Haitian bourgeoisie, then, derived most of its wealth from the circulation rather than directly from the production process, and since that circulation process was tied to the world market, the bourgeoisie's well-being depended entirely on the conditions of that world market, over which it had no control or influence.

The second consequence of the class formation described above was that the majority of the population lived in what Immanuel Wallerstein calls "semiproletarian households," which means that rather than relying primarily on income derived from wage-labor employment, most households derived their income partly from wage labor and partly, or mostly, from nonwage work such as production for self-consumption, petty commodity production, or production for sale in a market. Consequently, the level of remuneration for those workers involved in wage work was much lower than it would have been if the households had been fully proletarianized, because those involved in generating nonwage incomes lowered the wages of those employed in wage work, thereby reducing the employers' cost of production and increasing their profit margins (Wallerstein 1996, 26–27). Put differently, the semiproletarian character of Haitian households generated a large surplus or a reserve army of potential wageworkers that lowered the acceptable minimum wage of those able to find wage employment while raising the profit margins of firms that employed wageworkers. The failure of the Haitian bourgeoisie to transform the agricultural sector by proletarianizing labor relations in agriculture not only blocked any attempt to industrialize but also preserved the semiproletarian household structure and hence Haiti's low-wage labor characteristics that would become its primary mode of integration in the international division of labor in the twentieth century.

A third consequence of the class structure of Haiti was that the state itself became a source of accumulation and social advancement for those who controlled it. Since the state also depended primarily on the circulation process — through direct or indirect taxation—for its revenues, the state bourgeoisie entered into conflict with the private sector bourgeoisie to appropriate part of the surplus wealth produced by the working and farming classes. Because those in control of the state used it to enrich themselves as well as the sectors of the private bourgeoisie and middle classes allied with them, the state, in effect, became "privatized," that is, used as a source of prebend by officeholders.

The characteristics of the relations between state and dominant class summarized above are symptomatic of what I have called the "prebendary state" and others have referred to as the "predatory state" in Haiti (see Evans 1989;

Fatton 2002). Following Max Weber, I define the *prebendary state* as a regime where those who hold state power live off politics. In addition to their salaries, the rulers and officials of the state benefit from the perquisites of office, either in the form of bribes or outright appropriation of public monies from the various government agencies and state enterprises for private ends (Weber 1968, 86–95, 207–9). Or, as Peter Evans put it, the objective of those who control the predatory state plunder the resources of the state "without any more regard for the welfare of the citizenry than a predator has for the welfare of its prey" (1989, 562).

Under a prebendary regime, a fraction of the middle or dominant class controls the state by allying itself with a supreme ruler or dictator. Such a political regime takes on the characteristics of personal rule and of clientelistic networks through which jobs and political or public goods are provided and political functions are performed. As Robert Jackson and Carl Rosberg have argued, systems of personal rule do not respond to "public demands and support by means of public policies and actions," and personal rulers do not aim to implement public policies that respond to broad-based social interests (1982, 18). Put differently, rulers of prebendary states appropriate public resources for their own benefit and those of the class fractions allied with them, returning little to society in the form of public goods and services. The primary goal of officeholders is the maximization of self-interest rather than the social welfare. In such a system, corruption becomes generalized at all levels of the society, not only among state rulers but also among the various apparatuses of the state, public officials and functionaries, and all other sectors of society who attempt to subvert or ignore legal or ethical principles to maximize their self-interest. That is why clientelism and personal ties between the ruler, his supporters, and their extended networks become the only sources of cohesion within the state, rather than the relations between state officials and broad constituencies in the larger society (Evans 1995, 12). Prebendary states, then, are fundamentally antidevelopmental and antidemocratic, since the main objective of officeholders is their personal enrichment and prolongation of their rule rather than implementing public policies that respond to broad social needs even while simultaneously serving the interests of the dominant classes by expanding commodity production and the development of the society's productive forces.

From this, it follows that a prebendary state is a state that in effect becomes "privatized" for the benefit of those in power. In turn, the head of state, whether elected or a dictator, is impelled to monopolize and hold onto power indefinitely, if possible. This explains why, despite the attempts to create constitutional governments since independence, the coup d'état or overthrow of heads of state by force became the most common means of installing and removing governments from office in Haiti. This explains, too, why the army and military officers played such a prominent role in the political process. The dictatorial powers of the president rested primarily on the support of the armed forces, thereby creating the possibility for military officers to capture power and become heads of state. Of the twenty-three presidents Haiti had from 1804 to 1915 and the fourteen it had between 1934 and 2004, twenty-four were military officers, and twenty-eight of them were overthrown by popular uprisings or by coups d'état.[2]

Moreover, once political power became privatized, its holders could not tolerate any kind of opposition and hence sought to silence that opposition, either by neutralizing it politically or by exterminating it physically. This meant that neither the separation of powers characteristic of democratic governments, especially an independent legislature and judiciary, nor an organized and legitimate opposition could become institutionalized so as to check and hold those in power accountable. In turn, to the extent that an "opposition" existed, the tendency was for it to deny the legitimacy of those in power so as to substitute itself for the incumbents. Such a system, then, made it difficult if not impossible to institutionalize democracy or a peaceful and legal mechanism for the transfer of power from one group to another. As Kern Delince put it, the aim of a political opposition was "less to have an influence on the orientation of the decision of those in power than to put a brutal end to the very existence of the government" (1979, 40).

The reasons republicanism or democracy never became implanted and institutionalized in Haiti, then, can be explained by the class relations and structures, the balance of forces between them, and the political practices they gave rise to—namely the prebendary state—before and after independence. These structures effectively blocked the creation of a public sphere where differences—social, cultural, political, economic—could be articulated and mediated institutionally. That is why, as Jacky Dahomay (*pace* Jürgen Habermas) put it, a democratic consciousness based as it is on the development and exercise of written and positive law—of juridically defined and effectively applied sanctions legitimated through public discourse—could not become institutionalized in Haiti. As such, Dahomay argues, even if they existed on paper, judges in Haiti rarely officiated according to law, and "corruption, the arbitrary, the subordination of the judge to the personal power of the head of state and the irruption of extrajuridical, religious, or superstitious considerations in judicial decisions became common practice [among] Presidents who did not hesitate to intervene directly in the decisions of the courts" (2001, 18–19).[3]

For all that they sought to monopolize political power, however, historically state leaders in Haiti could not rule without entering into bargaining relationships and alliances with sectors of the economically dominant class. If the latter class always had to pay its "dues to the state to maintain [its] dominance," the holders of state power also had to reach compromises with the economically dominant class, "even while [they limited] the reach of representative institutions, including those that [represented] the dominant classes" (Trouillot 1990, 28). The Haitian ruling or dominant class, then, is comprised of two blocs: the economic, that is, those who own and control the means of production, including land, private businesses, and economic assets; and the political, those who control the government and apparatuses of the state and use them as their private prebend.

I will go further than Michel-Rolph Trouillot, however, and argue that while the state actors and the economically dominant class formed a "pact of domination" based on obligations of reciprocity between them, they were not necessarily operating on equal terms. If it is the case that state actors could and did act autonomously from and sometimes contrary to the interests of the economically dominant class, they nonetheless remained dependent on the economic ruling class and, by extension, the relations between the latter and the governments and bourgeoisies of the core countries. As the exporters of Haiti's agricultural or manufactured goods and importers of its durable and consumer goods, the Haitian economic ruling class served as the direct link between the Haitian economy and the world market. The members of the economically dominant class, then, and not the holders of state power, were the primary accumulators of capital in Haiti, and this fact always afforded them leverage over state actors rather than the other way around.

Moreover, the reproduction of the economically dominant class depended on its continued participation in the world market and its ability to accumulate wealth and capital and to bequeath those assets to their descendants. That was not so for state actors. Though they attempted to prolong their hold on power indefinitely, they could not automatically transfer their power to their offspring the way owners of capital could bequeath their wealth to theirs; and heads of state could remain in power so long as they had the support of other social actors, principally the military and police, the economic ruling class, and often influential external powers and actors. Thus, *pace* David Harvey, it could be said that the economic and state fractions of the dominant class pursued contrasting and conflicting logics that led them to perceive and express the pact of domination between them differently.

Since the core powers and their capital could establish a foothold in Haiti only with the consent of the government, however coerced, that fact afforded the state bourgeoisie considerable authority and leverage of its own vis-à-vis the economic ruling class, while reinforcing the government's subservience to and dependence on the core powers. But because the primary reason the core powers established relations with Haiti was to have access to its cheap labor and natural resources, state rulers who did not observe the "rules of the game" could be deposed and replaced by more compliant ones without displacing or threatening the private-sector bourgeoisie. The pact of domination, then, always involved a precarious balance of power between state rulers and the domestic capitalist class within the context of Haiti's subordination to and dependence on one or more core powers and those sectors of their capitalist classes with specific interests in Haiti. Depending on the specific geopolitical conjuncture of the world system and its expression in Haiti, the balance of power may favor one or the other fraction of the dominant class, but without altering Haiti's specific subordinate and subservient function in the international division of labor of the world system.

THE DUVALIER DICTATORSHIP AND BLACK NATIONALISM

A proper understanding of contemporary Haitian politics, especially the era of Aristide between 1991 and 2004, must begin with an analysis of the Duvalier and neo-Duvalierist dictatorships from 1957 to 1990. This is so for two reasons. First, the rise of François "Papa Doc" Duvalier to power in 1957 marked a significant turning point in the characteristics of the prebendary state system and in Haitian politics. And second, the transfer of power to Duvalier's son, "Baby Doc" Jean-Claude Duvalier, in 1971 signaled a new mode of integration of Haiti in the capitalist world economy and the surrendering of the formulation of economic policy to the international financial institutions—principally the World Bank, the International Monetary Fund, the Inter-American Development Bank (IDB), and the United States Agency for International Development. Thus, insofar as Aristide initially sought to change the structures of power and the practices of politics in Haiti, he necessarily had to contend with the pact of domination established between the Duvalier dictatorships, the Haitian economic ruling class, the United States and other core powers, and the international financial institutions they controlled.

With the help of the Haitian Army, François Duvalier was elected president in September 1957 after months of violence and armed clashes between supporters of the major presidential candidates—Louis Déjoie, Daniel Fignolé, Clément Jumelle, and Duvalier. These candidates sought to succeed President Paul Magloire, a former Haitian Army general who was forced from office in December 1956.[4] The struggle for power during the electoral campaign of 1956–57 was a major crossroads in Haitian politics. Of the thirteen presidential candidates, only three—Déjoie, Duvalier, and Fignolé—were of significance, because they represented the interests of the three major urban social classes: the mulatto bourgeoisie, the black bourgeoisie and the middle class, and the urban proletariat, respectively.

François Duvalier, a rural physician (hence the nickname "Papa Doc"), social scientist, cofounder of the black nationalist *Griots* group, member of the Ethnology Institute, and former member of Dumarsais Estimé's cabinet, carried the banner of the black nationalists. He drew his support from among the former members of Estimé's government, the black landowning bourgeoisie and speculators, black military officers, and the black middle class, especially those who benefited from employment in the public bureaucracy since the "Estimist Revolution" of 1946.

Duvalier did not seek to alter the class structure of Haiti and thus the social and economic dominance of the Haitian mulatto and black bourgeoisie. Neither did Duvalier aim to reduce the economy's subordination to and dependence on foreign capital. This fact revealed a fundamental contradiction in the black nationalist ideology as expressed in Haiti. While it attacked the racism and elitism of the mulattoes, it failed to link these practices to the global racism of the core countries toward those of the periphery. The nationalism of the fractions of the black bourgeoisie and middle class identified the mulatto bourgeoisie as the main enemy—not that bourgeoisie's or their own alliance with and subservience to foreign capital. As such, black nationalism in Haiti could never have been part of a progressive movement because it would have had to recognize the fundamental class basis of racial/color ideologies rooted historically in the conquest or dominance of non-European peoples by Europeans, reproduced in various ways in the peripheral societies to express and justify their own privileged positions in the hierarchical class structure. In short, for nationalism, of whatever stripe or color, to admit of class divisions and antagonistic interests among those it seeks to rally to its cause would be self-defeating.

Duvalier's and the black nationalists' objectives were to capture political power for the black bourgeoisie and middle class as a counterweight to the mulatto bourgeoisie's economic dominance. This would be achieved by forging an alliance with other class fractions under the leadership of the black bourgeoisie and middle class. The other classes that formed the power base of the Duvalier regime included members of the expatriate Levantine business groups, who were resented and socially excluded by the mulatto bourgeoisie; sectors of the medium-size farmers; the Vodou hierarchy; and elements from the urbanized lumpenproletariat. Duvalier had very little support among the urban working classes (Hector 1972, 51; Pierre-Charles 1973, 62–63; Nicholls 1979, 237–38; Voltaire 1982, 10–11).

For all Duvalier's antimulatto ideology, however, he did not exclude mulattoes who shared his views and objectives from his administration. Though they were small in number, several well-known high-ranking mulatto officers and members of the mulatto bourgeoisie were among the staunchest defenders of the Duvalier regime in its early years. This shows that ideologies of race or color cannot be reduced to the color of one's skin or to the class fraction one belongs to, but rather to one's self-identification, interests, and objectives. Duvalier saw himself as the legitimate heir of several black rulers, such as Jean-Jacques Dessalines (in power 1804–06), Louis F. Salomon (1879–88), and Dumarsais Estimé (1946–50). Duvalier's aim was not to do away with the mulatto bourgeoisie as a class, but to share power with it. As Frantz Voltaire noted:

> The black nationalist discourse has a double function: on the one hand it is a legitimizing ideology for the new protagonists on the political scene, and on the other hand it is a compensatory ideology for the faction of the petty bourgeoisie excluded from the system to whom it gives the illusion of a possibility of integration in the dominant oligarchic system. (1982, 5)

As Cary Hector pointed out, however, one needs to distinguish between the ideology of conquest of power and the ideology of power (Hector 1972, 52), that is, between black nationalism as a contesting and revanchist ideology and black nationalism as the ideology of the black bourgeoisie/middle class in control of the state. The former justified the claim to political power by Duvalier as the incarnation of the "historic mission" of the black elite to gain power in the name of the black majority against the exclusivism and elitism of the mulatto minority. Once in power, Duvalier moved to monopolize the political space by suppressing all competing political opposition. Marxism especially became a target, in all its variants. From 1958 onward, anticommunism and the open persecution of all "communists" (often used as a euphemism for anyone who opposed Duvalier) became a constant of the Duvalier regime (Hector 1972, 53).

Duvalier did not limit his attack to ideological and political opponents, however. To achieve the black nationalists' objective of a social and political balance with the mulatto bourgeoisie, the latter had to be removed from positions of power or authority in the apparatuses and agencies of the state, especially the military. To be effective against the mulattoes, however, the government's purge and repressive measures had to be ubiquitous and include all opposition or potential opposition, and it could know no bounds. Therefore Duvalier's first order of business was to consolidate his power within the state and over the society, and he spent the first seven years of his rule implementing that policy. The regime created a vast clientelistic network by taking over all the apparatuses of the state, including the military, and staffing them with

those loyal to Duvalier. All were under the supreme power of the chief executive, that is, Duvalier.

From 1957 to 1964, Duvalier unleashed a reign of terror hitherto unknown
on all opponents, real, potential, or imagined, and on the population in general. No institution within the state or the society was left untouched. By
1959, the legislature (the Senate and Chamber of Deputies) had been transformed into mere executors of Duvalier's will. He obtained from the Senate
special powers to rule by decree. Within the first six months of his presidency,
he arrested, tortured, killed, exiled, or drove underground the candidates who
opposed him during the electoral campaign and their prominent supporters. If
a suspected "enemy" of the regime could not be found and arrested, the members of his family, his relatives, his domestic servants—sometimes even his
pets or anyone with the same family name—might be arrested and killed instead. Entire families were killed by orders of Duvalier in the early months of
the regime's consolidation.

Duvalier subdued the media by arresting and torturing journalists, broadcasters, or publishers who criticized his policies, destroying their properties,
denying their studios access to electricity, compelling newspapers to print ed-
itorials written by the government, and forcing them to hire editors linked to
the Ministry of Information. Censorship was introduced in all forms of public communication. Trade unionists were arrested, and independent trade
unions and strikes were outlawed. Faculty and students at the State University of Haiti were also tamed, and all independent student organizations were
banned. Faculty and students at the university were henceforth chosen on the
basis of their loyalty to the president.

The Catholic Church, whose hierarchy was predominantly French, was tra-
ditionally conservative, opposed to the cultural and religious values and practices of the populace, and generally supportive of the mulatto bourgeoisie.
Duvalier expelled all foreign clergy and replaced them with Haitians. Even
though this decision led to Duvalier's excommunication by the Holy See in
1959 (rescinded in 1966), the substitution of Haitian for foreign clergy was
an important part of the ideological offensive of the regime against the mulatto bourgeoisie and was seen as necessary to consolidate its control over one
of the most influential institutions of society (Rotberg 1971, 201–23; Manigat 1964, 52–57; Nicholls 1979, 222–26; Diederich and Burt 1969, 108–10;
Heinl and Heinl 1978, 592, 610, 628).

Duvalier also transformed and neutralized the Haitian military in an effort
to thwart any possibility of a coup against him. To prevent the emergence of
powerful military strongmen capable of challenging his authority, Duvalier
frequently replaced those officers who had proved most loyal to him but who
were beginning to show signs of independence. Given also that the military

reflected the class divisions of the society, Duvalier attacked the power base of the mulatto elite by dismissing the entire general staff and the older officers with twenty or more years of service and by arresting others who were known supporters of his presidential rivals. He then promoted younger and mainly black officers who took an oath of allegiance to him. This bold measure at once got rid of most of the mulatto "old guard" officers trained during the U.S. occupation and who belonged to or backed the mulatto elite. At the same time, Duvalier took over from the army chief of staff the right to nominate the rural section chiefs, who would henceforth be devoted to him personally (Delince 1979, 127–28; Rotberg 1971, 202–3; Diederich and Burt 1969, 129, 199–202; Manigat 1964, 50).

Replacing the hierarchy of the military with black middle-class officers was not sufficient to guarantee Duvalier's absolute power, however. Distrusting the military for its historic role in the making and unmaking of governments, Duvalier wanted to build another source of armed power that he controlled personally and that could serve as a counterforce to the military. This new force took two forms: one was the formation of the Presidential Guard staffed by officers appointed by and directly under the orders of Duvalier; the other was the creation of a paramilitary organization originally called *Cagoulards*—because they wore balaclavas (*cagoules*) to hide their identity and were modeled after the *Zinglins* used by President/Emperor Faultin Soulouque (1847–1859) for the same purpose. The Cagoulards were later renamed the *Milice Civile* (Civilian Militia) and, after 1962, the *Volontaires de la Sécurité Nationale* (VSN, or Volunteers of National Security), but popularly known as the *Tontons Makout*. With 10,000 members, the *makout* force readily became much larger than the regular armed forces, including the police, which numbered slightly over 5,000 (Rotberg 1971, 205, 215).

The majority of the makouts came from the lumpenproletariat in the urban centers and from among the peasantry, Vodou priests, and section chiefs in the rural areas. As a paramilitary and mercenary force, the makouts possessed arbitrary powers that they used to terrorize the population, deprive them of their most elementary civil rights, and engage in all sorts of extortions. The makouts became the Praetorian Guard of the regime (Rotberg 1971, 215–16; Trouillot 1986, 163, 165, 181).

Under Duvalier, the terrorism of the state reached new heights. The regime distinguished itself from all previous governments in its unlimited and indiscriminate use of violence (Pierre-Charles 1973, 46). No one was spared: men, women, children, families from all classes, and even entire towns were subjected to the tyrannical and unpredictable violence of the state. By striking against all, anywhere, and at any time, the new violence became as symbolic as it was preventive. After 1965 when the regime had consolidated its power and created its vast and effective apparatus of repression and terror, it no longer needed to apply physical violence with the same degree of intensity as it did during the early years (Trouillot 1986, 177–80). As Trouillot observed, the Duvalierist violence

> did not seek the physical intervention of the State in the battlefield of politics; it aimed to create a void in that field to the benefit of the State. It wanted an end to that struggle for a lack of combatants in the sphere occupied by the totalitarian executive. (1986, 180)

By 1964, Duvalier had tamed the mulatto bourgeoisie and all other sectors of the society through his terrorist methods, extended his control over the educational and religious institutions, subordinated the regular armed forces to his own paramilitary forces, and transformed the other branches of government to respond to his dictates. The regime further strengthened its autonomy by expanding its means of wealth appropriation. As with preceding governments, the Duvalier government increased its revenues by imposing higher taxes on coffee exports and on the consumption of items of basic necessity. These taxes fell most heavily on the already poor rural and urban majority and made them poorer still. Mats Lundahl estimated that more than 40 percent of the farmers' potential income from coffee was appropriated through the increased taxes between 1964 and 1971 (Lundahl 1979, 397). By contrast, taxes remained very low or were not imposed on most of the imported luxury goods consumed by the wealthy (DeWind and Kinley 1986, 25–26).

In addition to taxation, the government invented many other schemes of wealth extraction, such as the sale and compulsory purchase of "economic liberation" bonds; obligatory contributions to the "Movement for National Renovation," for the construction of "Duvalierville," to a pension fund, for a literacy campaign, and for the creation of a national lottery; and even the collection of arrears from telephone users for the previous decade when the telephone system was inoperative. The government, however, did not increase its revenues only by collecting taxes or compulsory contributions by the citizenry. It also created new state enterprises or extended its control over existing ones, including the National Bank of Haiti; the Development Bank; the *Régie du Tabac*, which had a monopoly on the purchase, manufacture, and sale of tobacco products; a sugar mill in Les Cayes; the Organization for the Development of the Artibonite Valley; the Motor Vehicle Inspection Bureau; the National Railroad Company; and various communications, electricity, telephone, and air transport services. By 1962, the state sector represented about 18 percent of the gross national product (GNP) (Pierre-Charles 1967, 194–95; DeWind and Kinley 1986, 25–26; Rotberg 1971, 239–40). Thus, al-

though the Duvalier regime did not seek to expropriate or physically exter-
minate the mulatto bourgeoisie, its intervention in the economy and its appropriation of a major share of the national income strengthened its autonomy
vis-à-vis the bourgeoisie as a whole.

The wealth appropriated by these state agencies and enterprises not only
fed the coffers of the Duvalier family and those of the small circle of the
regime's hierarchy who were estimated to have taken $10 million per year
from the public treasury but also made it possible for the regime to pay the
paramilitary and security forces with the nonfiscalized funds derived from
some of the enterprises directly under Duvalier's control (DeWind and Kinley 1986, 28). Under Duvalier, then, the state became a key economic sector
that served as both a source of enrichment for the president, his family, and
the government's top functionaries and a source of income for the vast pool
of government employees, the military, and the security forces. The government employees and the members of the regular armed forces were paid out
of the fiscalized accounts, whereas the makouts and their leaders were paid
out of the nonfiscalized accounts of the state (Lundahl 1979, 382, 385–86;
DeWind and Kinley 1986, 28). Since Duvalier and his appointed functionaries controlled all branches and agencies of government and the public enterprises, the clientelistic system worked to ensure that only those loyal to the
regime found employment. Through its sheer weight in the economy and its
redistributive mechanisms, therefore, the Duvalier regime bought the allegiance of hundreds of thousands of people in the rural and urban areas.

With his effective repressive apparatus, his own sources of revenues, and
his vast clientelistic network in place, nothing stood in Duvalier's way to prevent him from making his regime permanent and hereditary. Duvalier, who
identified himself with the nation under the slogan "I am the Haitian Flag,
One and Indivisible," had himself "elected" president-for-life in June 1964
and then drafted a new constitution that granted him absolute powers. In this,
Duvalier did not differ from many of his predecessors who also sought to extend their presidency to life terms, including Jean-Jacques Dessalines (1804–
06), Henry Christophe (1806–20), Jean-Pierre Boyer (1818–43), Faustin
Soulouque (1847–59), Fabres Nicholas Geffrard (1859–67), and Silvain Sal-
nave (1867–69).

Where the Duvalier regime differed from its antecedents was in its ex-
tremes. It went further than most in its widespread and systematic application
of violence against individuals regardless of class, gender, or age. It also differed from prior dictatorships in its creation of an effective dual power structure directly controlled by the dictator; in its usurpation of all powers from
all branches of government and their concentration in the hands of the chief
executive; in its control over and remolding of the major ideological and

cultural institutions of the society: the Church, the Vodou hierarchy, the schools, the media; and in its use of its own nonfiscalized sources of income to maintain its *force de frappe*. The Duvalier regime, in short, succeeded in shifting political power in favor of the black bourgeoisie and middle class, and in consolidating its power in all the apparatuses of the state and in the most important institutions of society.

The Duvalier regime, however, did not represent a *qualitatively* different and "totalitarian" state as Trouillot argued (1986, 176–85). Neither was Duvalierism a "Creole" or "underdeveloped" variant of the fascism of Germany or Italy in the 1930s, as several authors have proposed (Manigat 1964; Pierre-Charles 1973; Roc 1968). The Duvalier regime shared many of the characteristics of a totalitarian or fascist state, such as its recurrent (racial) nationalism, its racist interpretation of (Haitian) history, the control over all the state apparatuses and the major cultural and ideological institutions by one center, its anticommunism, and its idolatry of a supreme leader. As an underdeveloped and peripheral economy, however, Haiti in the 1960s did not resemble in any way those of Germany and Italy in the 1920s and 1930s, and Duvalierism cannot be said to have represented the emergence of an antimonopoly capitalist or antiimperialist movement to resolve the crisis of finance and monopoly capital (Hector 1972, 59–62). Moreover, though control over the military and the state apparatuses was centralized in the hands of Duvalier to a much greater degree than under previous regimes, decision-making authority also stemmed from a single center under most of the preceding military- or civilian-led dictatorships and not from relatively autonomous branches of government. And if the regime of the father was characterized as totalitarian because of the exercise of total control by the chief executive, what of the regime of Jean-Claude Duvalier who, unlike his father, created a cabinet government and relegated more power to the army? In short, the distinction that Trouillot makes between the "authoritarian" regimes of the past and the "totalitarian" character of the Duvalier regime is one of degree, not of kind (Trouillot 1986, 160–66).

In my view, the significance of Duvalierism was not the form in which it exercised power, but rather that it expressed the rise of the black nationalists as the dominant political force, restoring the precarious balance that the black bourgeoisie and middle class had achieved with the mulatto bourgeoisie under Estimé but lost under Magloire. To consolidate that power, the Duvalier regime had to introduce new and "more drastic politico-organizational" techniques. "The victory of Duvalierism is explained by the effective conjunction of the ideological and political weapons that it alone could put together under the circumstance [of the crisis of 1946–56]" (Hector 1972, 63).

The Duvalier regime shifted the *balance of political power* toward the black bourgeoisie and middle class and achieved a greater degree of autonomy from the bourgeoisie as a whole. Those were its primary objectives. Control over the state apparatuses offered the only sure avenue for the social and economic advancement of the black middle class because of the limits of private-sector development and the exclusive barriers imposed by the domestic and foreign bourgeoisies. It did not intend or attempt to eliminate the economic dominance of the mulatto bourgeoisie as such nor the exploitative economic system on which that dominance rested. The regime simply sought to force the social and political accommodation of the mulatto bourgeoisie with the black bourgeoisie and middle class—in short, a pact of domination between them—as the only way for the latter to share the spoils of the extant economic system.

At the end of the first decade of the Duvalier dictatorship, the consequences of the regime's politics and policies were evident. It is estimated that the number of people killed during Duvalier *père*'s rule was as high as 50,000 (Prince 1985, 36). The terrorism of the state against its citizens; the corruption and extortionary practices of government officials from the highest to the lowest makouts; the reprisals against the mulatto bourgeoisie; the suppression of dissent, political parties, trade unions, and intellectuals; and the exile (forced or voluntary) of many of the most well-educated and professional cadres of the country, all had their toll in the overall decline of economic activity and in aggravating the already miserable economic conditions of the vast majority of Haitians. Rather than developing, the Haitian economy was regressing. In all sectors (agricultural, industrial, service, and tourism), Haiti experienced a marked decrease in productivity and investments, both domestic and foreign.

The standard of living of the majority of Haitians deteriorated significantly under the regime of Papa Doc. The per capita gross domestic product (GDP) declined from about $80 in 1950–51 to $74 in 1967–68, and the per capita income went down from $67 in 1962 to $62 in 1967. In 1967, Haiti had the highest infant mortality rate in the Americas (147 per 1,000), with 50 percent of children dying before the age of five; the lowest life expectancy (47.5 years); a generalized malnutrition and the lowest daily per capita consumption of calories (1,700) and protein (40 grams); a total of 332 medical doctors, or 0.68 doctors per 10,000 inhabitants (in contrast to about 1.5 per 10,000 persons in Guatemala, the next lowest); and 0.67 hospital beds for every 1,000 people (compared with 1.9 per 1,000 in the Dominican Republic). Only 2.6 percent of all houses (compared to 12.1 percent in Guatemala) and 21 percent of all urban residences (43 percent in Guatemala) had piped water, and only 0.1 percent had indoor plumbing. There were 17.4 kilowatt-hours of electricity per capita (compared with 164 for the Dominican Republic); 1 telephone per 1,000 inhabitants (compared with 63 in Barbados), almost all of them in the capital city; and 200 miles of paved roads and 2,000 miles of unpaved roads (Barros 1984, 1:37–38; Rotberg 1971, 6–11).

The cost of capturing and consolidating political power for the black bourgeoisie and middle class under Duvalier's leadership was therefore very high. In the process, Duvalier alienated the mulatto bourgeoisie and the United States, as well as the other Western European powers. Though he was prepared to lose the support of the mulatto bourgeoisie initially, he could least afford to do without the backing of some of the Western European powers and especially of the United States. It was therefore essential for Duvalier to maintain good relations with the United States—but not at the expense of his regime, its objectives, and its practices. In short, Duvalier accepted his dependence on foreign capital, but under certain conditions that he was not willing to compromise. Duvalier was willing to offer all the necessary advantages to foreign capital, such as tax exemptions, an abundance of cheap labor, and a climate of labor peace due to the suppression of all independent labor organizations and the banning of strikes. In return for these concessions, Duvalier expected to be given foreign economic and military assistance, especially from the United States, but without the latter interfering in how he governed the country. As Gérard Pierre-Charles aptly put it, the "essence of Duvalier's political economy [was to transform] Haiti [into] a second Puerto Rico. But this aspiration also [had] a pragmatic content. The North American investors would come to develop the industries, and mister President would exercise the administrative and repressive functions" (Pierre-Charles 1973, 65). Neither foreign investors nor the U.S. government responded as Duvalier had hoped until after 1966.

Through his clever exploitation of the United States' fear of communism and Haiti's proximity to Cuba, Duvalier finally managed to win U.S. support, though not to the degree he had sought. After the successful Cuban Revolution and the failed Bay of Pigs invasion by U.S.-backed Cuban exiles, Duvalier managed to get a reluctant United States to increase its aid package to Haiti. From 1958 to 1962, Haiti received a total of $70 million in gifts and loans from the United States despite the knowledge that the money would be used by the regime to reinforce the makouts and/or stolen by government officials. It was not until the "reelection" of Duvalier in 1961 and the continued corruption and brutality of the regime that Haitian-U.S. relations soured to the point where the administration of President John F. Kennedy suspended all economic and military assistance in 1963. The Kennedy administration, however, made no attempt to topple Duvalier, probably because of the recent debacle of the Bay of Pigs invasion. Haiti continued to receive only small amounts of aid channeled through international organizations, antimalaria cooperation from the United Nations, and surplus food distribution from the

United States. Duvalier turned to France, the other Common Market countries, and even to Czechoslovakia to fill the gap, but to no avail (Pierre-Charles 1973, 103, 107, 114; Rotberg 1971, 237–39; Diederich and Burt 1969, 379).

Despite the cold shoulder given to the regime by foreign governments, it survived. In fact, it could be said that in many ways the international ostracism of the Duvalier regime forced it to turn more to the citizens of Haiti to extract from them the revenues it needed to maintain itself in power. As mentioned earlier, the regime invented many novel ways to extort monies from the population and to divert the profits of state-owned enterprises for its own use. Those measures, combined with its absolute political power, put the regime in a stronger position to exert its autonomy, even if at great cost to the economy and society (Moïse 1980, 5). The Duvalier regime was willing to allow the economy to deteriorate rather than give in to the pressures of foreign governments to modify its repressive and corrupt practices. In the end, Duvalier succeeded in compelling both the reluctant mulatto bourgeoisie and the United States to accept his regime and to deal with it. After 1966, several factors combined to make an accommodation between the Duvalier regime, the mulatto bourgeoisie, and the United States possible.

Duvalier may have been a barbaric tyrant, but he was also staunchly anticommunist and knew how to exploit the East-West conflict. For the United States—which had failed to launch a successful invasion against Fidel Castro's Cuba, had drawn strong international criticism for overthrowing the democratically elected government of Juan Bosch in the Dominican Republic, and was getting more deeply involved in an unpopular war in Vietnam—it was far more desirable to acquiesce to the Duvalier regime than to alienate it further and push it to seek ties with the Eastern bloc, as Duvalier feigned. After the assassination of President Kennedy, the United States resumed its assistance to Haiti but through numerous inter-American or international organizations, such as the IDB and the Food and Agricultural Organization (FAO), rather than directly from the U.S. government. For its part, the Duvalier regime, now secured in its power, could rein in the makouts. Repression was no longer a daily necessity because the regime had succeeded in eliminating or intimidating the internal opposition or forcing it into exile. Thus repressive practices could be relaxed and targeted against designated "political activists," especially "communists"—the label attached to all those who opposed the regime, whether or not they belonged to a Marxist or socialist organization or identified themselves as such. The projection of this new image of political stability and less open repression paid off. In 1969 President Richard Nixon renewed full military and economic aid to Haiti, and the recovery experienced by the economy during the two years prior to the death of

François Duvalier could be mainly attributed to the improved political climate (Pierre-Charles 1973, 153, 158–59; Rotberg 1971, 248; Walker 1984, 206).

Besides winning renewed economic and military aid from the United States, the "new image" of the regime aimed at a reconciliation with the mulatto bourgeoisie, now politically tamed, and at encouraging foreign capital investment, now that a climate of political stability had been created. The reconciliatory moves toward the mulatto bourgeoisie also entailed a marked decrease in the antimulatto rhetoric of the early years. For its part, the mulatto bourgeoisie realized that the Duvalier regime concerned itself primarily with the monopoly of state power and not with the economic expropriation of the mulatto bourgeoisie, even though the regime tampered with the interests of that bourgeoisie by taking over some enterprises it once owned. Faced with the choice of joining the opposition, most of which was in exile, or acquiescing to the rapacious Duvalier dictatorship to protect its own interests, the mulatto bourgeoisie chose the latter. Besides, the regime's repressive policies toward workers benefited the bourgeoisie directly and offered other advantages such as tax evasion and participation in the generalized fraudulent practices of the government.

Foreign capital, too—especially that sector that relied on intensive labor production—saw many advantages in investing in Haiti. The abundance of cheap labor, the containment of all labor discontent, the generous fiscal concessions of the government, and the proximity of Haiti to the United States, all served to attract foreign assembly manufacturers to Haiti. Between 1967 and 1970, nearly 100 foreign companies, primarily from the United States, signed contracts to install plants in Haiti. Bauxite and copper production also increased, and tourism nearly doubled, passing from an annual average of 35,000 tourists between 1965 and 1967 to 51,156 in 1968 and 60,000 in 1969. The GNP, which in 1965–67 grew at an annual rate of 1.5 percent, jumped by 2.5 percent by 1969, its total value increasing from $366 million to $376 million (Pierre-Charles 1973, 161).

THE HEREDITARY DICTATORSHIP AND THE NEW "PACT OF DOMINATION" WITH THE BOURGEOISIE

By the time François Duvalier died and his nineteen-year-old son Jean-Claude succeeded him to the presidency in April 1971 (after the constitution had been amended to lower the age requirement for the presidency), a new pact of domination had been formed among the Duvalier regime, the black nationalist bourgeoisie and middle class, the mulatto bourgeoisie, and foreign capital. Jean-Claude Duvalier claimed as his objective the implementation of the proposed but as of yet unfulfilled "economic phase" of the "Duvalierist Revolution" (*Nouvelle Optique* 1972, 1). The government would act as the broker for the interests of the other two partners in the pact to promote the country's development.

The United States quickly endorsed the new regime as the best guarantee for stability. In 1972, the United States established new development assistance programs for Haiti. International aid agencies, including the World Bank, the IDB, the UN Development Program, the World Food Program, the FAO, the World Health Organization, the Organization of American States, the Inter-American Institute for Agricultural Cooperation, and about 130 private nongovernmental organizations, followed suit and resumed or started economic and other forms of assistance, as did France, Belgium, and Canada. Whereas total foreign aid during the 1960s amounted to $384 million in the form of official development assistance (multilateral and bilateral sources), it was $540 million from 1972 to 1981. From 1981 to 1985, net official development assistance (from all sources) totaled $657 million, and in 1985, overseas development assistance accounted for 8 percent of GNP. Nearly 80 percent of foreign aid came from the United States, the World Bank's International Development Association, and the IDB (DeWind and Kinley 1986, 30, 55–56; Walker 1984, 206–8; Prince 1985, 31; Voltaire 1982, 11; World Bank 1987, 244).

The partners in the triple alliance were not equal. The United States assumed the responsibility for financing the Haitian government through foreign aid, despite its awareness of the widespread fraudulent practices and misappropriation of public and aid monies by government officials. In return for this support, the Haitian government pursued pro-U.S. policies and opened the country to U.S. capital and products. The Haitian bourgeoisie also agreed to play its role as a subordinate partner to foreign capital by accepting the conditions imposed by the U.S. manufacturing assembly contractors and by collaborating with the regime. As Leslie Péan put it, the mulatto bourgeoisie came to accept the Duvalier regime as "second best."

> In the absence of an acceptable alternative, an "optimal" solution [was] to draw back and to coexist. The question [was] one of viable survival for a social class that always [stayed] close to reality but that [continued] nonetheless to question the political hegemony claimed by Duvalierism. (Péan 1985, 24)

The accession of Jean-Claude Duvalier to power caused some changes in the balance of forces within the regime itself. Conflicts developed between the "old guard," which coalesced around the widow of François Duvalier and the faithful servants of the late father who wanted to maintain the nationalist thrust of the regime, and the "new guard" of the "technocratic" cadres who served as advisors and cabinet ministers in the new government. The latter reflected the rapprochement with the mulatto bourgeoisie (Nicholls 1984, 260).

One of the first signs of change was the abandonment of the strident black nationalist ideology of the father's regime. This meant that the regime of Jean-Claude Duvalier no longer counted on the black bourgeoisie and middle class as its primary base of support, but instead sought to broaden that support to include the mulatto bourgeoisie. A clear indicator of the break with the nationalist ideology came in 1980 when President Duvalier defied his mother to marry Michele Bennett, a member of the mulatto bourgeoisie. As Rod Prince observed, the marriage "signified a fundamental change in the politics of Duvalierism as practised by Jean-Claude" (1985, 31).

The substance of Duvalierism, however, remained the same—that is, absolute control over the state apparatuses and the repressive forces to maintain power, this time with full backing from the United States. The alliance of the regime with the mulatto bourgeoisie and foreign capital revealed once again the real objectives of the subordinate black bourgeoisie and middle class: sharing the spoils of the extant economic system through the monopoly of state power. The abandonment of the black nationalist ideology, however, deprived the son's regime of its claim to power and hence undermined its ability to stave off the mounting challenge for a democratic alternative that emerged in 1980. Thus, although the rapprochement with the mulatto bourgeoisie appeared to widen the regime's base of support, it in fact weakened it politically.

One of the first signs of the realignment of forces came with the reorganization of the VSN (the makouts) and the armed forces to solidify the power base of the new regime. Under the guise of modernization, a new elite military force, the Leopards, equipped and trained by the United States, was created. To neutralize the power of the "old guard," Jean-Claude Duvalier increased the authority of the regular armed forces by integrating many of the most trusted members of the makouts into a regular corps of the army and by placing the entire VSN corps under the nominal and operational command of the army. This reorganization henceforth placed real power in the hands of the commanders of the Leopards, the Presidential Guard, and the Dessalines Barracks. By 1983, the armed forces numbered 7,000, the Presidential Guard 800, the Leopards 600, and VSN members about 10,000 (Pierre-Charles 1973, 171, 177–78; DeWind and Kinley 1986, 31; Prince 1985, 38).

There was yet another shift away from the practices of the father, who had centralized all decision making in his own hands and those of the makouts who marched under his orders. Jean-Claude Duvalier was made president-for-life by the new constitution of 1983 with the right to appoint his successor-for-life, a practice first introduced during the Saint-Domingue Revolution by Toussaint Louverture in 1801 when he appointed himself governor-general-for-life. Duvalier also continued to rule essentially by decree, since the legislature had only endorsed the government's decisions and never initiated any legislation. The essential difference introduced by Duvalier *fils* was the creation of a cabinet government and a National Planning Council (*Conseil National de Planification*, or CONADEP) composed of university-educated experts who were appointed to various ministerial posts. Though this new structure did not mean that the government would become more efficient and less corrupt, it transformed the regime "into a more ideologically orthodox dictatorship which [ran] on lines understood by [those] in charge of the United States" (Prince 1985, 33, 36).

The new structure did not signal the end of feuds between the "old dinosaurs" (the old guard's popular name) and the "new technocrats" over appointments to the ministerial posts, as the frequent cabinet reshufflings indicated. Though it was desirable to appoint ministers acceptable to Washington, they were not to take their responsibilities so seriously as to jeopardize or expose government corruption. This was the case, for example, with former finance minister Marc Bazin (a former World Bank official) who was dismissed in 1982 after five months in office for accusing the government of mismanagement and claiming that up to 36 percent of government revenues had been expropriated by unnamed individuals (Prince 1985, 34).

The Duvalier government, in fact, increased its mechanisms of wealth appropriation by intervening more deeply in the economy and encroaching further on the interests of the private-sector bourgeoisie. It did this in three ways: by extending the monopoly of state enterprises over the sale of items of basic necessity, by increasing taxes, and by creating new state enterprises to compete with or undermine private-sector enterprises producing primarily for the local market. As under Papa Doc, the *Régie du Tabac* continued to serve as the principal source of nonfiscalized funds for the regime of Baby Doc. In addition to the manufacture and sale of tobacco products and matches, the *Régie* appropriated the income derived from the taxes on many consumer items such as milk, herring, codfish, soap, and detergents (Honorat 1980–81, 5).

Two other state enterprises, the *Minoterie d'Haiti* and *Ciment d'Haiti*, had monopolies on the importation and sale of wheat and flour and of cement, respectively. To increase their profits, the government charged higher prices for those products than the consumers would have paid if they had been allowed to buy them on the open market.

Together, these three state enterprises brought tens of millions of dollars per year directly into the coffers of the regime to be used however the president and his close collaborators saw fit, while simultaneously increasing the cost of living for the already impoverished population. It was estimated that the *Régie* brought in $20 million per year, and that in 1982–83 and 1983–84 the *Minoterie* had a net profit of $10 million and $17 million, respectively (Péan 1985, 33).

In addition to the existing state enterprises that the Duvalier government took over, the regime created two new ones that also had a detrimental effect on the private sector and the national economy. These were the *Usine Sucrière Nationale de Darbonne* (USND), a sugar mill, and the *Société d'Exploration des Oleagineux* (SODEXOL), an oilseed company to produce edible and industrial oil products and other substitutes for milk and meat. The latter was jointly owned by wealthy potentates of the Duvalier regime, the Haitian government, and an Israeli-Panamanian consortium, and it benefited from a variety of fiscal privileges and exemptions. Both industries directly undermined already existing and profitable private enterprises and increased costs to consumers for their products (Péan 1985, 32).

In keeping with the practices of the prebendary system, the wealth generated by these enterprises was not used to expand or improve infrastructure development or social services to the Haitian population, but rather to enrich the potentates of the regime, support the makouts, finance the secret activities of the government, and bribe citizens to cooperate with the regime (Honorat 1980–81, 4–5). It was estimated, for example, that in 1984 the personal fortune of Jean-Claude Duvalier was $450 million and that of his mother was approximately $1.2 billion, which was more than Haiti's GNP in 1979 (Péan 1985, 33).

Moreover, high regime functionaries were not the only ones who participated in the corruption and misappropriation of monies; lower-level government employees down to the lowest makout participated as well. Entry in the clientelistic network in fact presupposed acceptance of and participation in these fraudulent practices, even though the small circle of close Duvalier associates appropriated the lion's share of the monies. In all the government ministries and their subdivisions, one's employment required the payment of a bribe to an official. For example, customs service workers stole goods from incoming shipments and resold them to the merchants who originally ordered them; workers from the public electricity company for a fee installed devices that reduced the meter readings of the amount of electricity consumed; telecommunications employees installed unregistered additional telephone lines; public water supply workers diverted water to certain residences by shutting off others under their jurisdiction; and building inspectors were bribed to overlook irregularities or additions made to buildings without construction permits (Godard 1983, 11).

The U.S. government and the international lending agencies were well aware of the fraudulent practices of the Duvalier family and Haitian government officials. In 1980 the International Monetary Fund (IMF) recommended that the Haitian government take drastic measures to end its misuse of public and nonfiscalized funds, implement fiscal reforms, and restore fiscal balance and the resources of the National Bank of Haiti (*Collectif Paroles* 1981, 7). The Haitian government responded by centralizing tax collection under the Internal Revenue Service and Customs, closing special accounts, unifying government spending in a single treasury account at the Central Bank, and implementing a new income tax, a general sales tax, a reference price system for the valuation of coffee exports, and a tax on luxury goods, alcoholic beverages, and cars. These reforms did little to reduce or end government corruption or eliminate the multimillion-dollar line item for "special obligations" in its annual budget. They were enough to satisfy the IMF, however, which gave its stamp of approval on renewed loans and assistance (DeWind and Kinley 1986, 93–94).

The United States and the international financial institutions it controls, such as the IDB, the World Bank, and the IMF, had committed themselves to supporting the Duvalier regime. This was because of Haiti's "strategic" location, sharing the Windward Passage to the Caribbean Sea and the Panama Canal with Cuba, and hence the "security interest" it represented for the United States (Hooper 1987, 33). Moreover, the Duvalier government followed a pro-U.S. foreign policy, offered important advantages to foreign capital investments in general and to U.S. investors in particular, and unquestioningly accepted the free market and development strategies offered as solutions to Haiti's problems. These strategies, of course, did not include ending the inherently corrupt practices that were the sine qua non of the regime's existence, even though they undermined the economy and hence the policy recommendations of the foreign backers.

Foreign capital, in other words, accepted the Duvalier regime for what it was and willingly took over from the Haitian government the tasks of building or expanding infrastructures, such as building roads, bridges, sewers, wharfs, power plants, water supply systems, and telecommunications facilities; providing social services, such as food and health care; and devising development projects in agriculture and industry, such as providing credit and technical assistance to the Agricultural Credit Bureau, the Institute for Agricultural and Industrial Development (IDAI), institutional development projects, and various regional agricultural organizations (Walker 1984, 211–14).

The United States Agency for International Development (USAID) and the World Bank became directly involved in designing and implementing Haiti's development strategy through successive five-year plans. From 1972 to 1986, three such five-year plans were devised and financed with foreign aid. About 65 percent of Haiti's development projects were financed with foreign aid for the

1972–81 period, and over 73 percent of all development expenditures were financed with foreign loans and grants. The 1982–86 Development Plan was 77 percent financed by international aid. Foreign aid funded 70 percent of public investments and 44 percent of domestic investments from 1976 to 1980 and largely financed the increases in GDP investments, from 10.6 percent in 1970 to 15.1 percent in 1980. Therefore, increases in foreign aid largely accounted for the growth rate in real GDP, which went from 3.8 percent annually during the 1970–75 period to 4.5 percent during the 1976–80 period (DeWind and Kinley 1986, 48; Hooper 1987, 33; Walker 1984, 207, 216; Péan 1985, 31).

Haiti lacks the natural resources that could have made it a target for massive capital investments from the core countries and hence placed the Haitian bourgeoisie and state in a stronger bargaining position vis-à-vis foreign capital. Its bauxite and copper reserves were relatively small and were exhaustively mined by foreign transnational corporations until they ceased operations, in 1972 for copper and in 1983 for bauxite. Drilling for oil proved worthless, and no other minerals had been discovered in sufficient quantities to attract investors (Barros 1984, 1:17). Agricultural production for export and industrial investments that rely on cheap labor supplies, therefore, constituted the main attractions for foreign investors. The latter type of investment became the basis of the development strategy adopted by the Haitian government and its foreign aid suppliers and planners.

Consistent with the objectives of the United States in the Caribbean, especially since the introduction of the Caribbean Basin Initiative by the Reagan administration in 1981, the strategy envisioned for Haiti aimed at integrating the Haitian economy more thoroughly with the U.S. economy. This was to be done by moving away from public-sector investments to supporting private-sector development and production for export. This entailed, on the one hand, investing in agribusiness production by diverting 30 percent of all cultivated land from producing for the local market to producing export crops, despite the knowledge by USAID experts that this would cause the expropriation and impoverishment of tens of thousands of small farmers. On the other hand, the strategy entailed establishing manufacturing assembly industries for export (DeWind and Kinley 1986, 48; Hooper 1987, 33). The first strategy failed to re-create large-scale plantation production for export for the same reason that all the previous attempts had also failed, namely, the highly inequitable distribution of land and resources among the rural population, the predominance of small farms and dispersion of the holdings of individual farmers, and hence their incompatibility with capital-intensive technology (DeWind and Kinley 1986, 69–70). However, the free-and-open-market agricultural strategy of the USAID, combined with the food aid programs, had disastrous consequences for Haitian farmers and Haitian agriculture.

The policies of food aid and cheap food imports from the United States encouraged by the USAID were designed to alleviate food surpluses in the United States. Though much of it entered the country illegally and with the complicity of Haitian government officials, the importation of such foodstuffs as rice, cooking oil, soya, and milk powder undermined domestic cereal and rice production because of the farmers' inability to compete with the cheaper imports. Cow and goat farmers were also displaced by the importation of cheaper poultry from Miami. Lastly, to prevent the spread of swine fever, the government, at the urging of the USAID, exterminated the entire domestic pig population and began replacing them with pigs imported from the United States (Caribbean Conference of Churches 1987, 5).

These policies and practices resulted in the overall decline of the agricultural sector as a whole. Whereas that sector had an annual growth rate of 1.1 percent for the period 1970–80, it had negative growth rates from then until the fall of the Jean-Claude Duvalier in 1986. Yet, the rural sector received the least attention from the government in terms of public expenditures: 54 percent of the total in 1976 went for 74 percent of the population, in contrast to 28 percent for Port-au-Prince alone, with only 14 percent of the population (Barros 1984, 1:124–26; DeWind and Kinley 1986, 108; Honorat 1980–81, 14; Talbot 1987, 8–9; Girault and Godard 1983, 8).

Thus, as in the past, although the vast majority of farmers were landed, their farms were too small and they faced too many adverse social, economic, and political circumstances to be able to produce enough to meet their own and the nation's needs. Seventy-eight percent of the rural population lived at or below the level of absolute poverty, in contrast to 55 percent of the urban population. In 1983, agriculture contributed 32 percent of the GDP and satisfied only 75 percent of the nation's food needs, thereby increasing the demand for food imports and food aid to supply the other 25 percent. By the latter part of the 1970s, Haiti was spending as much on food imports as it earned from its agricultural exports (Prince 1985, 43, 53; Honorat 1980–81, 15; DeWind and Kinley 1986, 109; 131; World Bank 1987, 230).

Only the second strategy—the establishment of manufacturing assembly industries for export—was successfully implemented, though it would exacerbate rather than alleviate Haiti's underdevelopment and poverty. The establishment of manufacturing assembly industries in Haiti was yet another form of a Caribbean-wide process of penetration of the region by U.S.- and European-based transnational corporations. More than 1,740 branches, subsidiaries, or affiliates of U.S.-owned corporations and more than 560 from foreign countries other than the United States dominated the Caribbean economies in sectors such as raw material and mineral extraction/refining, insurance, corporate finance and banking, tourism, and manufacturing assembly industries. Referred to as "industrialization by invitation," this new manufacturing assembly industry strategy was seen as an alternative to that of "import substitution" development advocated by the international financial institutions during the 1950s and 1960s. Even though the latter strategy led to the creation of many industries and increased manufacturing production in many Caribbean countries, it failed to reduce the need for imports of consumer goods, capital, and technology or to generate the growth of locally owned import substitution industries in the Caribbean that could successfully compete with foreign manufactured goods (Barry, Wood, and Preusch 1984, 6, 14).

During the 1970s and early 1980s, the assembly industries became the most dynamic sector of the Haitian economy. From accounting for 6.5 percent of total exports in 1970, the assembly industries represented 15.2 percent of total exports by 1977. By contrast, bauxite exports represented an average of 12.5 percent of the total during the 1970s (peaking in 1974), and coffee exports remained in the lead during the 1970s, accounting for more than one-third of total exports and about 25 percent of all export earnings in 1983 (Barros 1984, 1:69–71; Prince 1985, 45). By the end of the 1970s, manufacturing assembly exports accounted for about 25 percent of all the income generated in the manufacturing sector and about the same proportion of Haiti's export earnings and employed 80 percent of the workforce in the industrial sector (Grunwald, Delatour, and Voltaire 1984, 243; Péan 1985, 30–31).

The assembly industries produced finished or semifinished goods by using imported technology and raw materials. The principal goods produced by the assembly industries fell in the categories of electronic and electric products, textiles and garments, and sporting goods, mainly baseballs. The industries producing garments, electronic products, and baseballs constituted two-thirds of manufacturing production in Haiti, employed 75 percent of the industries' workforce, and accounted for 90 percent of the assembly industry exports (*Nouvelle Optique* 1972, 4; DeWind and Kinley 1986, 153, 158).

The main point to emphasize here is that the manufacturing assembly strategy did not alter the international division of labor between foreign and Haitian capital. That is, it did not give rise to an autonomous manufacturing bourgeoisie in Haiti that was able to compete with foreign capital. The reverse occurred. The sector of the Haitian bourgeoisie involved in the manufacturing assembly industries remained totally dependent on and subservient to foreign capital, assumed most of the costs and risks, and took in a lesser share of the profits.

The Haitian economy remained underdeveloped because the agricultural sector remained backward and dominated essentially by mercantilist relations of exchange, while foreign capital dominated the enclave-like manufacturing sector—the most dynamic sector of the economy—and repatriated the bulk of the profits. The triple alliance, in other words, failed to alter Haiti's dependence on production for export (of agricultural or of assembly of semifinished manufactured goods) and create a more diversified and integrated industrial base that could produce for export while simultaneously contributing to an expanded development of the national market and productive forces.

By the mid-1980s, Haiti had become the most impoverished country in the Western Hemisphere by any measure. Compared to the other Caribbean countries, Haiti had the highest infant mortality rate (123 per 1,000), the lowest life expectancy (53 years), the lowest literacy rate (23 percent), the lowest ratio of access of population to piped water in the urban and rural areas (21 and 3 percent, respectively, in 1982), and the lowest annual per capita income ($310) (Barry, Wood, and Preusch 1984, x–xi; World Bank 1987, 202, 258, 260). As already noted, about 78 percent of the rural population and 55 percent of the urban population lived under conditions of absolute poverty. By 1985, Haitians as a whole were consuming 20 percent fewer calories and 30 percent less protein (40 percent and 50 percent, respectively, in the rural areas) than the recommended daily amounts. Chronic malnutrition affected one-third of all children under five years old and, along with gastroenteritis, accounted for 90 percent of child deaths. Also in 1985, 90 percent of the population earned less than $150, and fewer than 20 percent of workers employed full-time received the official minimum wage of $3 per day. Only the approximately $125 million a year sent back to Haiti by the more than 680,000 Haitians living abroad (12 percent of the population) helped prevent a desperate situation from getting worse (Hooper 1987, 32–33; DeWind and Kinley 1986, 8–14).

By contrast, the Haitian bourgeoisie, which constituted only 1–2 percent of the population and derived its wealth from the exploitation of the rural and urban working classes, appropriated 44 percent of the national income, and 24,000 people owned 40 percent of the country's wealth. Between 1981 and 1985, President Jean-Claude Duvalier, his wife Michele, and their close collaborators were estimated to have stolen more than $505 million from the public treasury (Prince 1985, 51; Hooper 1987, 36).

By 1980, it became quite clear that the so-called economic revolution that was to follow the so-called political revolution implemented by François Duvalier would not materialize, and that the neo-Duvalierism of the son, defined as "Duvalierism reconsidered, corrected, and broadened" was a total failure (Chamberlain 1987, 17). Despite the massive amounts of foreign aid and the establishment of the assembly industries, the society and economy were in shambles. The top government officials, the foreign investors, the Haitian bourgeoisie, the clientelistic and technocratic cadres that supported the Duvalier regime, and the larger base of the makouts were the primary beneficiaries

of the regime's policies and practices (Moïse 1980, 5–6). For the vast majority, the three decades of Duvalierism had meant political repression and abject
poverty of the worst kind. The provincial cities were stagnating, and the countryside was paralyzed and was depopulating at the rate of 30,000 per year to
the cities, primarily Port-au-Prince. Thus, while the process of proletarianiza-
tion quickened, the limited industrial development in the urban areas offered
no viable alternative to the despoiled farmers. After migrating to the urban
centers only to face continued and grueling deprivation there, hundreds of
thousands migrated abroad as seemingly the only escape. As Alex Stepick
observed, this mass migration was neither economic nor political alone,
but stemmed from the very process of underdevelopment, the policies of the
nation-state, and the struggles for control of the nation-state (1984, 347). The
triple alliance, in short, exacerbated rather than resolved the social, economic,
and political crisis of the nation.

Within this context, an opposition mass movement emerged during the
1970s and especially after the aborted political opening of 1978–79 and the
renewed waves of repression of 1980. This movement signaled that the Duvalier regime no longer monopolized the political space and that the opposition was beginning to reflect aloud about the country's problems and their solutions (Moïse 1980, 5–7; 1990, 2, 423; Moïse and Olivier 1992, 70–72). This
movement drew particular significance from the fact that it was the first major political opposition movement since the 1915–34 U.S. occupation of Haiti
to emerge in the provinces before it spread to the capital city of Port-au-
Prince (Nicholls 1986, 1243). The domestic opposition movement, backed by
the Haitian immigrant communities in the United States and encouraged by
President Jimmy Carter's human rights foreign policy in 1976–80, compelled
the regime of Jean-Claude Duvalier to contemplate democratic reforms. The
dictatorship knew that it could not survive a free and open democratic contest
for power, however, and that it could maintain itself in power only through
force and by monopolizing the political space. In the dual tendency of liber-
alization and repression that marked the 1970s and 1980s, the latter prevailed
and proved once and for all that the dictatorship could not be reformed and
could not resolve the economic, social, and political impasse it had reached
(Moïse and Olivier 1992, 67–69, 85).

Once the popular movement gathered momentum in the 1980s, the Duvalier regime, which had seemed so powerful and unshakable, crumbled more
quickly than expected. The regime certainly had at its disposal the military
means to suppress the popular protest movement, but the conjuncture of 1986
was such that it could no longer revert to that practice. For its part, the domestic and external opposition movement, though primarily nonviolent, had
gained much momentum and legitimacy. It had become a force to be reck-

oned with, and it gradually succeeded in eroding the alliance among the bourgeoisie, the Catholic Church, foreign capital, and the U.S. government that had supported the Duvalier regime.

The alliance between the regime of Jean-Claude Duvalier and the bourgeoisie meant that the regime had to abandon the strident black nationalist discourse that solidified the dictatorship of François Duvalier among the black nationalist faction of the middle class. Thus, the regime of Jean-Claude Duvalier undermined its own base of support among the black middle class and gave rise to divisions between the "old" and the "new" guards. This loss of support among the black middle class also meant that the old methods of repression used by the father and justified by the black nationalist cause against the "mulatto threat" could no longer be applied effectively by the son. Equally as important, Jean-Claude Duvalier began to lose support within the ranks of the Duvalierist military officer corps, and reported threats of a coup d'état further weakened the regime (Dupuy 1989, 155–68; Ferguson 1987, 143).

Though the regime of Jean-Claude Duvalier had served the interests of the bourgeoisie primarily by suppressing the labor and peasant movements, the growing illegitimacy of the dictatorship compelled the bourgeoisie to distance itself from it. The bourgeoisie and the private-sector professional and managerial classes received encouragement from the mounting criticisms directed at the regime by the hierarchy of the Catholic Church. The openly political role of the Catholic Church after the crackdown of 1980 weakened the regime because of its considerable influence among all sectors of the population. Pope John Paul II himself encouraged the Church's opposition to the Duvalier regime during his visit to Haiti in 1983 by denouncing the regime's violence and declaring that "things must change in Haiti" (Wilentz 1989, 118).

By openly contesting the Duvalier regime and holding it accountable for its corruption and repression of dissidents, the Church opened the way for its most progressive sectors—in particular, the proponents of liberation theology and participants in the ecclesiastical base community movement known in Haiti as the *Ti Legliz* (Little Church)—to assail the dictatorship (and the entire system of exploitation which it presupposed) and to express their "preferential option for the poor."[5] By siding openly with the oppressed and impoverished population, the Church and the Ti Legliz movement played a significant role in furthering the political consciousness and mobilization of the masses (Delince 1993, 134–36; Midy 1991, 85).

For its part, the U.S. government faced two alternatives. It could either continue to back the discredited Duvalier dictatorship and risk a further radicalization of the opposition and the spread of anti-U.S. sentiment or it could abandon the regime and hopefully prevent another Cuba, Nicaragua, or El Salvador in the region. The United States chose the second alternative, compelled Duvalier to step down, and turned to the military to contain the opposition with the promise of democratic elections (Ferguson 1987, 121, 152; Hooper 1987, 30–31). Trouillot best summarized the role of "international interests" in Duvalier's ouster:

> Duvalier's departure . . . [was] a multinational exercise in "crisis management," a calculated break in the democratic path that the Haitian people had embarked upon. We may never learn the details of the negotiations [that led to Duvalier's departure], but negotiations there were. And we need not know these details, or fully investigate ex–U.S. Marine Colonel Oliver North's claim to have brought an end to Haiti's nightmare, to be certain of one crucial fact: Jean-Claude Duvalier was brought down by a high-level coup d'état executed with international connivance (1990, 226).

The "international interests" played the role they did primarily because the Duvalier regime was beleaguered by an opposition movement, completely isolated, and unable to solve the impasse it had reached.

NOTES

1. For a fuller analysis of the creation of the new ruling classes in Haiti during the revolutionary period and after independence, see Dupuy 1989, 51–113.

2. The United States occupied Haiti between 1915 and 1934, and those in charge of the occupation handpicked two of the four presidents during that period. Also excluded in this count are the five provisional governments between December 1956 and September 1957 when François Duvalier was elected president with the support of the military.

3. Dahomay is on much stronger ground when he locates the absence of a democratic or republican tradition in Haiti in the class relations, structures, and practices of power in Haiti rather than in the transcendental Hegelian notion of the *immediacy* of the slave revolution. This immediacy and the personalistic power it gave rise to rested in the fact that the slaves were recognized as objects rather than as "free men" and were subjected to a naked, extralegal power. To this, the slave "opposes a dialectic of liberation that poses liberty in its nudity, that does not have time to think in terms of mediations that open on the totality of the social" (14–15). As such, then, the revolution gave rise to a "*liberation* from the servile condition and not the institutional conditions of *liberty*." It is because of the absence of such institutional conditions of liberty in the young Haitian state, then, that "the values that drove the problematic of liberty . . . were those of heroism and the institutional weaknesses of the Haitian state were inevitable" (13–14). Insofar as the "reign of *immediate* liberty prevailed," it

"could not but lead to a specific type of political power, that which became individualized in the will and capriciousness of chiefs" (15).

In my view, Dahomay and others who share a similar perspective (e.g., Jean and Maesschalck 1999) have gotten the Saint-Domingue Revolution and the concept of liberty the slaves articulated all wrong. Suffice it to say here that their essentially idealistic interpretation of the slaves' concept of liberty is at odds with Dahomay's attempt to locate the tendency toward authoritarianism in the concrete class relations and structures generated by the struggle for power during and after independence, as it is with my own.

4. For a detailed analysis of the political history of Haiti since the end of the U.S. occupation in 1934, see Dupuy 1989, 143–55.

5. The "preferential option for the poor" is discussed in the next chapter.

Chapter Three

The Prophet Armed: The Popular Movement for Democracy and the Rise of Jean-Bertrand Aristide

PRELUDE TO JEAN-BERTRAND ARISTIDE

From the fall of the hereditary Duvalier regime in February 1986 until March 1990, Haiti experienced an unparalleled political crisis marked by the rise and fall of four military-dominated governments and an unrelenting popular struggle for a democratic alternative. Complex struggles during that period lay at the root of the general crisis and paralysis of the country. On the one hand, the Duvalierist forces attempted to retain and consolidate their control over the state apparatuses and the government. On the other hand, the broad-based popular movement fought to create a democratic government that would prioritize the multiple needs and aspirations of the impoverished majority for a just, egalitarian, and participatory society. The policies of the United States overarched the struggles of the opposite camps and must be considered among the balance of forces operating within Haiti.

Two tendencies were evident within the forces favoring democratic change. On one side were certain sectors of the Haitian bourgeoisie and the professional and managerial middle classes who had abandoned the pact of domination with the Duvalier dictatorship but feared the masses. Sensing the winds of change and believing that they stood to benefit from the creation of a democratic order, the "enlightened" sectors of the dominant class sought to establish a representative democracy to legitimize the rule of the bourgeoisie and preserve its privileges. Their objective, then, was to create a minimalist democracy. On the other side was a plethora of social groups and forces representing a broad cross-section of society, including professional and political organizations, workers' associations and trade unions, women's groups, religious and lay community organizations, neighborhood committees, and peasant organizations. This array of social forces represented various interests that together amounted to demands for land redistribution, jobs, workers' rights, human rights, and a more equal distribution of income and resources—in other words, a maximalist democracy. Though decentralized organizationally and ideologically divergent, these forces represented the broad popular movement for a more inclusive and participatory democracy that sought to transform an exclusionary social system dominated by a small wealthy elite and a rapacious and tyrannical dictatorship supported by the core powers (especially the United States, France, Canada, and the international financial institutions).

Those who wanted to preserve the status quo of the previous three decades opposed both expressions of the democratic movement. They included principally the social groups for whom total control of the military, the state, and the public sector enterprises and bureaucracy—that is, the prebendary state system—represented the only guarantee for safeguarding the power and privileges they acquired during the thirty-year Duvalier dictatorships. They constituted the neo-Duvalierists who fought to perpetuate Duvalierism without the Duvaliers, and which included both hardcore and more moderate factions of the ancien régime. Allied to the neo-Duvalierists was the tiny—but wealthy and powerful—sector of the haute bourgeoisie that benefited from the dictatorial regimes and opposed any change that would threaten their class privileges, along with conservatives in the United States who saw the military as the only force capable of preventing the emergence of a democratic movement that challenged the existing class system.

My objective here is not to analyze in great detail the four-year period between Duvalier's downfall in 1986 and the election of Aristide in 1990.[1] Rather, I want to focus on the characteristics of the broad democratic movement and what it made possible.

The popular movement that emerged after 1986 differed in several respects from the one that confronted the Duvalier regime before then. This broad social movement took many different organizational and political forms. It included several political groupings, professional associations, democratic coalitions and human rights organizations, radicalized community-based religious groups, women's organizations, neighborhood committees and civic action groups, trade unions, peasant cooperatives, and a plethora of newspapers, journals, and radio programs expressing a broad range of views and agendas of the popular opposition movement. The emergence of an independent media played a singularly strategic role in the opposition movement. As Franklin Midy argues, the independent press, within which radio broadcasts played a prominent role, implanted the idea of independence from the absolute power of the state. It launched the struggle for freedom of information and expression by informing the population of events and issues that the government tried to suppress. By allowing the transmission of news, events, and ideas that expressed the grievances, aspirations, and critiques of the powerless and the victims of the dictatorships, the independent press became engaged politically and played a key role in the national struggle for democracy (Midy 1991, 78–80).

The national scope of the opposition movement expressed a decline in the dominance of the capital city of Port-au-Prince as the hub of political activity. The views and struggles waged by this broad and varied movement taken together represented nothing less than a call for the restructuring of Haiti into a democratic, just, and egalitarian society (Soukar 1987, 19; Pierre-Charles 1988, 65; Ferguson 1987, 160). As Gérard Pierre-Charles put it, this popular movement was a

> truly democratic revolution that began in the minds and hearts of the people prior to the mass uprisings against the Duvalier regime. It [was] an ongoing process born from the belly of the system of oppression that has made the Haitian people the most exploited and poorest of the hemisphere. (1988, 65)

The characteristics of this broad and decentralized democratic movement meant that no single political organization or individuals would emerge as its identifiable leaders. This was the most important virtue of that movement for, without identifiable leaders, the cadres and participants of the movement could not be easily targeted and eliminated. Hence, the movement as a whole could withstand and survive the repression directed against it by would-be dictatorships that succeeded the Duvalier regime. The absence of a centralized organization and an identifiable leadership also meant that, apart from a broadly shared consensus against would-be neo-Duvalierist dictatorships, the opposition movement did not articulate a unified alternative vision or a national political platform for a reconstructed Haiti (Moïse and Olivier 1992, 87). Nonetheless, the aggregated demands advanced by the popular movement amounted to nothing short of a call for a radical democratic reconstruction of Haitian society.

It is in this context that one can measure the significance of the creation in January 1987 of a broad, left-of-center, social democratic coalition known as KONAKOM, the *Komité Nasyonal Kongrès Oganizasyons Démokratik* (National Committee of the Congress of Democratic Organizations). KONAKOM's objective was to create a popular, progressive, and democratic government as an alternative to the discredited dictatorial system that benefited the privileged few (Soukar 1987, 13, 53; Chamberlain 1987, 20). As it became the most active opponent of the *Conseil National de Gouvernement* (CNG, National Council of

Government)—formed after Duvalier's exile by the "connivance" of the U.S. government, the Haitian military leaders, and the hierarchy of the Catholic Church—and the most articulate proponent of progressive alternatives, KONAKOM prevented the centrist and right-of-center political leaders and their parties or political groupings[2] from monopolizing the political discourse. The determined struggles waged by KONAKOM and the issues it put on the agenda played a large role in the new constitution that was drafted and approved by an overwhelming majority of voters in the March 1987 referendum.

The 1987 Constitution was the most progressive Haiti had ever known.[3] Calling for the creation of a parliamentary democracy, it barred former close collaborators of the Duvalier regime from running for or holding public office for a period of ten years. Going beyond the traditional liberal provisions, the constitution embodied several social democratic principles and articles that conformed to the concepts of social and economic justice discussed previously. It called for a thorough agrarian reform and declared that health care, housing, education, food, and social security were fundamental human rights, in addition to those of personal liberty and freedom of thought, religion, and political association. In yet another significant acknowledgment of the historical exclusion of the majority of Creole-speaking Haitians, the constitution declared Creole an official language along with French, the language of the educated and propertied classes.

To deter the consolidation and prolongation of power indefinitely by the president of the republic, the new constitution counterbalanced his or her power with that of a prime minister chosen from the party having a plurality of seats in both houses of the National Assembly (the Senate and Chamber of Deputies). The presidential term was set at five years, with the possibility of a second term only after an absence from office of five years. A system of checks and balances and of power sharing among the president, the prime minister, and the two houses of parliament was instituted to prevent the monopolization of power by the executive. Ministers and secretaries of state had to be chosen jointly by the president and the prime minister and, once formed, the government had to be approved by the two houses of the National Assembly. The president still had the power to appoint high state functionaries, but often this was to be done with the approval of the Senate, as was also the case for nominating the commander of the army, chief of police, and ambassadors, among others.

As it preserved the right to private property, the constitution did not undermine the privileges of the propertied classes, but it did strike at the heart of the Duvalierist system and its traditional means of perpetuating itself in power. As Claude Moïse concluded, the greatest innovation of the 1987 Constitution was that it sought to redistribute power among the three branches and redefined their relationships, while also creating autonomous institutions and new regional and local assemblies to achieve a certain degree of decentralization of political power (Moïse 1990, 467). Even though the constitution embodied the principles of a representative democracy, which historically has been compatible with and conducive to the rule of the propertied classes, it opened the door to progressive reforms aimed at moving toward a more egalitarian and redistributive maximalist democracy that responded to the interests of the disempowered and impoverished majority. The constitution not only embodied lofty principles in the abstract but also registered the aspirations and the struggles of the heterogeneous forces opposed to the continuation of dictatorship of any kind. It was a

> product of all the conflicts of interests, the sociopolitical demands, and, above all, the relations of forces between the diverse social and political sectors, as well as the points of formal agreement. It [was] a project of popular participation in creating a society with a new kind of relationship between the state and the people—in other words, a democracy. (Pierre-Charles 1988, 71)

In this context, the demand for its adoption and implementation was nothing short of revolutionary, and the Duvalierist forces understood it as such.

The progressive forces regrouped around KONAKOM realized that they could not force the CNG out of office and that the electoral route offered the best opportunity to oust the Duvalierist forces from the government and the state apparatuses once reform-minded and democratic forces gained control of them. It was at this point that fifty-seven organizations within KONAKOM formed the *Front National de Concertation* (FNC, National United Front) to contest the parliamentary and presidential elections scheduled for November 29, 1987, and nominated Gérard Gourgue, the former CNG minister of justice, as their presidential candidate. Though Gourgue was a moderate and a centrist, the FNC chose him as its candidate anyway because of the belief that he could defeat the other two major candidates, Marc Bazin and Louis Déjoie II, who were more right-of-center and were supported by the bourgeoisie and the United States. Nonetheless, Gourgue's choice as the candidate of the left-of-center FNC was controversial within the organization and reflected the conflicting tendencies within it (Soukar 1987, 16).

Because of these internal conflicts, the FNC never issued a political platform that spelled out its program of government. Though moderate forces had prevailed in the choice of Gourgue, several left-of-center organizations, such as the *Blòk Inyon Patryotik* (BIP, Patriotic Unity Bloc) and *Komité Inité Démokratik* (KID, Democratic Unity Committee), continued to militate within it. Even though the FNC had not declared itself socialist, the very presence of organizations like these two within it sufficed for the CNG and the U.S. State Department to tag it a leftist/communist front. The FNC's candidates for the legislature and the presidency were seen as dangerous and, thus, had to be prevented from winning. Well before November 1987, it had become clear to many activists and observers of Haitian politics that the CNG would not allow the elections to take place. Ironically, the same forces who opposed the CNG and represented the spearhead of the struggle for democracy that would bring Aristide to power in 1991 would oppose him from 2000 to 2004, but this time by entering into an alliance with neo-Duvalierist forces and supported by the United States, France, and Canada.

A public opinion poll conducted in Port-au-Prince in August 1986 indicated that Gourgue was not the candidate who was most popular, most well known, or most likely to win the elections. To the contrary, Bazin, the right-of-center leader of the *Mouvement pour l'Instauration de la Démocratie en Haiti* (MIDH, Movement for the Establishment of Democracy in Haiti), was seen as the best-known presidential candidate in the country and the one most likely to win. He was also thought to be the favorite candidate of the United States and the CNG. Bazin was followed in the opinion poll by presidential candidates Sylvio Claude, a centrist and leader of the *Parti Démocrate Chrétien d'Haiti* (PDCH, Christian Democratic Party of Haiti), and Hubert de Ronceray, a former Duvalierist and leader of the *Parti de la Mobilisation pour le Développement National* (PMDN, Mobilization for National Development Party) (Laguerre 1987, 15–18).

These findings notwithstanding, the CNG, the military, and the Duvalierist forces in general considered the constitution and the elections scheduled for November 29, 1987, to pose a real threat to their continued political dominance and privileges. The Duvalierists, both within and outside the government and the military, had become socially isolated. The candidates who represented the interests of the bourgeoisie, like Bazin and Déjoie, had joined with the candidates representing other social interests and the Left to demand the application of the famous Article 291 of the 1987 Constitution, which barred all former close collaborators of the Duvalier regime from seeking office for ten years. All the presidential candidates agreed that the elections should be organized and supervised by the independent *Conseil Electoral Provisoire* (CEP, Provisional Electoral Council). The sectors of the bourgeoisie that had broken with the Duvalier regime supported the holding of free elections because they were confident that one of their candidates would win them, thereby allowing that class to reassert its political influence, legitimize its dominance, and attract new foreign investment and foreign aid in Haiti. Moreover, the legitimacy gained from the elections would allow the bourgeoisie to contain the more radical fringes of the democratic movement, by force if necessary, by branding them as extremists and antidemocratic.

For the neo-Duvalierist forces, the holding of free elections that they could not control and that excluded their candidates from participating represented a major threat to their continued hold on the government and the state apparatuses as the only means to "guarantee the continuity of the interests established by the last thirty years of dictatorship" (Louverture 1987, 8). Faced with the certainty of losing the elections, the neo-Duvalierists vowed to wage a civil war if their candidates were prevented from running for office—as they were when the CEP published the list of eligible candidates on November 2, 1987. It then became clear that the CNG intended to sabotage the elections scheduled for November 29.

In addition to refusing all logistical and other support to the CEP, the CNG allowed soldiers and *makouts* to unleash a wave of terror throughout the month. When on election day the people still defied the threats and turned out to vote en masse, soldiers and makouts opened fire on them, killing at least twenty-two and wounding another sixty-seven. The CNG immediately canceled the elections and disbanded the independent CEP. Gen. Henri Namphy, the head of the CNG, justified its actions on the grounds that, if the elections had been held, the CEP would have handed victory to a candidate of the Left—a claim for which there was no basis in fact (Louverture 1987, 8–16; Saint-Gérard 1988, 81–83; Chamberlain 1988, 1). Former U.S. ambassador to Haiti Brunson McKinley sided with Namphy when he accused Gourgue of being "at least a Communist front man, if not a Communist himself," and declared that the CEP was "being run by foreign leftists" (Wilentz 1989, 327).

Whoever (other than the military's choice) would have won the elections, whether from the bourgeoisie or from the Left, would have been perceived as a threat by Namphy and the Duvalierists and would not have been allowed to take office. As with both Duvaliers, Namphy understood quite well that dictatorship was the only means of retaining power and that only someone who could be controlled by the military could be "elected" president. For its part, the U.S. State Department, which had historically relied on dictatorial regimes to preserve the existing social system and prevent the coming to power of elements potentially inimical to U.S. interests, mildly protested the election-day massacre and continued to defend the CNG as the best guarantor of democracy in Haiti (*Caribbean and Central America Report* 1988, 6). The Reagan administration, always apprehensive about the Left and more partial to dictators in the region, was not willing to force the Haitian military to accept a democratic alternative.

The CNG had achieved its objective. The Duvalierists were kept in power, but at great cost. The election-day massacre completely illegitimatized the CNG nationally and internationally. The four so-called major presidential candidates—namely, Marc Bazin, Louis Déjoie II, Sylvio Claude, and Gérard

Gourgue—joined together to create the *Comité d'Entente Démocratique* (CED, Democratic Agreement Committee) to condemn the CNG, demand the restoration of the independent CEP, and oppose and abstain from any new elections organized and supervised by the CNG. The U.S. Congress as well as other foreign aid donors cut off all nonhumanitarian economic and military assistance to the CNG, although the Central Intelligence Agency continued to train, finance, and equip the *Service d'Intelligence National* (National Intelligence Service) as well as paying key members of the Haitian military. Such payments continued until shortly after the coup d'état against President Aristide in September 1991 (Weiner 1993).

Responding to these pressures, the CNG decided to hold new elections on January 17, 1988, but this time under its own appointed Electoral Council. Chosen by the CNG as its candidate, after prodding by the United States and Jamaica, Leslie F. Manigat was "elected" president on January 17 with less than 10 percent of the electorate voting in what all independent Haitian and foreign observers agreed were fraudulent elections (Chamberlain 1988, 2). As a staunch anticommunist, a member of the International Christian Democratic Party, and a person with connections in other Caribbean countries (notably Venezuela and Jamaica) and the U.S. intelligence and conservative political communities, Manigat was seen as the perfect man for the job. As with the elections in Honduras and El Salvador, the United States, still captive to its Cold War mentality, sought to have elections in Haiti that would yield a weak president who would remain subservient to a powerful military. Despite acknowledging that the elections were fraudulent, the U.S. State Department welcomed Manigat's "election" as a positive development that would "move Haiti in a democratic direction" (*Haiti Beat* 1988, 11).

Manigat lasted less than five months after he took office in February 1988. Relations between Manigat and the military soon soured. Contrary to expectations, Manigat was unable to deliver on his promise to win the renewal of military and economic assistance, and hence some sort of legitimacy, from foreign aid donors. In an attempt to increase revenues, he initiated a policy of fighting contraband trade and sought to pursue legal actions against Jean-Claude Duvalier to recoup the hundreds of millions of dollars allegedly stolen by him. Both of these actions threatened vested interests within the armed forces. Moreover, Manigat seemed unable to do anything about those powerful military officers who were implicated by the U.S. State Department in international drug trafficking.

Thus, in an attempt to remove some top military officers and consolidate his power, Manigat appeared to align himself with the very officers opposed by the State Department. Reacting to this apparent move against them, the same officers of the former CNG who had chosen him for the presidency backed a coup d'état organized by noncommissioned officers in June 1988. Though the Reagan administration publicly decried the coup, it was the first to recognize the new military government with General Namphy again as its head (Wilentz 1989, 335–36).

Namphy, who claimed that Haitians were not yet ready for elections and democracy, declared that his government would rule by decree. He subsequently abolished the 1987 Constitution, which he condemned for having introduced "elements that are foreign to Haiti's history and traditions" (*Haiti Observateur* 1988; *Haiti en Marche* 1988d). Though Namphy had been accepted by the army as the president of the new military government, deep divisions remained within the higher ranks of the army. Several factions, and factions within factions, rivaled each other to capture the presidency and control the military establishment, with none of them favoring turning power over to an elected government. As Amy Wilentz put it, the Haitian army was "a collection of gangs run by individual *gwo nègs* (strongmen)" (1989, 372).

Knowing the precariousness of his support within the military hierarchy, Namphy quickly moved to ally himself with some of the most notorious henchmen of the Duvalier regime responsible for countless crimes, including the election-day massacre in November 1987. He also reintegrated many former makouts into the army to increase his base of support among the rank and file (*Haiti en Marche* 1988b; Wilentz 1989, 337–38). To intimidate the democratic opposition movement, Namphy unleashed a campaign of terror against various sectors—especially the progressive peasant organizations struggling for land reform and the radical liberation theology movement led by the influential priest Father Jean-Bertrand Aristide—that had strong roots in the urban working-class and poor communities.

General Namphy's actions made it clear that he aimed to consolidate not only his own power but also that of the worst elements of the Duvalier regime. Had he succeeded, the makouts would have regained their prominent positions in the army and in the other state agencies as well. That possibility, coupled with the increasing brutality of the second Namphy government, sparked another coup d'état on September 17, 1988. Namphy was forced to leave Haiti, and the noncommissioned officers who led the coup installed Gen. Prosper Avril as Haiti's new president.

As soon as he took over, Avril sought to consolidate his power by forcing fifty-seven top-ranking officers and potential rivals to retire. Seeing an opening provided by the "soldiers' rebellion," citizen vigilante groups from working-class and poor neighborhoods unleashed a new wave of "uprooting" the makouts. All over Port-au-Prince, bands of makouts, particularly those who had participated in the bloody Sunday, September 11, 1988, massacre at Father Aristide's church at Saint Jean Bosco, were hunted down, beaten, and killed. The demand for immediate justice in the capital echoed throughout the provinces, and for a moment it appeared as if the country was on the verge of another popular uprising (Wilentz 1989, 363; *Haiti en Marche* 1988a).

The "soldiers' rebellion," however, proved ephemeral. General Avril, in effect, used the rank and file to his own benefit. By allowing them to get rid of Duvalierist officers and makouts loyal to his rivals in the officer corps, Avril was in a stronger position to avert possible countercoups and could proceed to consolidate his own power—which he swiftly did. Having gotten rid of some of the most powerful Duvalierist officers, Avril then moved against those who helped put him in power. Charging that soldiers were plotting a coup d'état against him on October 15, 1988, Avril arrested fifteen noncommissioned officers, among them one of the leaders of the coup of September 17 that overthrew Namphy. By striking at the anti-Duvalierist forces among the rank and file and noncommissioned officers, Avril appealed to his "right flank" among the Duvalierist officers and civilians allied to him, who also opposed the "democrats" whom they saw as their ideological enemies (Wilentz 1989, 379).

Avril, as a former financial manager for the Duvalier family and a personal aide to the younger Duvalier before he rose to prominence, had no intention of breaking with Duvalierism. An astute politician and tactician, Avril had learned from his long association with François Duvalier that to remain in power he had to be ready to sacrifice his friends and strike at his enemies or enlist others to do his dirty work for him. He demonstrated this skill very early in his career as president (Wilentz 1989, 379; *Haiti en Marche* 1988a).

In addition to his constant vigilance and political maneuvering, Avril, like many of his predecessors, kept himself in power by buying loyalty from others. This took many forms, including augmenting the salaries of public employees and the soldiers of the Presidential Guard; misappropriating the profits of the public enterprises; and all sorts of favoritism, such as allowing certain officers and even soldiers to buy goods from public enterprises or military warehouses at subsidized prices and resell them on the market at substantially higher prices. Another practice consisted of granting to certain favorites of the government a share of the goods imported by the government, such as rice and sugar, which they resold to the merchant who in turn retailed them on the national market. Among the nefarious consequences of these practices was an increase in the deficit of the government budget by $60 million in just one year (*Haiti en Marche* 1989b, 1989c). The preservation of these practices and the spoils of office notwithstanding, the White House and the State Department were not yet ready to abandon Avril, for fear of the alternative.

The inclusion of Duvalierists and non-Duvalierists in his thirteen-member ministerial cabinet also reflected an attempt on Avril's part to placate simultaneously his Duvalierist constituency, some sectors of the bourgeoisie, and the more moderate opposition. Avril also sought to satisfy the undaunted opposition movement (which demanded the scheduling of new legislative and presidential elections) and to win the renewal of military and economic aid from the U.S. Congress (which insisted on the holding of free elections as a precondition for the renewal of such aid). In November 1988, Avril decreed the formation of an Electoral Council that would be in charge of drafting an electoral law and of organizing and supervising the elections. Contrary to the 1987 Constitution, which required that the members of an electoral council be nominated by independent and representative institutions (such as the Catholic and Protestant churches, the Association of Journalists, and human rights organizations), the members of the new Electoral Council were to be nominated by Avril's government and chosen from the nine provinces of Haiti. Such a decision guaranteed that only individuals loyal to Avril would be appointed, undermining the credibility of the council from the start (*Haiti en Marche* 1988b).

When the new CEP issued its electoral calendar in September 1989, it was not at all surprising to see that it reflected Avril's expressed desire to spread out the elections into three stages, starting with the municipal, followed by the legislative, and finally the presidential. The process was to begin in April 1990 and end with the presidential elections in November 1990. Having the voting spread out in three stages and at different times would undoubtedly make it easier for Avril to manipulate their outcome while keeping his promise to hold "free" elections (*Haiti en Marche* 1989a).

The U.S. Congress refused to renew economic and military aid to the Avril regime because it remained unsatisfied with Avril's performance. In addition to demanding the scheduling of new free and fair elections, Congress included many other preconditions for the renewal of aid, which Avril could not meet. Among the more important were the reinstatement of the 1987 Constitution, respect for human rights, disarming the makouts, ending corruption in the public administration, greater cooperation with the United States in the "war on drugs," and accepting the preeminence of civilian over military rule. Congress, at this time, was far ahead of the Reagan White House in its willingness to push for a democratic alternative and raise the cost to the Haitian military for not conforming to its dictates.

The puzzling question was, why were Congress and the members of the Congressional Black Caucus who played a key role on the question of aid to Haiti so determined to press their demands with Avril when they had supported the Duvalier regimes and the CNG despite their refusal to hold elections, their deplorable human rights records, and their widespread corruption? The answer could be that, having been deceived and embarrassed by Namphy, they were not willing to fall for Avril's promises and wanted to see concrete and sustained action on his part before resuming U.S. aid.

Two other hypotheses are more plausible. The first had to do with the international conjuncture of 1985–89, when the emergence of *glasnost* and *perestroika* in the Soviet Union in 1985 and the momentous "democratic revolutions" in Eastern Europe in 1989 signaled the demise of Soviet Communism and the Soviet bloc and the end of the Cold War. Closer to home, the Sandinista government in Nicaragua was facing a major economic crisis caused largely by the U.S.-financed Contra war; it was compelled to move considerably to the right economically in 1988 and adopt a stringent structural adjustment program to curb inflation and the rising debt burden by cutting social spending and social services, lowering wages, and allowing unemployment to rise. Politically, the Sandinistas were also on the defensive and agreed to hold internationally supervised elections in February 1990.

Similarly, in a dramatic rethinking of their strategy after their early 1989 "strategic counteroffensive," the Farabundo Marti National Liberation Front (FMLN) in El Salvador decided to seek a negotiated end to the civil war and form a broad multiclass coalition with the aim of participating in national and presidential elections. This left Cuba as the only socialist government in the region, and the aim of U.S. policy was to isolate the Castro regime as the only nondemocratic government in the hemisphere. Congress, therefore, did not want to allow a dictatorship to reestablish itself permanently in Haiti. It saw free and fair elections as the only way to legitimize governments in the region. The U.S. Congress, if not yet the White House and the State Department, understood that military dictatorships were no longer needed to assure U.S. dominance in the hemisphere and that the Cold War containment ideology could no longer serve as an ideological cover for supporting such dictatorships. The premises of the post–Cold War "New World Order imperialism" foreign policy guidelines of the United States were beginning to be formulated by Congress in shaping its policy toward Haiti.

The second hypothesis is that in Haiti the democratic Left had not yet reorganized itself to face new elections by coming forth with a presidential candidate capable of challenging the other center-right candidates. If elections were held soon, one of those candidates was likely to win, with a good chance that the winner would be Marc Bazin, the United States' favored candidate. Bazin, who had shown his willingness to compromise with the military, would not likely pursue widespread criminal indictments against military officers and might not even challenge the preeminence of the military as an institution in Haitian politics.

Even if the Left won the elections, it would be powerless to implement the social and economic reforms that, when adopted by other progressive governments in the past, irritated the United States and provoked its covert or overt interventions to undermine or overthrow those democratic governments. The beginning of the end of the Soviet bloc, the discrediting of socialism as an alternative to capitalism, and the global shift to anti-statist and pro–free market policies advocated by the "Washington Consensus" meant that a left-of-center government in Haiti would have little choice but to come to terms with the "rules of the game" of international capitalism. It would have nowhere else to turn for support. Even if the Left in Haiti had not yet understood that the principles of self-determination, a by-product of the Cold War, died along with the latter, for the U.S. Congress, the United States had nothing to lose and everything to gain by pressing for elections in Haiti. So, it decided to distance itself from the Avril regime.

Avril could not meet the demands of the U.S. Congress. Controlling the government, the state apparatuses, the military, and the public bureaucracy was the principal base of power, privilege, and social promotion for the neo-Duvalierists and their middle-class supporters. To allow free elections that would inevitably end up in victory for some sector of the democratic opposition, which could then introduce reforms in the public administration and the military to curb corruption and disarm the makouts, was tantamount to class suicide for the neo-Duvalierist forces. And without the neo-Duvalierists, Avril was nothing.

Sensing that Congress might be serious about its conditions for the renewal of financial aid and that his government was becoming increasingly isolated nationally from the bourgeoisie, the Catholic Church (which had renewed its criticism of the government's human rights abuses), and the moderate opposition once willing to enter into a dialogue with him, General Avril reinforced his ties with the Duvalierist "old guard." At the same time, in a move reminiscent of Namphy's tactics to strengthen his power, Avril talked of "safeguarding the sovereignty of the nation" against foreign interference in the internal affairs of Haiti, an obvious reference to his displeasure with the U.S. Congress's recalcitrance on the aid question. He also hinted that the soldiers of the army might hold a plebiscite to have him remain as president for five years or more.

No one took Avril's nationalist pronouncements seriously. His regime, like those of his predecessors, had no legitimacy. As with the previous dictatorships, only force, not rule by popular mandate, could maintain Avril in power. The end of his administration was marked by a renewed wave of random murders, armed robberies, and repression of targeted sectors of the democratic opposition—including the arrest, torture, and assassination of leaders of independent trade unions, political organizations, and peasant cooperatives—by the military and paramilitary gangs of *attachés* (*Haiti en Marche* 1989e; *Haiti Observateur* 1989a, 1989c).

The climate of insecurity created by these practices was designed to spread panic among the population and disarm the opposition. These tactics were similar to the ones adopted by the CNG when it faced an opposition movement determined to struggle for the election of a civilian government as a precondition to a transition to democracy. This was precisely the situation confronting Avril. The opposition had launched a call for unity against dictatorship, and different organizations formed alliances to consolidate their forces. Twenty-five political organizations, including many of the left-of-center and radical groups, joined together to form the Common Front Against Repression. Bazin's center-right party, the MIDH, formed an alliance with the center-left *Parti Nationaliste Progressiste Révolutionnaire Haitien* (PANPRA, Progressive Revolutionary Nationalist Haitian Party), led by socialist Serges Gilles, and the *Mouvement National Patriotique–28 Novembre* (MNP-28, National Patriotic Movement–November 28) to form the *Alliance Nationale pour la Démocratie et le Progrès* (ANDP, National Alliance for Democracy and Progress). Six other parties also called for the unconditional departure of the Avril government and temporary transfer of power to the Cours de Cassation (Haiti's highest court of appeal) in accordance with the constitution (*Haiti en Marche* 1989d; *Haiti Observateur* 1989b, 1989c).

Avril responded by stepping up his attacks against the opposition between November 1989 and January 1990. He also sought unsuccessfully to obtain financial support from Taiwan. Rebuked by all sectors, Avril eased up on his repressive measures and called for a dialogue with the "moderate opposition," but to no avail. Washington and Paris remained silent and indifferent to these moves, with the former insisting on its demand to restore constitutional rights and the electoral process, and the latter canceling a planned visit to Haiti by the French minister of cooperation and development. Most sectors of the opposition renewed their call for unity and for Avril's departure, and the ANDP, which was most moderate in its demands and had been willing to dialogue with the regime, remained steadfast with its conditions for participation in the elections. These included respecting the 1987 Constitution, allowing the return of exiled political leaders, modifying the electoral calendar to hold presidential and parliamentary elections simultaneously, and having those elections supervised by the United Nations. More damaging still for Avril was the resignation of his ambassador to Washington, who declared that the recent violations of human rights by the regime made the holding of free elections and a transition to democracy impossible in Haiti. Similarly, in a sermon delivered on February 14, 1990, the bishop of Jérémie, Monsignor Willy Romélus, declared that elections were impossible under Avril and called for his departure (*Haiti en Marche* 1990f; Maguire 1991, 11–12). Completely isolated, discredited, and illegitimatized, Avril received the famous "phone call" from U.S. Ambassador Alvin Adams,[4] who compelled him to re-sign and leave Haiti on March 12, 1990 (*Haiti en Marche* 1990a).

The fall of the Avril regime was a major defeat for the neo-Duvalierist forces and a significant victory for the broad democratic opposition and for U.S. diplomacy. Had the White House and the State Department decided to oppose Congress and renew economic and military assistance to his regime, Avril might have weathered the storm of the opposition movement with stepped-up repression and consolidated his power. Likewise, had the popular opposition movement not been united against Avril and the preceding regimes, and had it not shown its determination to press for a democratic al-ternative despite the brutality and large-scale repression it suffered at the hands of the successive military governments, the concentration and prolon-gation of power by the Duvalierist forces after 1986 would have been a fait accompli.

It was not a given that the fall of Avril would lead to the formation of an interim civilian government and the organization of democratic elections un-der international supervision. Here again, the unity of the opposition move-ment, at least in terms of its desire for a democratic alternative, allowed it to seize the moment and take advantage of the opening created by Avril's defeat. Moreover, the internecine conflicts within the higher ranks of the army split it in such a way that no military officer dared seize power. The combination of the absence of another military strongman capable of taking power and the momentum of the democratic opposition led to the creation of an innovative transitional power-sharing formula that neutralized the neo-Duvalierists (for a time) and paved the way for the organization of the December 1990 elections.

The democratic opposition, temporarily unified under the umbrella of the *Assemblée de Concertation* (Unity Assembly), formed a transitional govern-ment. The government comprised a provisional president chosen from among the Supreme Court justices, a nine-member ministerial cabinet, and a Coun-cil of State that included representatives of the eleven political parties that formed the Unity Assembly, plus the *Komité Tèt Ansanm pou Onè Respè Kon-stitisyon* (Unity Committee to Honor and Respect the Constitution) headed by Father Antoine Adrien. An accord signed on March 4, 1990, between Pro-visional President Ertha Pascal-Trouillot, a former justice of the Supreme Court, and the Council of State made it clear that the latter would exercise overall control and vigilance over the government.

The Council of State was empowered to approve most decisions made by the provisional government before they could take effect. They included the nomination of the ministerial cabinet; all decrees issued by the president; all treaties, agreements, and international conventions negotiated by the provisional government that were not binding for the democratically elected government-to-be; and the overall economic and political orientation of the provisional government. Equally as important, the Council of State retained the right of veto over presidential decisions and the right to a vote of no confidence against the government (by a two-thirds majority of the members of the council). By contrast, the provisional president did not have the power to dissolve the Council of State (*Haiti en Marche* 1990c).

In practice, relations between the president and the Council of State soured as Pascal-Trouillot tried to usurp the prerogatives of the Council of State and exercise power independently. Contrary to the stipulations of the March 4 accord, President Pascal-Trouillot nominated members of her cabinet and heads of state agencies and even issued presidential decrees without consulting the council. The greatest rift between the executive branch and the Council of State occurred over the return to Haiti from exile of some notorious henchmen of the Duvalier regime, including Roger Lafontant, former interior minister under Jean-Claude Duvalier (1982–85) and head of the *Tontons Makout*, and Gen. Williams Regala. Haitian and international human rights organizations accused Lafontant of supervising the torture of prisoners and persecuting members of the clergy and the press. Regala was accused of complicity in the massacre of voters during the November 1987 elections (French 1990; Chamberlain 1990a, 7; *Haiti en Marche* 1990b).

Standing behind the principle that the separation of powers prevented the interference of the executive branch with the judicial system, Pascal-Trouillot deferred the enforcement of the warrants to the courts. The courts, in turn, passed the responsibility on to the police, who refused to act. Infuriated by this game of "passing the buck," the Council of State responded by issuing a deadline for the provisional president to resign if she did not take action against Lafontant and Regala. The intervention of the U.S. ambassador and a split within the Council of State, however, allowed Pascal-Trouillot to survive. Those members of the council who were also presidential hopefuls believed, along with the CEP and the U.S. ambassador, that to force the resignation of Pascal-Trouillot and dissolve her government was dangerous adventurism that would set back the electoral process. They therefore dissociated themselves from the call for her resignation (Chamberlain 1990b, 7).

For their part, the Duvalierists understood quite well the significance of the Council of State in the present conjuncture. As a product of the popular struggles and expressing the aspirations of the democratic forces, the primary objective of the council was to create the conditions for the organization of elections and the transition to democratic government. To this end, the council intended to be guided by the articles of the 1987 Constitution. One, Article 191, called for the formation of an independent CEP that was empowered to develop the electoral laws and to organize and supervise the elections. This the Council of State did. The president of the CEP declared that it would apply the famous Article 291 of the constitution that barred former close and zealous collaborators of the dictatorial regimes from exercising any public functions for a period of ten years following the adoption of the 1987 Constitution. The massacre of voters in the November 1987 elections had been the response of the Duvalierists to the strict application of this article, and it was anticipated that they would do so again this time around.

Taking the offensive, the neo-Duvalierists attempted to deepen the rift between President Pascal-Trouillot and the Council of State by reviving the "color question" and depicting Pascal-Trouillot as an heiress to Papa Doc Duvalier, and the Council of State as the representative of the reactionary mulatto bourgeoisie. Not satisfied with propaganda alone, the neo-Duvalierists stepped up their violence by attacking the Council of State and assassinating one of its elder members in a failed attempt to kill the council's president (*Haiti en Marche* 1990e; Chamberlain 1990a, 7). The CEP was not to be intimidated, however. The Council of State was encouraged by the U.S. government's willingness to finance much of the election and its warnings to the Haitian military high command that it would not tolerate another coup d'état or interference with the electoral process. The United Nations and Organization of American States decided in early October 1990 to send unarmed observers to supervise and provide security during the voting process, and the Caribbean Community countries offered support and practical help as well. With such international backing, the CEP finally set the presidential and parliamentary elections for December 16, 1990 (Danroc 1990, 109–11, 306; Chamberlain 1990b, 7).

ENTER JEAN-BERTRAND ARISTIDE

The scheduling of elections for December 1990 demonstrated the resolve of the opposition movement and the pro-democratic forces to put an end to dictatorship and build a modern and democratic Haiti. Not everyone in the pro-change camp, however, saw the upcoming elections in the same light. For the sectors of the privileged classes who understood the necessity of a democratic government, the elections represented an opportunity for a pro-bourgeois candidate to gain political power and form a legitimate government that could also contain the more sweeping demands for change emanating from the grassroots movement. For the more progressive and left-of-center organizations, the elections represented a major dilemma. Some activists opposed the elections altogether and argued instead for the formation of a coalition government that would reflect the various sectors of the progressive popular movement. Other organizations and activists engaged in a divisive debate about the desirability and possibility of democratic elections under conditions of continuing violence against the Council of State and the popular democratic forces by uncontrolled sectors of the military and makouts who acted with impunity. While that debate went on, the neo-Duvalierist party, the *Union pour la Réconciliation Nationale* (URN, Union for National Reconciliation), put forward its standard-bearer, Roger Lafontant, as its candidate for president.

At that point, Jean-Bertrand Aristide responded to the challenge by declaring his own candidacy for the presidency. Having made that decision, Aristide did not withdraw his candidacy when, as anticipated, the CEP later disqualified Lafontant from running for the presidency along with several others, including former president Leslie Manigat. Aristide had emerged since the overthrow of the Duvalier regime as the single most important symbol of resistance to the ignominious and kleptomaniac neo-Duvalierist dictatorships. His humble origins also set him apart from most other candidates from well-to-do backgrounds and played a major role in his identification with the impoverished majority and their allegiance to him.

Born in 1953 to a property-owning peasant family of modest means in Port Salut in southern Haiti, Aristide soon moved to the capital city of Port-au-Prince, where he began his education with the Salesian Order at the age of five. Having decided to become a priest very early in his life, he entered the Salesian seminary in Cap-Haitien in 1966. After completing his seminarian studies at the age of twenty-one, he spent his novitiate in the Dominican Republic and went on to study philosophy, psychology, and theology in Haiti, Canada, Greece, Israel, and Italy. By 1975, long before his ordination in 1982, Aristide had defined his position vis-à-vis the traditional Church: his pastoral work would prioritize the poor (Aristide 1990, 33–58).

This "preferential option for the poor" is a basic tenet of liberation theology. It implies not only identifying with the poor and their suffering but, more importantly, the commitment to work alongside the poor and join them in their struggle for liberation (Boff and Boff 1990, 2–9; Gutiérrez 1990, 12–14). This commitment is grounded not only "in the social analysis we use, or in human compassion . . . [but] in the final analysis, in the God of our faith. It is a theocentric, prophetic option that has its roots in the unmerited love of God and is demanded by this love" (Gutiérrez 1990, 14).

It is in this context that Aristide's option for the poor led to the unfolding of "the connecting thread of a theological view which surely brings one back to the one God, that of the excluded, manipulated by the more privileged to maintain an ancestral domination over the poor" (Aristide 1992b, 69). This stance inevitably put Aristide on a collision course with the Catholic Church hierarchy, for it led him to another conclusion, namely, that the Catholic Church in Haiti either compromised with the dictatorships or at least preached acceptance of these regimes. Henceforth, his relationship with the Church in Haiti and with the Vatican would be one of increasing divergence and confrontation. Returning to Haiti in 1985 after nearly six years of study abroad, Aristide found a country "in a state of general mobilization for change" (Aristide 1992b, 66). Having already become an ardent proponent of liberation theology, Aristide soon emerged as one of the most outspoken leaders of the radicalized ecclesiastical base communities movement, known in Haiti as *Ti Kominotés Légliz* or *Ti Légliz* (TKL, literally "little church").

The fusion of mysticism, martyrdom, and anti-*makoutism* added a messianic character to Aristide, whose humble origins appealed to the masses and won him their immediate devotion. As Gérard Pierre-Charles, Claude Moïse, and Émile Olivier have observed, Aristide emerged at a time when the population—crushed by the abject exploitation of the dominant classes, downtrodden by the violence of the dictatorships, and steeped in its own religious mysticism—was ready to accept a savior (Pierre-Charles 1991, 18; Moïse and Olivier 1992, 147). Through his words and actions, Aristide expressed some of the characteristics of charismatic authority. He had developed what Arthur Singham argued was needed by a charismatic leader: a keen understanding of the cultural and social relations that governed the lives of the ordinary people, and the ability to express their grievances in national terms and to exploit his personal relationship with the people to build a mass movement (1968, 148).

As Max Weber argued, the charismatic hero does not obtain his authority from established orders or official enactments. Rather, it is through his actions, by performing miracles or heroic deeds, that the charismatic leader proves his powers. The recognition of a charismatic leader by his followers "derives from the surrender of the faithful to the extraordinary and unheard of, to what is alien to all regulation and tradition and therefore viewed as divine." When thus established, this charismatic authority is not subject to formal laws and regulations, but rather derives its "objective laws" from "the highly personal experience of divine grace and god-like heroic strength and rejects all external order solely for the sake of glorifying genuine prophetic and heroic ethos" (Weber 1978, 2:1114–15).

His or her formal qualities notwithstanding, a leader acquires and exercises charismatic authority in concrete social contexts and at specific historical moments. As such, charismatic authority is always socially and historically contingent. Aristide developed his charismatic powers in the specific context of the post-Duvalier period, the democratic opening occasioned by the dictator's departure, and the popular movement for a democratic Haiti. The significance of this point cannot be overlooked. Aristide did not create the mass movement but rather was created by it. That is, the popular movement against the neo-Duvalierist forces created the conditions for a charismatic persona like Aristide to rise to the occasion and capture its essence like no one else could. Through his sermons at Saint Jean Bosco church and his radio broadcasts, Aristide inspired his followers, the poor, and the population at large, gave them hope, explained to them the nature of the system that imprisoned and impoverished them, and galvanized them into action against the neo-Duvalierist forces. His attacks were not limited to the Duvalierists and the makout system only but were also directed at the United States (which he referred to as the "cold country to the north"), the Catholic Church hierarchy, and the bourgeoisie for their collaboration with the dictatorships and their roles in the exploitation and oppression of the people (Sontag 1990; Wilentz 1990, x–xx).

Aristide likened Haiti to a prison, where the rule of the game was that the "prisoners" (i.e., the poor and oppressed) were presumed guilty by virtue of being poor. They must accept their "prison sentence" (their poverty) without protest, without discussing their social conditions with their fellow prisoners, and without organizing to defend their rights and their interests for fear of worse cruelty or death (Aristide 1990, 34).

In Aristide's view, the Duvalierists intended to maintain power at any cost and, to that end, they deployed permanent violence and repression against the population. The Duvalierists sought to preserve power not simply for its own sake but also because it enabled them to plunder the public treasury for their own benefit. The Duvalierists ran the state and the government like an organized gang, with the Duvalier family originally at its head. Yet, even with the Duvalier family gone (which Aristide likened to the "king" and "queen" in a chess game), the "bishops," "knights," and "rooks"—the lower officials of the regime—remained to take over and perpetuate the system. The military commanders linked to the system had become a mercenary force. The lower echelons, particularly the rural police and section chiefs, benefited from the system principally by extortion and by terrorizing the population (Aristide 1990, 26; 1992b, 70–71).

The Duvalierists, which Aristide often simply referred to as the *makouts*, formed an alliance with the moneyed and propertied oligarchy and protected its interests. In return, part of the profits of the oligarchy went to finance the makouts. The Haitian bourgeoisie, which included the landed and commercial-industrial oligarchy and represented a tiny fraction of the population, was in reality nothing more than a comprador bourgeoisie that mediated between foreign capital and the national economy. Its primary concern was to enrich itself by exploiting the people as much as possible and without regard for their welfare (Aristide 1990, 6–9; 1992b, 71, 74–76). The whole system was shored up by the imperialists from the "cold country to the north" through their military and financial aid. In short, the government and the oligarchy were devoid of any meaningful development or social project, save that of enriching themselves and maintaining the population in their state of ignorance and misery (Aristide 1990, 7–8; 1992b, 71, 76).

Aristide reserved his most detailed and biting criticism for the hierarchy of the Catholic Church. As a liberation theologian and a leader of the TKL movement, he opposed and struggled against the Church hierarchy because it sided and colluded with the bourgeoisie and the dictatorships to exploit and oppress the poor and working people. The Church leaders also sought to suppress the growth of the TKL movement among the rebelling rank-and-file priests and the work they were doing among the poor (Aristide 1992b, 58–60).

The structure of the Church, Aristide maintained, was similar to that of a multinational corporation, like United Fruit, Gulf & Western, or National City Bank. The pope, as the chief executive officer, presided from the headquarters in Rome over the branch plants—the dioceses and churches—all over the world. The principal task of the pope, qua chief executive officer, was to protect the international interests of the corporation and to ensure its efficient operation, uninterrupted growth, and profitability. His role was also to maintain cohesion and prevent dissension among the shareholders and the managers (the archbishops and the bishops) and the rank-and-file employees (the priests and nuns who execute the orders from above). What sets this multinational corporation apart from all the others (and, in a sense, makes it more powerful) is its possession of a secret weapon that allows it to maintain the allegiance and passivity of the final consumers, the people. "That weapon is belief, the long-established belief of the people . . . in the word of the Church" (Aristide 1990, 20–21). Aristide continued:

> The man in Rome and his colleagues are able to wrap company policy up in the proud yellow and white [flag] of the Church. They can pronounce and prettify actions using the beautiful words of the Bible. They can dress up their officers and parade them around the Church as men of God. They can take the policies of United Fruit, Gulf & Western and the National City Bank, all multinational corporations like the Church—with the same interests—and package them along with their own policies, and call that package truth. (1990, 21)

The reactions of the Church hierarchy and the dominant classes to Aristide's views further reinforced the bond between him and his followers. As the popular struggles against the post-1986 military rulers intensified and Aristide gained a prominent leadership role in them, the Church hierarchy, the conservative sectors of the bourgeoisie, the United States, and the military governments saw him as a dangerous "radical firebrand." The Church authorities tried to silence him by transferring him to a parish outside of Port-au-Prince, but each time, his supporters responded by occupying his church at Saint Jean Bosco and the Port-au-Prince Cathedral, forcing the authorities to back down. Failing to achieve their objective with these measures, the Salesians, with the approval of the Vatican, finally expelled him from the order in 1988 for preaching violence and class struggle (Sontag 1990; Wilentz 1990, xv). Drawing an analogy between himself and Jesus Christ, Aristide said later in response to his expulsion that "it doesn't really matter whether I have a church or an order, after all. Jesus Christ, you'll remember, was not a priest" (Sontag 1990).

Aristide's defense against the government's and the Church's accusation that he was preaching class struggle and revolution was that, under certain circumstances, it was legitimate for the people to defend themselves against the brutality and systematic attack by the powers-that-be. As Aristide saw it, the conditions that existed under the rule of the post-Duvalier military governments, which had reacted viciously to the popular movement for social change and democracy, demanded that the people defend themselves. Aristide maintained that it was the privileged classes (including the military rulers and the Church hierarchy) who, through their greed, selfishness, indifference, and unwillingness to share wealth and power with the poorer classes, must bear responsibility for the "class warfare" they accused him of advocating (Aristide 1990, 15–17).

Turning the argument against his accusers, Aristide offered a simple choice to the privileged classes (i.e., those he referred to as "eat[ing] at the great table"): either they avoid class warfare by agreeing to share their wealth and power with the poor or they accept the alternative. "They must accept the simple fact that it is they, and not I and my colleagues, who are advocating war" (Aristide 1990, 17). The image that Aristide often evoked in his discourse was that of the bourgeoisie sitting "at a vast table covered in white damask . . . and eating steaks and pâté and veal flown in from across the water . . . while the rest of my countrymen and countrywomen are crowded under that table, hunched over in the dirt and starving" (Aristide 1990, 9). This situation, Aristide argued, was violent and one day would lead the people under the table to "rise up in righteousness, and knock the table of privilege over, and take what rightfully belongs to them. Brothers and sisters, it is our mission to help them stand up and live as human beings" (Aristide 1990, 9).

Pushing his analysis further, and in keeping with the materialist or historico-structural perspective that liberation theology borrowed from Marxism (Boff and Boff 1990, 27–28), Aristide sought to explain the "laws" that governed human communities in the extant relation of forces:

Life unveils a politics that does not look for the common good but which is based on the relations between exploited and exploiters. The exploiters justify and legalize the exploitation of a majority by a minority. From this human reality whence emerges a negative force, because it does not correspond to the common good and is opposed to justice, there also emerges an opposite force. We thus have the force of politics in which the weak suffers the exploitation of the strong, and the divine force from which the weak rises to reestablish an equilibrium of justice. In other words, theology and politics bring us at the heart of history. (Aristide 1992a, 17)

Aristide's view here corresponded to the classic tenets of liberation theology, which locate the primary cause of poverty and oppression in the socioeconomic organization of capitalist society, whereby some (the workers) are exploited, while others (the underemployed, unemployed, and other marginalized groups) are excluded from the production process altogether. This exploitation and exclusion result in denying the poor access to adequate food, housing, health care, and education, as well as respect for their personal dignity, self-expression, and freedom (Boff and Boff 1990, 26; Gutiérrez 1990, 8).

At this point, it may be useful to make a distinction between liberation theology and Marxism. For Karl Marx and Friedrich Engels, the working class was the only class that could emancipate all of human society because its structural location in the relations of production made it possible for it to abolish its own as well as all other modes of wealth appropriation. All dominant social classes in history, Marx and Engels argued, sought to consolidate their rule by subjecting the rest of society to their forms of wealth appropriation. They succeeded in becoming ruling classes and subordinating other classes because theirs were either movements of emergent minorities or movements led in the interests of minorities. By contrast, the proletariat, because it was the "lowest stratum" in capitalist society with no other classes below it to exploit, "cannot stir, cannot raise itself up, without the whole superincumbent strata of official society being sprung into the air" (Marx and Engels 1978, 482).

As Ellen Meiksins Wood also argued, the working class and its struggles remain at the center of the Marxist theory of social change because it locates the exploitation and political oppression of the working class in the relations of production characteristic of capitalist society. The Marxist proposition that the working class is potentially the revolutionary class is not a metaphysical abstraction, but stems from the materialist premises of the theory (Wood 1986, 14). From this, it also follows that:

(1) the working class is the social group with the most direct objective interest in bringing about the transition to socialism; (2) the working class, as the direct

object of the most fundamental and determinative—though certainly not the only—form of oppression, and the one class whose interests do not rest on the oppression of other classes, can create the conditions for liberating all human beings in the struggle to liberate itself; (3) given the fundamental and ultimately unresolvable opposition between exploiting and exploited classes, *class struggle* must be the principal motor of this emancipatory transformation; and (4) the working class is the one social force that has a strategic social power sufficient to permit its development into a revolutionary force. (Wood 1986, 14–15, emphasis in original)

Marxism is concerned first and foremost with the creation of a socialist society. The liberation of the working class—by the working class itself—is the necessary (if not sufficient) precondition for the emancipation of other oppressed groups. Only by becoming "masters of the productive forces" (Marx and Engels 1978, 482) can the working class carry out the fundamental, structural changes in the social relations of production as well as in the political relations of domination.

Although liberation theology is also concerned with the "this-worldly" social emancipation of the poor and the oppressed, it remains committed to the spiritual or prophetic aspects of liberation. This latter aspect is, in fact, its guiding principle. In its more "classist" interpretation, liberation theology borrowed heavily from the Marxist tenets summarized above and prioritized the exploitation, oppression, and struggles of the "socioeconomically oppressed" over other forms of oppression and discrimination, such as racist, ethnic, or sexual oppression. In the words of Leonardo and Clovis Boff:

> The socioeconomically oppressed (the poor) do not simply exist *alongside* other oppressed groups, such as blacks, indigenous peoples, women—to take the three major categories in the Third World. No, the "class oppressed"—the socioeconomically poor—are the infrastructural expression of the process of oppression. The other groups represent "superstructural" expressions of oppression and because of this are deeply conditioned by the infrastructural. . . . This shows why, in a class-divided society, class struggles—which are a fact and an ethical demonstration of the presence of the injustice condemned by God and the church—are the main sort of struggle. (Boff and Boff 1990, 29)

Being poor today has increasingly come to mean standing up and struggling for justice, peace, freedom, and more democratic participation in society, as well as "organizing 'to live their faith in an integral way,' and being committed to the liberation of every human being" (Gutiérrez 1990, 8). Liberation theology is "about liberation of the oppressed—in their totality as persons, body and soul—and in their totality as a class: the poor, the subjected, the discriminated against" (Boff and Boff 1990, 28–29). The "selective affinity" between liberation theology and Marxism reflected in these ideas meant that, like the Marxist premise that the workers themselves must be the agents of their own liberation, liberation theology defined the poor not simply as objects of charity or as passive victims of their oppression but as the active agents of their own liberation (Löwy 1993, 36; Boff and Boff 1990, 25–28).

The "selective affinity" or compatibility between liberation theology and Marxism does not mean that liberation theologians cease being concerned with its prophetic mission or that it abandons its faith in the God of Jesus Christ or in the Catholic Church's magisterium (Dussel 1992; Löwy 1993). As Boff and Boff put it, because of its materialism and atheism, Marxism "can be a companion on the way, but . . . never *the* guide, because [there is] only one teacher, the Christ" (1990, 28, emphasis in original). So, while liberation theology and Marxism may be compatible at some level, they remain at odds in other essential respects.

There are, then, at least two currents within the liberation theology movement. In the first, more classist current, liberation theologians like the Boffs see the working class as the primary agents in the emancipatory project. In the second, more populist current, proponents like Aristide view the poor, the exploited, the excluded, and the marginalized—not the working class—as the agents of social change. Whereas the classist interpretation implies that nothing short of a socialist society organized primarily in the interest of and led by the working class will result in human liberation, the populist interpretation opens itself to a compromise. It adopts what could be called an "agnostic" position on the type of alternative social order that could render justice and equality to the poor and the oppressed.

Aristide not only adopted the populist and agnostic version of liberation theology but also tended to emphasize its prophetic side in his writings and sermons. He used liberation theology to justify the "this-worldliness" of the liberation of the oppressed Haitian masses. As he put it:

> The liberating faith allows the believer to be in deep communion with the God who is present, in good as in bad times. . . . God of life, he lives for all. Such is the God of Jesus Christ in whom we believe. This theological dimension certainly sustains a people struggling against corruption with neither economic nor arm power. It is thus fair to believe that the relation of forces . . . manifests itself clearly at the heart of this drama. It is the theological force resisting the political forces which use money and weapons to fight the poor. The God of the Haitian people is called the force of resistance, resistance against the *macoutes* and against all wrongs. (Aristide 1992a, 67)

Aristide's adherence to the more populist and prophetic interpretation of liberation theology notwithstanding, the fact that he advocated social justice and equality for the poor and the oppressed earned him the bitter enmity of the military rulers, the bourgeoisie, and the Church hierarchy. These groups were not in the least interested in the subtle theoretical or theological differences—if they were aware of them at all—between the classist and the populist tendencies within a doctrine that they simply considered dangerous and threatening to their interests. To them, Aristide was simply a "communist." He had allied himself with, and become the champion of, the poor. As such, there was no possibility of compromise or of forming a "pact of domination" with him, as had been possible with the Duvalier dictatorships. Unlike the latter who sought an accommodation with the mulatto bourgeoisie to share in the spoils of the extant class system, Aristide's objective was to empower the poor and make them the equals of the dominant classes—an objective that could be achieved only by transforming the class system and redistributing wealth and resources to the poor. As far as the dominant classes (the private and state bourgeoisies, the military, the Catholic Church) and their foreign backers were concerned, then, the only way to deal with Aristide was to destroy him. That fundamental perception and distrust of Aristide would not change even after he came to power and it became clear that despite his populist and theological radicalism, his interests as well as those of the cadres who formed the leadership of his Lavalas movement and government pushed them to form a "pact" with the dominant classes.

On three occasions, the government of General Namphy tried to assassinate Aristide, but each time he escaped unharmed.[5] For Aristide, all these assassination attempts were a demonstration of a weak force vanquishing a strong one, a victory not only for himself but for the Haitian people in general (Aristide 1990, 62). They also represented God's energy manifesting itself in the people. In reference to the incidents mentioned above, Aristide wrote:

> Thus would God have us walk through the valley of death and find ourselves, our voyage at the end, at the sunlit crossroads of life; so would God have us travel nightmarish highways of rain and gloom and murder only to pull into a carefree village at sunrise in our exhausted car with four tires flat; so would God have us fight for life in the battlefields of blood and entrails, and harvest life from fields of bones and ashes. There in the wasteland when you had not thought to find life, you will suddenly find the signs of God's renewal, blooming and flowering and bursting forth from the dry earth with great energy, God's energy. (1990, 64)

Aristide emerged stronger than ever from his confrontations with the Church and the military and earned the reputation of being the nemesis of the makouts and Duvalierism. He came to be seen, in fact, as the icon of antimakoutism. Equally as important, by appearing to be undaunted by these assassination attempts, Aristide proved his prophetic quality to his followers. He defied and confronted the forces of evil and emerged victorious. It was understandable, then, that he galvanized the population behind him when he decided to run for president. For them, Aristide, who had already been known through his radical sermons and his pastoral work, was the only one who could stand up to and not compromise with the makouts and who, guided by the light of God, could rid the country of the Duvalierist scourge that had terrorized and devastated the entire society (Moïse and Olivier 1992, 147).

The decision to run for president represented a major about-face for Aristide. As recently as April 1990, Aristide had asserted that he was free of the disease known as "presidentialitism"—that is, the "incurable sickness" to become president of Haiti—that afflicts many Haitian politicians (Aristide 1992b, 140). Up until two weeks before he declared his candidacy, he believed that the elections, desired by the United States, would solve nothing for the Haitian people. He had remained one of the strongest proponents of "linkage" among the leftist opposition leaders, meaning that genuinely democratic elections could not be held until the criminals of the Duvalierist regime had been brought to justice (Aristide 1992b, 136; Hérard 1990, 3).

The entry of Roger Lafontant in the presidential race and his own rethinking of the political conjuncture of September–October 1990 led Aristide to change his mind. He offered three reasons for his decision to run for president. First, he argued, by insisting on the arrest and trial of those Duvalierists accused of crimes and by boycotting the elections until this demand was met, the Left was falling into a trap that would allow one of the "acceptable" and "electable" conservative candidates (supported by moderate Duvalierists like Provisional President Pascal-Trouillot, the privileged bourgeoisie, and imperialism) to win. The United States wanted the elections, and a sector of the bourgeoisie wanted to recuperate the dictatorship for its own benefit. Despite the inactions of the provisional president, Aristide believed that she was more moderate than the hardcore Duvalierists like Namphy or Avril. Even if her intentions regarding the elections were unclear, the Council of State and the United States were determined to hold them.

From Aristide's point of view, the elections would be held no matter what, and unless a candidate "from the people" entered the race, the field would be open only to those who would maintain the status quo. He also realized that, because these elections would be supervised by international observers, their outcome—and the winner—would have unprecedented legitimacy. In the words of Aristide, "Woe betide the non-participants!" (1992b, 138). Without a strong candidate from the people who could galvanize and unify them, the bourgeoisie could establish a formal democracy that would exclude the lower classes, allow it to form an alliance with the moderate neo-Duvalierists, and rule without any vision of a reconstructed Haiti or a commitment to justice and equality. Aristide concluded that in this way the "obscure forces, relieved of their mafia components, could dominate anew and perpetuate themselves" in power (1992b, 138–41).

The second reason Aristide gave for participating in the elections pertained to the divisions he saw within the pro-democratic and anti-makout camp. Splintered into various factions, the pro-democratic forces would divide the electorate and thus facilitate the victory of the pro-makout forces. That is why, in his view, there was a need for one candidate from among the people to be chosen, to move forward with the people in the same direction. "Only one solution imposed itself to us: unity. The unity of all those men and women who had said no to the return of the *macoutes* to power and yes to the democratic transition" (Aristide 1992a, 30).

The third reason stemmed from Aristide's sense of his own role as a political leader and his relationship with the oppressed masses. Even though it had been suggested to him (long before 1990) that he run for president, Aristide maintains that he had always refused because he considered himself a spokesman for the oppressed, whose role it was to raise their political consciousness (1992b, 140). Because no name had emerged from among the left-wing parties who could defeat the challenge posed by Lafontant and the other Duvalierists, as well as the other elite- or foreign-backed candidates, Aristide believed that he had an obligation to the people to declare his candidacy—even though his aversion to the presidency and his sense of himself as an opposition leader pushed him toward saying no. But the people, with whom he had formed a close bond long ago and who considered him "a shield [and] a free and disinterested spokesman," would consider it a betrayal if he declined. "My candidacy was akin to a reflex of self-defense," Aristide claimed. "My place at the heart of the popular demands was reassuring. . . . I would accept the responsibility, I would be the candidate of all my known and unknown companions of misery" (1992b, 143).

Although Lafontant was the precipitating factor that finally led Aristide to make his decision, he made it clear that his candidacy was more a counterforce to the Duvalierist system as such and not due to the risk of this or that Duvalierist becoming president. This is why he decided to stay the course even after Lafontant and Claude Raymond, two of the most hardcore "barons" of Duvalierism, were disqualified by the CEP from running for president. Aristide had a problem with "the system that produces these individuals. Even if Lafontant leaves, we cannot say that we are saved. It is like with Jean-Claude Duvalier. Article 291 is not for Lafontant only, it is to ban all Duvalierists" (*Haiti en Marche* 1990d).

As a charismatic liberation theologian, Aristide ultimately came to see his candidacy as a messianic mission, and herein resided the fundamental roots of his undemocratic, paternalistic, and authoritarian political practice, as I will show. "It has often been written that I considered myself more and more as a prophet," Aristide wrote, "[but] I only had the impression of obeying the word of God and of being the representative of communities which, themselves, were certainly prophetic" (1992b, 143). Denying that he was the Messiah, and asserting that he owed whatever political vision he had to "those who have walked beside me," Aristide nonetheless went on to draw an analogy between Jesus Christ and himself, as he had done on earlier occasions. Unlike others who saw in Jesus a divine being, Aristide viewed him as a fully human being from whom the divine emerged.

> He was so human that he was God. . . . That is why I accepted finally to discover, to experiment with the complementariness between the priest and the president. If the people put forth so much energy for their priest-candidate, it is because they distinguish the human capable of bringing about a new political partition and to advance toward another land of justice, love and respect. (1992b, 143–44)

Aristide made the same point in still another way. The historical irruption of the poor onto the political scene, he argued, was that of God rising up in the life of the poor. It was a process whereby the people's

> faith in God transformed itself into a lever that lifted a whole people against a whole range of false promises made by the traditional candidates. Having found the crystallization of this God at the center of its own reality, that of the poor fighting for liberty; having discovered the communion of the poor building a whole new world, the people transformed itself into a theophany which was the manifestation of this God. This living God that guides. The God who advises. The God who accompanies. The God who anthropomorphises himself so that the Haitian people can theomorphise themselves. (1992a, 20)

With this fusion of politics and theology, of the secular and the sacred, the enlightened people chose the one who incarnated simultaneously the political authority and the power willed by God. Aristide continued:

> It is this collective thrust that imposes a political choice. Theology is no longer an ensemble of credos, but a force which pushes toward a better world. One does not recite credos, one lives by this force. Lived in this manner theology goes beyond the singular to articulate the plural. The ensemble of the Haitian people found a voice that expressed the different dimensions of a history, while making of the collective the sign of each. They all wanted to find a candidate

who responded to their taste, to their choice. The gaze of all, brothers and sisters, converged in the same direction. . . . The light of God had to be discerned to render unto God what God was due. Reality had to be scrutinized to find in it the concrete gestures expressing this unity to be offered to a unique God. Thus, the people found a candidate to provoke with it the irruption, the manifestation of this divine face reflecting the human reality. On the 18th of October, the chosen candidate understood that he also had to live this theological density by accepting to espouse the collective causes and demands, thereby rejecting his first choice [of turning down his candidacy]. (1992a, 21)

These lengthy citations from Aristide were necessary to make the point that the explanation for becoming a presidential candidate was to be found not solely in the secular reasons but primarily in his own sense that it was his theological duty to do so. Aristide, in other words, could have chosen to remain true to his earlier stated position not to run for office and instead thrown his support behind another candidate. If he had decided to enter the race simply to counter the threat posed by Lafontant, he could have withdrawn after the latter was disqualified. But Aristide justified his decision to stay in the race even after Lafontant's disqualification on the grounds that his opposition was to the Duvalierist system as such, and not only to some of its ardent adherents.

It does not follow, however, that only by running for president could he successfully challenge that system and cause its demise. It could be argued, in fact, that given Aristide's stature as a clergyman and as a popular charismatic leader revered by the masses, he could have played a far more constructive role in the struggle for change, as he had already demonstrated. An opposition leader can adopt uncompromising stances precisely because he or she does not have the responsibility to govern and, especially in a democratic order, be held accountable (ultimately to and by the voters) for his or her decisions and actions. By contrast, an elected president must make compromises with opponents to neutralize their opposition, win their support, and govern effectively. Occupying public office would necessarily place constraints on Aristide's policies and lead him to accommodate the very social forces who controlled the social order that he and his movement sought to change in order to prevent them from undermining or even toppling his government. Aristide said many times that he rejected the idea of running for president because he considered his role to be a formative one, that is, to raise the people's political consciousness and struggle with them to achieve their liberation. Did he also reflect on the implications of his candidacy along the lines suggested above? Or did he believe that as president he could govern without having to compromise his beliefs and goals, to subject himself to the checks and balances of democratic government, and to come to terms with what were bound to be very obstinate and predictably hostile opponents?

The only viable explanation for Aristide's decision to run for president is that he really believed he had a theological or prophetic responsibility to do so and that this belief led him to put aside potentially restraining arguments. To understand this point, it may be necessary to return to the meaning of the phrase "option for the poor" that lies at the root of liberation theology. As Gustavo Gutiérrez explained it, the commitment to the liberation of the poor is not an "option" in the sense that an adherent of liberation theology is free to make or not to make this commitment. It is the sine qua non of liberation theology, for its ultimate objective is to achieve "salvation in Christ in terms of liberation." The praxis of liberation theology is one of "solidarity in the interest of liberation and is inspired by the gospel." This is what allows liberation theology to remain faithful "to the message of the God who acts in history to save a people by liberating it from every kind of servitude." Liberation theology implies three kinds or levels of liberation: liberation from conditions of oppression and marginalization "that force many to live contrary to God's will for their life"; personal transformation that allows one to "live with profound inner freedom in the face of every kind of servitude"; and "liberation from sin, which attacks the deepest root of all servitude; for sin is the breaking of friendship with God and with other human beings" (Gutiérrez 1990, 12–13, 16, 24–25).

It is precisely his adherence to these principles that led Aristide to claim:

We had said many times for many years, notably since 1985, that we were not candidate [for political office], but that we were ready to respond to the people's will and thus to the will of God. Walking with the people and in communion with it, our faith, on the 18th of October, transformed itself into a political choice fed at the source of a theological life. . . . Son of the people, united with the people, with the people during the past five years, we refused to take part in the activities of the political parties as far as being a member of political parties or a supporter of a political leader. But, having gotten to the 18th of October, a choice had to be made to remain faithful to its [the people's] theological and political choices. (1992a, 22)

Invoking the will of the people as an expression of the will of God—the poor as the "elect" of God who will save those who listen—as the underlying justification for his candidacy gave Aristide's decision the air of inevitability and, indeed, of obligation. This justification becomes all the more significant in light of the fact that, before he declared his candidacy on October 18, there had been no known "organized voices" among the people that called for Aristide to run for president. Indeed, two of the base organizations from Aristide's parish of Saint Jean Bosco—namely, *Solidarité Ant Jèn* (SAJ, Solidarity Among Youths), created in 1985 to unite the youths from the poor neighborhoods of

Port-au-Prince in the struggle against the Duvalier dictatorship, and the *Konbit Véyé Yo* (Vigilance Committee), created in 1986 to pursue the work of political conscientization and the process of uprooting the makout system (Aristide 1994b, 205–6) — joined with others like *Tèt Kolé pou Yon Mouvman ti-Peyizan* (Solidarity with the Small Peasant Movement) to criticize publicly Aristide's decision to participate in the elections (*Haiti en Marche* 1990d).

Aristide seemed to have been aware of this problem. He acknowledged that, even though the voices heard on the radio broadcasts that called for his candidacy were few, those that reached his heart and ears directly, but silently, were much more numerous by comparison. He continued:

> The more we tried to touch the roots of this depth, the more we found ourselves at the heart of a collective soul, that of a people which expresses itself in gestures, in words, but equally in eloquent silences. One must know this people to understand it. One must know its psychology to touch the conscious and unconscious mechanisms which underlay its silently eloquent discourse. (1992a, 25)

Aristide, in fact, did not need to show a groundswell of support for his candidacy to decide to enter the presidential race. Since he claimed that he was doing so because he believed that this is what the people wanted, he only had to explain why such a demand was not expressed publicly and massively before October 18, 1990. The only explanation was the mystical and theological argument. Recourse to this type of argument, however, is dangerous and opens itself to demagogy and arbitrariness. Any leader can claim to be in touch with and understand the "soul" of a people and "hear its silent discourse" and, thereby, justify any number of acts on those grounds without having to account to anyone or follow democratic principles and practices.

Aristide vindicated his claim to be the people's choice by offering this proof: Soon after he accepted the candidacy, the percentage of voter registration increased from 35 percent to 90 percent in the space of a few hours. The surge in voter registration did not happen as quickly as Aristide claims, but an estimated 92 percent of the 3.2 million eligible voters did ultimately register to vote, and there is no doubt that this was caused by Aristide entering the race for the presidency (Chamberlain 1990a, 5).

Another expression of his popularity could be seen from the throngs who attended his campaign rallies throughout the country. Aristide, in short, gambled on his popularity, and he won incontestably. For him, this was yet another demonstration of God's work:

> The hand of God was not hidden that day. . . . [G]uided by him and in communion with him, our theological reality was able to project the choice of the

people and of a man. Choice of a man, choice of his people; choice of the people, choice of its man. People of God, man of God, together they only obeyed their God, by rendering unto him what was due him. (1992a, 25)

Whatever justifications he offered for his decision, Aristide could not run for office without the cover of a political organization. He had not yet formed his own political organization and had to find a home in one already active on the political scene. The recently formed *Front National pour le Changement et la Démocratie* (FNCD, National Front for Democracy and Change) had asked Aristide to run under its banner. The FNCD, which regrouped fifteen left-of-center organizations (including KONAKOM and the KID), had initially chosen Victor Benoit, the leader of KONAKOM, as its presidential candidate. However, it became evident that Benoit lacked the popular appeal to defeat the other well-known candidates, particularly Marc Bazin, the leader of the well-financed and well-organized right-of-center MIDH, and the candidate of the ANDP, who was then considered the front-runner.

Aristide, for his part, wanted to avoid being seen as an opportunist and was reluctant to displace Benoit as the FNCD's candidate unless Benoit withdrew his name (Aristide 1992b, 142). Pressured by the KID, the FNCD apparently went over Benoit's head to nominate Aristide and compelled Benoit to agree (reluctantly, if not angrily) to withdraw his candidacy. He reportedly did so "for cause," that is, because of the need to counter the threat posed by the makout forces, and not because he favored Aristide's nomination. Benoit and his organization, KONAKOM, then left the FNCD (Charlier 1990, 9; Chamberlain 1990a, 5; Sontag 1990).

Though he became the candidate of the FNCD, Aristide never considered himself beholden to that organization. Aristide, in fact, entertained a jaundiced view of the existing political parties, even those on the Left like the FNCD that were close to his political views. He saw them basically as "talk shops" that held congresses, engaged in legitimate but Byzantine discussions in which he did not participate, had difficulties coming up with a unified candidate, and whose proliferation rendered them ineffective (Aristide 1992b, 141). For Aristide, the FNCD served merely as a conduit and legal cover for his candidacy, and nothing more. His allegiance was only to the people and to his soon-to-be baptized *Opération Lavalas* (OL, Operation Lavalas, meaning "cleansing flood") movement, which he believed was more significant than the FNCD (or any other political organization then in place) and of which he was the self-proclaimed leader.

The issue goes deeper than Aristide's sense of the limitations of the extant political parties. He believed that he had formed a special bond with the masses and that he incarnated their aspirations and had become their spokesman. Since he believed that the will of God was manifested in the will of the people, it follows that accepting their call on him to pose his candidacy was an expression of God's will. He believed also that he stood above all other political actors or organizations that lacked this symbiotic relationship with the masses. In short, Aristide became persuaded that the "prophetic" people had propelled him onto the historical stage and that only he and his Lavalas movement could bring about the transformations they demanded. And it is here, in the charismatic persona and relationship between Aristide and his followers, that one is to locate the seeds of what I will call the hybrid nature of Aristide's politics, that is, a mixture of authoritarian and democratic tendencies that conflicted with one another and gave Aristide's presidency the aura of unpredictability. Indeed, it is precisely the authoritarian tendency or temptation, made more immune to deterrence by Aristide's belief that the people, and God, were always behind him, that would prove disastrous for him in both 1991 and 2000–04.

As Jonathan Hartlyn argues, hybridity is a type of regime, or rule, that shares both authoritarian and democratic tendencies, with the latter having an uneasy coexistence with and being undermined by the former. As Hartlyn puts it:

> This kind of democracy often appears to rely primarily on the goodwill of the leader at the top, constrained by fears of political instability or domestic and international pressure, rather than on agreement regarding a set of democratic "rules of the game." Enhancement in all three of the key elements of democracy [the rule of law, the right of public contestation, and the enfranchisement of all adult citizens] would require a decline in [hybridity]. Until then, political democracy remains fragile because of the attitudes and behaviors of key political actors and because of the weakness of both effective political intermediation and the rule of law. (1998, 16)

For Aristide, Lavalas was not to be confused with a political party restricted only to those who adhered to its principles. Rather, it was an idea and a movement open to all those who wanted to join with the people to bring about change, regardless of their class location or institutional affiliation. As Aristide wrote:

> One does not adhere to *Lavalas* as one becomes a card-carrying or a dues-paying member of a party. One joins freely a movement which transforms the eternal vassals, the serfs into free human beings. We are all free human beings. *Lavalas* was the chance of all men and women. . . . It was the opportunity for the army, a mercenary institution yesterday, to become united with its people. It was the chance of the bourgeoisie to opt for a democratic transition rather than a violent revolution. It was the chance of the Church to come closer to its

people. . . . The idea of Lavalas—the torrent that cleans everything in its path—
was growing in the [peoples'] opinion: unity, the unraveling, the cleansing of a
shameful past, eradicating the roots of the Macoute system. To unravel. To uproot. To be born again. (1992b, 142)

He went on to say: "Our program is simple. . . . We say no to the corruption
and terror of the past and yes to the mobilization of the people—yes to
change, change that we undertake ourselves" (Sontag 1990). From these ideas
came the slogan that would become the refrain of the Lavalas movement,
and which was heard for the first time on October 8, 1990, in a broadcast on
Radio Antilles: "*Yon sèl nou fèb; ansanm nou fò; ansanm, ansanm nou sé
Lavalas*" (Alone we are weak; united we are strong; all together we are a
cleansing torrent).

Lavalas had its roots in the ecclesiastical base communities, or TKL,
movement. Its principal sociological and demographic base was among the
urban youths and the marginalized and urban poor, but not among the working class as such. Lavalas also regrouped diverse grassroots organizations
from the rural areas and provincial cities that were formed after 1986; peasant organizations, principally among them the *Mouvman Peyizan Papaye*
(MPP, Papaye Peasant Movement); and many civic and political-educational
networks, professional cadres, and progressive elements from the private sector and from the Haitian diaspora (Pierre-Charles 1991, 16–17; 1993, 222–
23). Lavalas, in short, could be thought of as a broad popular front that aimed
to dismantle the prebendary and discredited dictatorship and build a democratic state that prioritized the demands of the excluded and exploited majority and their full participation in deciding the agenda of their communities
and of the nation.

Even though Lavalas brought together many political groups and tendencies and relied on the mobilization of the organized and unorganized popular
sectors for its eventual electoral success, it was not at all clear how the various constituents of the movement expressed their ideas and demands within
the movement. No efforts were made before or after the elections to create a
structure that coordinated and integrated the groups and organizations that
were part of the Lavalas movement (Oreste 1992, 4). The Lavalas movement
published its vision of a new and democratic Haiti and the economic development model it would adopt in two documents, *La chance qui passe* and *La
chance à prendre* (Opération Lavalas 1990b, 1990a), but these documents
were known only by a small circle of intellectuals, the literate members of political organizations, and other literate political observers. The leaders of
Lavalas held no congresses to discuss, amend, and ratify the program of government proposed in these two documents. Moreover, Lavalas never revealed

its internal organizational structure to the public. Lavalas, in fact, had no formal structure. It was neither a political organization nor a political party, with clearly defined principles of membership, rules of decision making, methods of choosing the party leadership, and responsibilities of the leadership to the constituent members and vice versa. As such, it is difficult to know the mechanisms by which it developed its ideas and its overall orientation, or who spoke for the movement and with what authority.

To be sure, one may attribute this failure to the fact that the legacy of more than thirty years of dictatorship, the climate of violence in which the electoral campaign occurred, and its short duration of only two months did not make it possible to develop an organization that followed democratic principles and procedures. It could be argued also, as Kern Delince does, that political parties have never existed in Haiti because the extant dictatorial system could not tolerate autonomous political organizations that could challenge its political monopoly. Even if they were not always banned legally, political organizations in Haiti have historically existed in a hostile environment averse to their evolution. This explains why in Haiti the practice has been for citizens and political activists to throw their support behind an influential or powerful leader whose authority they accept and from whom they expect assistance and protection in return (Delince 1993, 142). This historical practice is at the root of the authoritarian and personalistic domination and clientelist relations of Haitian politics, and a fundamental principle of the prebendary state system.

This latter tendency prevailed in the case of Aristide and his Lavalas movement. As I just mentioned, the primary social base of Lavalas came overwhelmingly from urban youths (especially from Port-au-Prince), the marginalized, and the urbanized poor. The members of these "marginalized cities," as Alain Gilles has argued, confront conditions of permanent poverty and other factors such as illiteracy, inadequate health care, housing, and employment. Moreover, these cities are characterized by a perpetual movement of groups of rural migrants from different regions and social backgrounds. Under such conditions, the sense of social rootedness or neighborliness is either absent or weakly developed, as are the bonds of solidarity that workers often form in the processes and units of production. Consequently, Gilles concludes, the populations of these marginalized cities tend not to develop a specific class consciousness, and they analyze society not in terms of group or class conflicts, but more as a generalized opposition to society as a whole. They are thus more open to a religious or messianic interpretation of their social problems and become very receptive to populist charismatic leadership and domination (Gilles 1991, 109).

It should not be surprising that Lavalas recruited its mass base from among the members of the "marginalized cities" of Haiti; that it would express the characteristics of a fluid and loosely knit organization; or that Aristide's charismatic and messianic leadership was precisely the sine qua non of his symbiotic and paternalistic relationship with the impoverished masses. This much was candidly admitted by the leadership of the *Organisation Politique Lavalas* (OPL, Lavalas Political Organization) in an internal document written in June 1992, nine months after the September 1991 coup that overthrew Aristide. The above characteristics, they argued, emerged from the

> impulse of a powerful popular movement in favor of change and democracy and from the personalistic and charismatic nature of the political leadership. . . . They rest on the force of popular demands and the popularity of one man, who incarnated it, and not on adherence to an explicit political group or program. (Organisation Politique Lavalas 1992, 6)

In the absence of such mechanisms of control and accountability and a program debated and approved by the rank-and-file of the movement, there was a danger that anyone could speak and anything could be said in the name of Lavalas. Given the personalistic nature of the leadership, however, it is reasonable to conclude that Aristide, along with a cadre of close advisors and intellectuals, made all the decisions, wrote the documents, and spoke for the organization and the movement it claimed to represent. While ostensibly representing the aspirations of the majority and struggling for an inclusive democracy, Aristide and Lavalas did not depart from that all-too-Haitian and all-too-Caribbean tradition of "one-manism," whereby class politics and factional interests become personalized and the leader substitutes himself (or herself) for those he claims to represent and arrogates to himself the right to speak and set goals for them (Lewis 1987, 165–66). More universally, this phenomenon is known as the cult of personality. This was the case regardless of Aristide's popularity, regardless that his candidacy was backed by some of the best-organized groups as well as the unorganized sectors who together represented various cross-sections of the population, and regardless that his progressive theological and secular views corresponded to the real aspirations and demands of the excluded majority.

Despite its undoubted democratic aspirations, Lavalas was not a democratically structured organization, and neither did it seek to adhere to or foster a democratic practice. Within Lavalas, Aristide and a close network of advisors led without direct accountability to a defined constituency vested with definite powers and responsibilities. Even more dangerously, Aristide justified his leadership in theological terms before his ratification by the people in the December elections. Lastly, Aristide and the leadership of Lavalas decided on programs and goals without subjecting them to popular debate and ratification by the constituent organizations or groups ostensibly represented within the movement. Thus, it was not only his theological interpretation of politics that nurtured Aristide's authoritarian tendencies but also the personalistic character of his leadership and of his relationship with his followers.

Before the elections, then, the most that can be said is that Aristide benefited from the support of many sectors of the popular opposition movement, centered on the desire to rid the country of the makout system and its legacies. The demand for an inclusive and institutional democracy, social justice, land reform, equality, dignity, jobs, health care, education, and welfare services — in short, for a maximalist democracy — were very much part of the political discourse. These demands were shared by many organizations that considered themselves part of the Left, not only by those who adhered to the Lavalas movement. Nevertheless, the landslide victory of Aristide in the December 16, 1990, elections — in which he captured 67.48 percent of the popular vote — confirmed his unquestioned popularity. It was a popular mandate for him and the government of his prime minister-to-be to implement the hoped-for transformations of the old regime and create a just, equal, and democratic Haiti.

The analysis thus far of Aristide the liberation theologian and charismatic leader makes it possible to draw the following conclusions. Aristide and his Lavalas movement symbolized and expressed the desire of the Haitian masses for a just and democratic Haiti, freed of the legacies of the tyrannical and rapacious Duvalier dictatorships and their successors. Aristide had become the prophet who "looked at reality with the eyes of God, . . . the one who after having discovered the truth in reality was not afraid to unveil that truth, to proclaim that truth at the risk of his own life" (Midy 1988; also cited in Moïse and Olivier 1992, 151).

As Claude Moïse and Émile Olivier argue, Aristide's liberation theology linked an interpretation of the Gospel with a radical stance in favor of the poor and their struggle. This discourse not only identified the actor (Aristide) and the subjects for whom he spoke (the impoverished masses) but also the enemies who must be extirpated in order for justice to be done (1992, 151–53). Aristide had clearly identified the enemies of the people as the Duvalierists and the makout system they created, the bourgeoisie, the hierarchy of the Catholic Church, and the imperialists from the "cold country to the north." In short, Aristide had become

the savior, the redeemer. . . . Henceforth the protagonists expressed themselves in terms of justice, of morality, of dignity, of change that transcends social classes. To echo these demands, to give voice to the voiceless, rekindle hope, take into account the will of the masses to accede to the status of citizen, these are the manifest aspects of the Aristidean discourse. (1992, 153–54)

As Moïse and Olivier acutely observe, the danger of a mass movement that relied on the mediation of a charismatic leader was that, while he or she may serve a useful purpose in defining a political project and in galvanizing popular support for its realization, this could quickly lead to disaster when the charismatic leader turned into an idol. To prevent this from happening, they argued that two conditions had to be met. The first was that between the leader and the masses there must exist a structured organization controlled by enlightened and responsible people. The second was that the charismatic leader must be an "enlightened visionary" who understood the complexity of the present conjuncture, and, conscious of his or her limits and essentially formative role, exercised his or her responsibilities without losing sight of the democratic objective: namely, to allow the citizens to take charge of their problems and propose their own solutions (Moïse and Olivier 1992, 154).

A third argument can be added. To ensure that the citizens take charge of their problems and determine their own political agenda, a political party must be democratically structured. This means that accountability of the leadership to the rank and file, the *demos*, must be built in, as must be the mechanisms by which the leaders are chosen and changed by the party rank and file.[6] This is the only way to prevent leaders, no matter how enlightened or noble their intentions, from substituting themselves for the masses and becoming authoritarian rulers or dictators. The above point is amply demonstrated by the experiences of the "vanguard parties" that transformed themselves into "ruling parties" and imposed the "dictatorships of the party" or of the "maximum leader" (i.e., the former Soviet-bloc countries, as well as in China, North Korea, and Cuba).

It is clear that the conditions for democracy did not exist within the political organizations in Haiti in 1990. No leader, including Aristide, had succeeded in federating and democratizing the various political tendencies and organizations that claimed to be part of the democratic movement. Aristide drew his inspiration from and behaved according to the tenets of liberation theology. He was a charismatic leader who had a direct relationship with the masses whom he had galvanized and who, in turn, idolized him and became his faithful followers (Moïse and Olivier 1992, 154–60). Both he and his Lavalas movement claimed to be above ordinary politics and political parties because they responded to the will of the deified people and, hence, the will of God. Worse, and even more dangerous, however, was that once Aristide's Opération Lavalas emerged as the dominant political force and the other popular organizations and left-of-center coalitions, especially the FNCD, accepted Aristide as their leader, they in effect surrendered their autonomy and their ability to criticize Aristide, to serve as checks and balances to his powers, and to articulate independent agendas.

As Jean Alix René has observed, once Aristide took over the leadership of the popular movement, the mobilization of the people no longer revolved around a clear social, political, and economic agenda but "around the persona of Aristide the popular leader, the chief who possessed a superhuman power and was able to substitute himself for the popular organizations" (2003, 136). Moreover, René argues, in addition to forming the basis of the clientelistic system predicated on the paternalistic relations between the prophetic and protective "father" (Aristide) and the "children" (the masses), Aristide's populist discourse pretended to create a new "pact" with the masses to "give them a place at the table next to the [privileged] minority," but in fact hid the reactionary character and the class interests and ambitions of that sector of the petite bourgeoisie and the weaker fraction of the bourgeoisie that Duvalierism excluded from power (2003, 162–63).

As Laënec Hurbon observed further, rather than doing away with clientelism and the cult of personality, the Lavalassian power, which he calls "anarcho-populist," would reinforce it. For "once allegiance to the charismatic leader becomes decisive in obtaining positions in the cogs of the administrative apparatuses, all the gates are open for the cult of the chief, a bit mutatis-mutandis as in the good old days of macoutism. This time around, however, there would be no hierarchy; to be on the right side, it would suffice to proclaim oneself of the people or a true Lavalassian" (2001, 52).

Insightful as these observations are, I believe it is necessary to distinguish between clientelism as a systemic feature of the prebendary state and "anarcho-populism" as a political strategy. *Clientelism*, as we have seen, refers to the use of the institutions of the state for private gain rather than for the public good, whereas, Hurbon points out, *anarcho-populism* refers to a political strategy whereby the charismatic leader (in this case Aristide) adopts a hands-off attitude toward the masses and allows or even encourages them to act with impunity in the name of the movement (Lavalas) that is identified with him (Hurbon 2001, 52). To be sure, insofar as the leader needs to secure the allegiance of the masses, anarcho-populism necessitates a clientelistic or patronage network. But clientelism, or a prebendary state, per se need not be based on, or give rise to, anarcho-populism. The Duvalier dictatorships were surely clientelistic and repressive, but no one ever suggested they were also anarcho-populist.

The real challenge for Aristide, then, was whether the priest-turned-prophet would also be able to make the transition to democratic president. For if, as I argued in chapter 1, power is relational and contingent, that is, an expression of the relations and balance of forces between actors and the resources they can deploy toward one another in a specific time and place to advance their (personal, class, or group) interests—even against the will of others—then one cannot conclude that it was a given that Aristide would substitute an authoritarian or anarcho-populist power for a democratic one even if, as I have suggested, that tendency was already present. In fact, as I will show in the following chapters, during the first seven months of Aristide's first term (February–September 1991), Aristide and his government exhibited both democratic and authoritarian tendencies, hence hybridity. While he made it clear symbolically that he sought to empower the people and encouraged them to mobilize and organize themselves to advance their interests, he did not engage in or encourage acts of reprisals against the private-sector bourgeoisie or attempt to suppress press freedom or silence his opponents. He took action against the army and sought to dismantle the repressive institutions of the dictatorships (e.g., the section chiefs system), proposed a reformist economic policy, and attempted to streamline the public enterprises and even to curb corruption. But he did engage in extrajudicial acts by mobilizing his supporters and threatening the judges in the trial of Roger Lafontant if they did not render a verdict to his liking. He also called on the masses to defend him when he realized that a coup d'état against him was imminent.

Thus, one could argue, with the popular mandate he received in December 1990, Aristide sought to advance his agenda while creating a space for the participation of all sectors of society in public life, especially the hitherto excluded majority. That the dominant classes—the Duvalierists, the military, and the private-sector bourgeoisie—saw this as a threat to their interests was not Aristide's fault. At the same time, his inflammatory class rhetoric, and the ease with which he turned to extrajudicial or anarcho-populist strategies when things didn't go his way or to defend his presidency against direct threats, reinforced the impression that Aristide was unpredictable and hence dangerous.

If for a brief moment in 1991 the balance of forces was in favor of Aristide, conditions were very different during his second term (2001–04). In 1991 Aristide had a strong popular mandate and a mobilized population behind him, but by 1994 that movement had dissipated as a result of the severe repression of the three-year rule of the military junta led by Gen. Raoul Cedras. Aristide also came to power in 2001 with his legitimacy and that of his party in control of parliament challenged. Having governed in 1991 with a divided parliament that blocked his initiatives and lacking the backing of a mass movement, Aristide was determined the second time around to marginalize his political opposition by winning at least two-thirds of the seats and hence have a veto-proof parliament. Irregularities in the vote counting for the Senate seats led the opposition parties that fared poorly to declare the entire parliamentary elections of 2000 to have been fraudulent and to boycott the presidential race as well.

By 2000, Aristide no longer enjoyed the support of the middle-class factions that had opposed the Duvalierists and the coup against him. On the contrary, those middle-class parties, in particular those that were regrouped under the former FNCD, joined with the *Organization du Peuple en Lutte* (OPL, Organization of the People in Struggle)—a faction of the Lavalas Political Organization that broke with Aristide in 1996—and other political parties to form a broad coalition against Aristide. Known as the *Convergence Démocratique* (CD, Democratic Convergence) and supported by the United States and the European Union, its stated objective was to remove Aristide from power, and it even called for the reinstatement of the Haitian Army that Aristide had disbanded in 1994. Moreover, the United States, the EU, and the international financial institutions imposed an economic embargo against the new Aristide government by suspending all economic aid. Feeling threatened and on the defensive, Aristide tried to negotiate his way out of the political crisis with the opposition at the same time that he politicized the police and called on his armed gangs of supporters known as *chimès* (in Creole or *chimères* in French—who took their name from mythical fire-breathing monsters) to intimidate his opponents.

As violence and human rights violations escalated, Aristide increasingly lost legitimacy and became even more beleaguered. Within his government, corruption became rampant as rival factions of his party vied for control. The autonomous and uncontrolled chimès, linked to the chief executive through patronage (clientelism), also factionalized into pro- and anti-Aristide gangs that sought to establish their own fiefdoms in their neighborhoods. Eventually some took up arms against Aristide and created an opening for former members of the armed forces and their affiliated paramilitary death squads to usurp the armed insurgency and force Aristide out of power and into exile in February 2004.

Thus, it could be said that from 1996 onward, but especially after the elections of 2000, the democratic space opened in 1990–91 was supplanted by the tendency toward authoritarianism and anarcho-populism *strictus sensus*. The descent into lawlessness, however, was not Aristide's doing alone. The foreign-backed opposition, as well as the attitude of the United States, the Europeans, and the international financial institutions toward the Aristide government also pushed him down that path. In short, then, the closure of democracy and the opening toward chaos and the arbitrary resulted from the dialectics of power relations in the post-1996 to 2000 period, as much as the democratic opening of 1990–91 resulted from a different dialectic. Those differences will be the subject matter of the next chapters.

NOTES

1. I have done this elsewhere (Dupuy 1997, 47–69). Much of the discussion that follows here is drawn from that analysis.

2. See Kern Delince 1993, 144, for a useful discussion of the distinction between political parties and political groupings. Instead of political parties it is more accurate to speak of political groupings in the context of Haiti.

3. The 1987 Constitution is reprinted as appendix 2 of Moïse 1990.

4. Ambassador Adams, in fact, went to Avril's residence to tell him to leave Haiti. Be that as it may, the phenomenon of the "phone call" (or "visit") from U.S. ambassadors has come to be used as a euphemism in popular Haitian political discourse to mean the decision taken by the White House to oust a particular dictator or president from power. It is a tacit acknowledgment among Haitians that real power in Haiti rests with Washington and that nothing of major significance happens in Haiti without the consent of the United States. The long history of U.S. meddling in the internal affairs of Haiti lends credibility to this claim. But it also tends to be taken as a given. It ascribes omnipotent powers to the United States and serves as a substitute for critical analyses of concrete situations and the changing power relations within and between countries.

5. The first incident occurred in August 1987 at Pont Sondé when gunmen opened fire on a crowd attending a Mass celebrated by Aristide to commemorate the peasants who had been massacred by the military and agents of the large landholders at Jean-Rabel that July. Several shots were aimed directly at Aristide, missing each time. Then, on the way back to Port-au-Prince that same evening, Aristide and the other priests who had accompanied him to Pont Sondé were ambushed by armed gunmen at an army post near the village of Freycineau, but they managed to escape. The third and most bloody attack against Aristide occurred in September 1988, while he was celebrating Mass at his church at Saint Jean Bosco. During the ceremony, gunmen opened fire on the worshippers, attempted to kill Aristide, and burned down his church. The Sunday massacre left between ten and twenty dead and eighty wounded. Here again, Aristide, protected by his followers, escaped unharmed (Aristide 1990, 37–46, 52–55; Sontag 1990).

6. To be sure, no amount of rules and regulations can prevent a leader from usurping the democratic process and establishing complete control over an organization. But these rules and regulations provide a mechanism by which the members of an organization can enforce democratic practices by legitimately sanctioning those who seek to violate them. The same principle applies to society at large. Democratic practice can be sustained insofar as there are institutions and actors with sufficiently binding authority and legitimacy to enforce compliance and make the cost of noncompliance higher than conformity to the rules of the game.

Chapter Four

The Prophet Disarmed:
The First Lavalas Government
and Its Overthrow

FEBRUARY 1991 TO SEPTEMBER 1991:
PRELUDE TO A COUP D'ÉTAT

Jean-Bertrand Aristide was sworn in as president on February 7, 1991, under foreboding conditions. From the outset, the most powerful political actors in Haiti feared Aristide's objectives and lined up against him. He needed to win some of these actors over to his side to have the slightest chance of success.

Because it envisioned the creation of a more egalitarian society, the Lavalas government threatened the most fundamental interests of the prebendary Duvalierist state. As such, it was to be expected that the neo-Duvalierists would oppose Aristide and try to overthrow him. For its part, the Haitian bourgeoisie generally (and especially the small but powerful monopolist faction that collaborated with the Duvalier and post-Duvalier dictatorships) feared and despised Aristide. It was imperative for the Lavalas government to convince the bourgeoisie and the professional strata that it was in their interest to break with Duvalierism and side with the new government because they would have more to gain under the new system than they would by staying with the old regime factions.

Aristide had a chance of succeeding only if he could neutralize the business elites and prevent them from undermining his government by withdrawing their financial support and opposing the government's initiatives. To do this, Aristide had to woo the business elites by forming as broad a consensus and inclusive government as possible, but without abandoning his commitment to the reforms outlined in the Lavalas Project to be discussed below. The Lavalas government also had to speak frankly to the masses about the objectives of the new government: to tell them that this was a liberal and not a revolutionary project; to explain to them why they should accept the compromises it called for with the propertied and privileged classes; and to show how, even with such compromises, they would still benefit more under the new order. Framed in the language of chapter 1, Aristide had to convince the masses that although his government would not be able to create a maximalist democracy that would reverse the nautonomic conditions under which the majority of the population had been kept for nearly two centuries, it would nonetheless make strides in that direction by prioritizing their needs without undermining the rights and privileges of the bourgeoisie and middle classes.

Aristide had to know that he was walking a tightrope without a safety net, from which the slightest error might send him tumbling down. Yet his behavior during the next seven months showed that he failed to understand this point. President Aristide, Prime Minister René Préval, and his ministers spoke often to various constituencies to explain the government's actions and policies. The president granted many interviews, gave press conferences, spoke at organized rallies and official ceremonies, and made radio and television addresses. But when they spoke, the president and his ministers did not always do so with one voice, and they did not explain clearly their objectives or their actions.

While the government ministers were left to elucidate their program in technical terms and spoke mainly to the press, the intelligentsia, and the bourgeoisie, Aristide took most of the responsibility for speaking to the masses. Yet, he often gave contradictory messages—sometimes to the same audiences. At times he sought to reassure the bourgeoisie and the middle classes, and at other times he chastised and threatened them. When he spoke to the masses, he sometimes appeared to mollify them and at other times energized them by adopting a defiant and even revolutionary posture against his opponents. This dual strategy, typical of hybrid regimes as discussed previously, gave the impression that the government was proceeding on an ad hoc basis: improvising, unsure of itself, and contradictory. This inconsistency could not but create confusion among both supporters and detractors of the government and ultimately played into the hands of its enemies. Confusion can be tolerated from a government in power when the stakes are not high and when the government has enough confidence in its policies and enough resources at its disposal to preserve its base of support and fend off the opposition. But in a highly charged atmosphere, such as the one confronted by the Aristide government, where the stakes were high and where its enemies were waiting for the slightest mistake to attack, Aristide simply could not afford to confuse the various sectors of the population about his intentions.

In many ways, the impressions created by Aristide and his government—of being uncertain and unprepared—were inevitable. Aristide and his government promised much, and they were beleaguered from the outset by a dilapidated public treasury, an economy in ruins, unforeseen crises that demanded immediate attention, threats and hostilities from the neo-Duvalierists, reticence and opposition from the bourgeoisie and parliament, and increasingly militant demands from below to deliver more quickly on its promises and move faster and go deeper with the reforms. Everything was a priority in Haiti. The Lavalas government needed time to sort out what deserved the most urgent attention and to devise strategies to deal with the chaotic and seemingly intractable conditions it inherited (Moïse and Olivier 1992, 161). Neither the impatient popular supporters of the government who wanted immediate results, nor its undaunted enemies would give it that time. The contradictions within the government's economic program and the difficulties of the president and the government in getting their messages out coherently would ultimately exacerbate the tensions among the bourgeoisie, the military, the masses, parliament, and the government. All these factors combined created the opening for the neo-Duvalierists to strike.

The Haitian and foreign press also engaged in hyperbole against Aristide. For example, an editorial written for the *Wall Street Journal* by one of the editors of the New York–based conservative Haitian weekly *Haiti Observateur* wasted little time in warning the Haitian bourgeoisie and the United States that

> if US experts expect some miraculous free-market conversion by the lifelong socialist, they likely will be disappointed. According to one source who accompanied Father Aristide as he visited the home of a wealthy Haitian family on election day, the president-elect walked out of the house with a look of astonishment. "Wow!" Father Aristide is reported to have exclaimed. "What a house! I'm pretty sure this could house 12 families." (Joseph 1990)

Howard French, a long-time *New York Times* correspondent whose columns influenced opinions among the U.S. intelligentsia and policymakers about Haiti, reminded readers of Aristide's "scathing oratory" against the United States and the Haitian bourgeoisie and that among his "most fervent backers" was a wealthy but staunchly anti-American businessman of Palestinian descent, Antoine Izméry. Although French suggested that Izméry may be "slipping out of the President-elect's inner orbit of advisers," he pointed out that Izméry continues to have Aristide's ear to assure himself that "he [Aristide] is not softening" (French 1991c). Conservatives at the Heritage Foundation in the United States joined the chorus and urged the Bush administration not to deliver the $82 million in aid earmarked for Haiti by warning that, as with the Sandinistas in Nicaragua in 1979, Aristide would use the aid money to establish a "communist dictatorship in Haiti" (Wilson 1991).

The anxiety about Aristide among the bourgeoisie did not limit itself to ex-aggerations about an impending communist dictatorship, but extended to deeds as well. During the two months preceding his inauguration, businesses reduced their inventories by emptying their warehouses and slowing down imports. Many exporters made plans to relocate their operations to the Do-minican Republic as they anticipated unrest in Haiti (Hockstader 1991a).

Then came the first strike by the neo-Duvalierists. Roger Lafontant, who had pledged that Aristide would not take office, launched an attempted coup d'état on January 6, 1991, with fifteen collaborators, arresting Provisional President Pascal-Trouillot and forcing her to resign. The real target of the coup was Aristide, who managed to escape being captured by Lafontant (FBIS 1991b). Soon upon learning of the attempted coup, thousands of Aris-tide supporters took to the streets to oppose it. For two days, they erected bar-ricades and blocked access to the airport, attacked Lafontant's headquarters and killed many of his supporters (some by the infamous "*Père Lebrun*"[1] practice of placing a burning tire around the victim's neck), burned two su-permarkets, and severely damaged businesses owned by individuals with ties to Lafontant. The mobs also ransacked the papal nuncio's residence and burned the historic cathedral of Port-au-Prince and the residence of the Con-ference of Catholic Bishops. The attacks on Church properties were in re-sponse to a January 1 homily by the pro-Duvalierist archbishop of Port-au-Prince, Msgr. François Wolff Ligondé, who many people thought encouraged the neo-Duvalierists to act. Echoing the conservative hysteria about Aristide, Monsignor Ligondé called him a "socio-Bolshevik" and warned that under his government Haiti would become a dictatorship, but reassured his listeners that "this too shall pass" (FBIS 1991j; Farmer 1994, 158).

Faced with a general uprising against Lafontant's coup, General Hérard Abraham, the army's commander-in-chief, ordered the army to crush the coup and arrest Lafontant and his collaborators. But Abraham did not make his move until twelve hours after the attempted coup began, and only after the U.S. and Venezuelan ambassadors, among others, pressed him to do so. They made it clear to him that, unless the army intervened, the masses might turn against him and the army as well (Hockstader 1991a; Krauss 1991; French 1991d).

That same month, on January 27, another rumored coup attempt to free La-fontant provoked a violent response by the population, and on February 3, a fire allegedly set by a makout burned Aristide's orphanage, Lafanmi Selavi (Family Is Life), killing four of its young residents. In all, at least 125 people died in street violence and clashes with the army and police during the seven weeks preceding Aristide's inauguration on February 7, most of them during the January 7–8 angry popular response to Lafontant's attempted coup (D'Adesky 1991; Hockstader 1991b).

In this context, one can understand the two very important speeches Aristide gave on January 9 and at his inauguration on February 7, 1991. In the first speech, Aristide told the masses who had defied the coup that he understood their disappointment at not having captured the "powerful Macoutes today so that they do not destroy you tomorrow." He warned them, however, not to be provoked by others into committing acts for which they would be blamed. He called on the masses to remain vigilant, and on the officers and soldiers of the army to join with the people to arrest the terrorist makouts to prevent them from destroying the newly born democracy (FBIS 1991b).

This speech and subsequent statements by Aristide made it clear that he considered the violent actions of his followers to be a legitimate defense against the makouts who attempted to usurp power by force and whose impunity "begets the crumbling of society, where gun-toting people do not let unarmed people exercise their rights." Until there was a system of justice that could prosecute those who hitherto committed crimes and assassinations with impunity, Aristide maintained, he would not condemn the people for taking the law into their own hands and "necklacing" the makouts, because "one must understand what is happening and what is meant by that action" (FBIS 1991aa).

This bold stance told the masses that Aristide stood with them, but it reinforced the suspicions of the bourgeoisie, the United States, and other foreign governments about his encouragement of mob violence as a weapon of intimidation against his opponents. Those fears were heightened still further in Aristide's inaugural address on February 7, when he let it be known that his agenda in favor of the poor remained a priority. He called for unity among all Haitians and a "marriage" between the army and the people to oppose the makouts and those who are against democracy. He also asserted that the electoral victory of December 16, 1990, tore off "the veil of confinement skillfully draped around the isolation of the people." He made clear his intention to organize the Lavalas movement that brought him to power to implement the changes the people demanded.

> From now on, this historical mobilization and avalanche organization, imbedded with the stamp of Haitian genius, will regenerate the nation. It is at this new cornerstone of history that the decisive emergence of strength asserts itself, now that the people's will is irreversible. It is at this new cornerstone of history that begins the demystifying speech of collective voices denouncing with the deep resonance of the language spoken by the whole population a language of imposture, of stolen speech, gloriously conquered indeed on the day of independence, but perfidiously conjured again later (FBIS 1991z; Aristide 1992a, 103).

The time had come for "the situation to really change." For this to happen, and echoing views he had espoused as an opposition leader, Aristide announced that "the boiler must not burn only on one side"; that the poor people must "share in the country's wealth"; that those "still sitting under the table . . . [must be] sitting around the table"; that "donkeys [must] stop working for horses (poor people [must] stop working for rich ones)"; and that "whether they like it or not, no matter what, stones in water [must] get to know the pain of stones in the sun (rich people [must] know the struggle of the poor)" (FBIS 1991z; Aristide 1992a, 101–4).

To symbolize that there had been a change and that, henceforth, the poor and excluded masses would be included and prioritized, the new president chose a peasant woman to put the presidential sash on him. The next morning, President Aristide served breakfast to hundreds of homeless people and street kids invited to the National Palace. For the wealthy Haitian elites who abhor the Haitian people whom they derisively refer to as *moun pèp* (the common people), *moun endéyo* (the country or rural folks), or *gwo zòtèy* (big toes—because they often go barefoot), that is, the socially excluded, illiterate, and uncivilized masses, these gestures alone justified all their hatred of Aristide, whom many among them contemptuously called the "ugly little Nigger from the ghetto" (*Haiti en Marche* 1991h). In effect, through these acts, Aristide signaled that he was shunning the bourgeoisie to form a new pact of domination with the masses, on whom he relied to defend him against his enemies.

In an important sense, Aristide's hardened position resulted from the events preceding his inauguration, that is, when it became clear to him that his government would operate under a constant threat from the makouts and without the bourgeoisie's support. Lafontant's attempted coup and the people's immediate and violent reaction placed Aristide in a quandary and brought to the surface the contradictions inherent in Aristide's views. The bourgeoisie, the United States, and the foreign and domestic media expected Aristide to reassure them that—the makout threat notwithstanding—he would now behave as the president of all Haitians, as the prince and not the prophet, and renounce "class struggle" and mob violence. They blamed him for not stopping or condemning the counterviolence of his supporters against the attempted coup makers. U.S. officials, in their typical condescending attitude, "became increasingly disenchanted with Aristide during that period of turmoil" (Marquis 1993). "There can be no excuse for using the failed coup attempt as an excuse for exacting vengeance," a U.S. State Department spokesman stated bluntly after the events of January 7–8 (French 1991c). Jean-Jacques Honorat, a staunch foe of Aristide and director of the human rights organization *Centre Haitien de Défense des Libertés Publiques* (CHADEL, Haitian Center for the Defense of Public Liberties) funded by the National Endowment for Democracy among other foreign organizations, who later would serve as de facto prime minister (October 1991–June 1992) after the coup d'état of September 1991, went further and claimed that Aristide was "inciting people to riot! We have all the ingredients here for a new fascism. Human rights violations have been as severe in the last month as they were under Duvalier" (Farmer 1994, 166).

Aristide knew that the bourgeoisie and the United States were not with him and that they would use the slightest mistake or provocation on his part to side with the neo-Duvalierists against him. He understood that he could count on only the masses and that it would be suicidal for him to condemn them for defending him against the makout threat. To keep the masses mobilized and on his side, he continually projected a defiant attitude toward his opponents. By adopting this posture and condoning their acts of violence, however, he further alienated the bourgeoisie and the United States, who feared Aristide and the masses more than they did the makouts. The makouts acted on direct orders from their superiors and hence their behavior was more predictable, but since there was not an institutionalized hierarchical relationship between Aristide and his supporters, the latter could act on their own with their actions condoned afterward. Their behavior was therefore much less predictable.

Aristide's option for the masses, his distrust of the bourgeoisie and of the United States, and theirs of him made it impossible for him to substitute the prince's clothing for the prophet's. It reinforced his inclination to "go it alone" and shun any attempt to form a broad consensus government. Aristide was now president, but the events preceding his inauguration forced him to behave as if he was still the leader of an opposition movement. He never abandoned that modus operandi during his brief seven months in power.

Feeling threatened and on the defensive, Aristide and his followers closed ranks. No single political party had won a majority in the National Assembly in the two rounds of elections held in December 1990 and January 1991. The *Front National pour le Changement et la Démocratie* (FNCD, National Front for Democracy and Change), under whose banner Aristide ran for the presidency, captured forty seats (thirteen senators and twenty-seven deputies) and constituted the largest bloc in parliament. Bazin's Alliance Nationale pour la Démocratie et le Progrès came in second with twenty-three seats (six senators and seventeen deputies). Although eight other parties and some independent candidates split the remaining sixty-three seats, none won more than eight seats alone (FBIS 1991m).

That left Aristide free to choose his own prime minister in consultation with the presidents of the Senate and the Chamber of Deputies, rather than having to choose a prime minister from the majority party as mandated by Article 137 of the 1987 Constitution. Aristide went with his close and trusted friend, the engineer-agronomist turned baker and fellow militant anti-Duvalierist René

Préval, as his prime minister. After winning confirmation from the Senate, Prime Minister Préval, who also held the posts of interior and national defense minister, formed a cabinet comprised of friends and allies of Aristide from the progressive wing of the university-educated and professional intelligentsia (FBIS 1991kk). The formation of a cabinet that excluded representatives from other political parties and the FNCD coalition that backed Aristide's candidacy occasioned immediate criticism from the FNCD and other political leaders that Aristide would favor his supporters rather than seek broad consensus for his policies (FBIS 1991w; Hockstader 1991b). That decision would prove to be one of the several harmful, yet easily avoidable, errors of Aristide's presidency.

Two weeks after Aristide's inauguration, Prime Minister Préval outlined the immediate priorities of his government to the National Assembly on February 17, 1991. They included feeding the population and providing a minimum of health and preventive services, attenuating the high cost of living for the impoverished masses, restricting public spending, curbing corruption, controlling the collection of taxes to prevent tax evasion, launching infrastructure projects to increase employment and facilitate private sector investments, decentralizing Port-au-Prince to encourage investments in the provinces, providing subsidies and technical assistance to the peasants to increase self-sufficiency in food production, and regulating and streamlining the public enterprises. The government also contemplated bringing to justice those accused of having committed crimes against the people (e.g., assassinations, massacres, and theft) since 1986 and conducting a literacy campaign over the next three years to reach approximately three million people between fifteen and forty years of age (*Haiti Observateur* 1991c).

The government planned to form an Inter-Departmental Council that would work with the various ministries to study and recommend policies to achieve the government's administrative, political, economic, and cultural objectives. An *Institut National de la Réforme Agraire* (INRA, National Institute of Agrarian Reform) would also be created to implement the intended agrarian reform and establish a system of credits to the peasant farmers and new peasant organizations that would represent their interests within the INRA (*Haiti Observateur* 1991c).

The prime minister made it clear that the newly installed government would not seek a radical transformation of the existing economic system, but would modernize it by reforming the corrupt state institutions. This would make it possible for the government to perform its class-mediating role and absorb many of the costs of capital accumulation and economic development.

Prime Minister Préval outlined his program of government to the Haitian parliament in late February (*Haiti Observateur* 1991c). The government's program was also elaborated it in the *Cadre de Politique Économique et Programme d'Investissement Public* (Economic Policy Framework and Public Investment Program) that the *Ministère de la Planification de la Coopération Externe et de la Fonction Publique* (Office of Planning for External Cooperation and Civil Service) and *Ministère de l'Économie et des Finances* (Office of Management and Budget) submitted to the International Monetary Fund (IMF) in April 1991 (Haiti 1991).

It is wrong, therefore, to say, as Claude Moïse and Émile Olivier and others do, that "Aristide had no program" and that the "*Lavalas* team was not prepared to govern" (Moïse and Olivier 1992, 160–61). The problem was not so much a lack of a program as it would be the ability of the government to translate it into concrete public policies that it could then implement. The government's program was to be implemented over the five-year mandate of Aristide as president. Aristide and his government, however, lasted in office only seven months. No government anywhere could be expected to implement its program in such a short time, no matter how well crafted it was or how well prepared its leaders were. It takes time for any new administration just to get organized. This is especially so in a democracy, where the government in power must engage in the give-and-take of parliamentary politics. It is even more so in a country like Haiti that had just freely elected its first democratic government, where there did not exist a tradition of democratic governance to draw upon, and where the government that came to power by majority vote was despised by political, military, and economic elites for whom dictatorship was the sine qua non of their existence and who sought to undermine and overthrow that government. This does not mean that the Lavalas government was simply a passive victim of the forces of reaction or that its contradictory actions did not exacerbate the tensions with its enemies. It is simply to say that the Lavalas government came to power under foreboding conditions and that these conditions resulted from the contradictions and conflicts among the contending forces as well as those within the Lavalas government itself.

In a speech he gave at the United Nations on September 25, 1991, just five days before he was toppled by the Haitian military, Aristide outlined his views on democracy in the form of the "Ten Democratic Commandments." Starting from the premise that the pedagogy of a democratic praxis enlightened by liberation theology is informed by the lived experience of the poor (the second democratic commandment), Aristide listed three rights he considered to be fundamental human rights alongside the universal human rights to life, liberty, and the pursuit of happiness: the right to eat and the right to work (fourth commandment) and the right of the impoverished masses to demand what they are owed (fifth commandment). This meant justice and respect for all and an end to the social injustices suffered by Haitians nationally and internationally (Aristide 1992b, 193–223; 1994b, 128–47).

To guarantee these rights, Aristide argued that his government would be based on the principles of "justice, participation, and openness" and that it would "respect the individual and individual rights; respect private property and private initiatives; and respect the rights of workers" (Aristide 1994b, 158–60). In addition to these principles, three other conditions had to be met to implement the government's economic objectives over the next five years. Collectively characterized as a "transition from misery to poverty with dignity," they included the decentralization of the political structures to increase popular participation in decision making at the rural, communal, departmental, and national levels; a literacy campaign; and agrarian reform (Aristide 1994b, 160–61). In short, in this speech, Aristide gave the impression that he envisioned nothing short of a maximalist democracy for Haiti. That speech, however, was purely rhetorical. What's more, it contradicted the overall more moderate orientation of the program of government Prime Minister Préval had presented to parliament.

The government's development model was a variant of the basic needs or growth-with-equity model that emerged in the Caribbean during the 1970s and 1980s. It also conformed to the classic vision of West European social democracy adapted to the poverty and underdevelopment of Haiti. The growth-with-equity model developed in the Caribbean as an alternative to the free-market capitalism found in most societies of the region and the state socialism established in Cuba since 1961.[2] Claiming that the Lavalas movement was based on the principles of popular participation, openness in government, and social justice, the Lavalas development model prioritized the needs of the most destitute and neglected sectors of the population and the economy to make possible a transition from "misery to poverty with dignity" and to equate development with democracy (Opération Lavalas 1990b, 15–30). It sought to create not only a state of laws that respected individual liberties but also a just and equitable society that targeted the most basic needs of the population (Haiti 1991, 2–4). As Suzy Castor, then a member of the cadres of Lavalas, succinctly put it, the Lavalas model may be conceived of as a modernizing economic development project based on social justice and a politics of redistribution (1991, 34). One could also say, however, that in the tradition of Haitian programs, the Lavalas model was more theoretical than implemental, more a platform drafted by the Lavalas cadres than a program that the government would have carried out even if it had had the time to do so.

The alternative development program proposed by Opération Lavalas drew from two documents written by the cadres of the Lavalas movement known as *La chance qui passe* and *La chance à prendre* (Opération Lavalas 1990b,

1990a). These two documents offered an original reconceptualization of the Haitian economy and the principal sources of its wealth and culture.[3] The core of the Haitian economy and society, it argued, are the rural and agricultural sectors, yet these sectors were the most neglected and would require the most massive intervention on the part of the state to unleash the new processes of growth with equity (Opération Lavalas 1990b, 56–58). Since I have analyzed the Lavalas development model in great detail elsewhere (Dupuy 1997, 93–113), and since it was not implemented during Aristide's first term that lasted a mere seven months, I will only summarize its broad outlines here.

The overall objective of the model was to lay the foundation for a more independent, integrated, and equitable pattern of development. This strategy neither opposed private property ownership nor sought to assign to the state the leading role in economic development through extensive nationalization of key sectors and control of the "commanding heights" of the economy. Nor did the program imply that class and social inequalities would not continue to exist. It sought to minimize the most negative consequences of the free market and capitalist system by calling on the state to play a greater protective and redistributive role in favor of the agricultural sector, the peasantry, the working class, the informal sector, the small entrepreneurial petite bourgeoisie, women, the young, and the poor and by mediating the conflicts among the various classes in general (Opération Lavalas 1990a, 21–25).

In the context of the experiences of Cuba since 1961, Jamaica under Michael Manley (1972–80), Grenada under the New Jewel government of Maurice Bishop (1979–83), and Nicaragua under the Sandinista government (1979–90), the Lavalas development model appeared quite moderate. However, in the context of Haiti, with its long tradition of dictatorial rule and the most abject forms of exploitation since its independence in 1804, the Lavalas development model seemed quite radical.

It must be reiterated that, while it stressed the need for a redistributive policy to improve the living standard of the impoverished peasantry and urban majority, the Lavalas program did not challenge the institution of private property and the leading role of the private sector in economic development. Rather than substituting state or collective property for private property, it intended to promote the expansion of the latter among the small farmers through the creation of small- and medium-size agro-industrial and craft enterprises. It also prioritized those industries that produced primarily for the national market, but without downplaying the significance of production for export and of the assembly-manufacturing enclave. The program recognized the existence of divergent and contradictory class interests, but it suggested that, by assuming the burden of its redistributive policies, the state could mediate among them and satisfy both the particular interests of the bourgeoisie and the general interests of the majority through a program of national development.

In terms of the discussion in chapter 1, it could be said that the Lavalas development model fell in between a "maximalist" and a "minimalist" definition of democracy, more akin to a moderate than a radical version of social democracy, because it emphasized the redistribution of income and resources rather than making access to basic resources and income (e.g., food, health care, education, adequate shelter) a right to which all citizens were entitled. The model took as a given the continued existence of private ownership of the means of production and the market economy. As Michael Kaufman argued in the case of Jamaica in the 1970s, the social democratic project shared with modern liberalism the view that the injustices of capitalism could be corrected through the actions of a state under the control of an enlightened and technocratic leadership (1985, 59–60). The Lavalas model agreed with the liberal view that capitalists had a right to appropriate the profits of their enterprises because they would presumably save and reinvest them productively (Przeworski 1985, 43). It fell to the state to assume the role of redistributing income and resources to other social strata. The social democratic model envisioned by the architects of the Lavalas program, like the democratic socialist program proposed by Manley in Jamaica, insisted on class reconciliation as a "vehicle for the gradual reduction of class divisions" (Kaufman 1985, 60).

The Lavalas program held the liberal democratic premise that the bourgeoisie, especially the sector that invested nationally, had an essential role to play in the new democratic order because the private sector was best capable of generating economic development. The class compromise it called for, therefore, would occur primarily on the terms of the bourgeoisie since it was the logic of capital, efficiency, and profit that would guide the reforms the program contemplated. Rather than asking the bourgeoisie to make concessions, the liberal state with its progressive technocratic intelligentsia would modify the class injustices and the conflicts they generated. Thus, insofar as the program intended for the government to play a greater role in the economy and preserve its public enterprises, it would also serve as the basis of the clientelistic relations between the government and its mass base while promoting the interests of that fraction of the middle class that comprised the functionaries, legislators, and intellectual cadres of the new government.

The Lavalas model sought to defend the interests of all sectors of society while remaining faithful to the rules of the game established by the owners of capital and the international capitalist system. Although the program conformed to many of the tenets of the international financial institutions, it differed from them in some fundamental ways as well. On the one hand, the program intended to streamline and rationalize the public sector to make it more efficient, more market responsive, financially solvent, and less reliant on government subsidies. It assigned a leading role in economic development to the private sector rather than to the state and kept Haiti open to free trade and production for export through the assembly-manufacturing industries. It wanted to grant land titles to the peasants who held state-owned lands, thereby divesting the state of its holdings and creating market relations in land. Moreover, the Lavalas government was determined to curb corruption and waste in the public sector, implement a better and fairer system of taxation, reduce the rate of inflation, rationalize the public administration and service agencies, eliminate tax exemptions on imports, and impose a minimum tax on all previously exempted imported goods. In short, the government aimed at reducing the public deficit by controlling and restricting spending as much as possible and increasing revenues through various reform measures.

On the other hand, the program also differed significantly from the overall orientation and recommendations of the international regulatory agencies. In contrast to the latter, the project did not envision selling state enterprises to private buyers, but privatizing primarily their management to make their operation more fiscally independent and more market responsive. The program prioritized the needs of the most neglected sectors and impoverished strata of the population and intended to reallocate resources and services to them. It focused on the necessity to reform and subsidize the agricultural sector as the basis for Haiti's version of growth with equity, and emphasized production for the domestic market over production for export. It sought to improve the competitiveness of Haitian agriculture and export industries by increasing the efficiency of the enterprises. It also intended to raise the wages and productivity of workers rather than relying on the low-wage strategy of the international financial institutions and the United States Agency for International Development (USAID). Lastly, though the program realized the necessity to maintain Haiti's ties to the U.S. economy, it advocated greater regional and South-South economic and political relations to increase Haiti's autonomy and counteract the dominance of the United States.

Although the program did not advocate state control over the commanding heights of the economy and assigned the leading role to the private sector, it contemplated playing an interventionist, *dirigiste*, and even protectionist role in economic development. This was not a state-led or state-dominated model, but was more interventionist and more social democratic than the "market-friendly" model advocated by the World Bank. The social democratic project sought to balance the interest of classes within Haiti and to negotiate Haiti's historical subordination to foreign capital and the rules of the international capitalist division of labor by balancing those interests with its own model of growth with equity. This was decidedly a novel approach that would test whether the so-called New World Order imperialism would allow a hitherto client state of the United States to experiment with its own homegrown model of democracy and economic development.

TOWARD A COUP D'ÉTAT

In late February 1991, the National Assembly approved a bill based on several articles of the 1987 Constitution (especially Article 295) that gave the first elected president the power to implement within six months all necessary reforms in the public administration and the magistracy (FBIS 1991k). Aristide and his prime minister were well aware that the announced measures would not stand a chance of implementation unless Aristide first neutralized the traditional power bases of the prebendary state system. This meant reforming the military institution and dismantling its paramilitary organization variously known as *makouts*, *zenglendos*, or *attachés*. Without this, Aristide argued, there would be no justice and no security; and, without security, there would be no investment of capital or economic development (Caroit 1991). This explains why Aristide decided, starting with his inaugural address, to "strike at the head" of the army by requesting the retirement (or reassignment to obscure posts) of several top-ranking officers who had controlled the armed forces under past regimes and by promoting or commissioning new officers thought to be more supportive of democratization (Aristide 1992b, 160; FBIS 1991z; AW/NCHR/CR 1991, 4; Slavin 1991). Among the presumed reform-minded officers was Col. Raoul Cédras (who would become the leader of the coup against Aristide in September 1991). Cédras was promoted in July 1991 to the rank of brigadier general and named interim commander-in-chief of the army to replace General Abraham, who was pressured to resign (*Haiti en Marche* 1991b).

In addition to the reshuffling at the top, the reforms contemplated for the army included three essential measures: separating the army from the police, disarming the paramilitary organization, and dismantling the *chèfs seksyon* (section chiefs) system. Historically, the police force in Haiti was a division of the army, and the section chiefs, who reported to the local subdistrict army commanders, functioned as a rural police force. They recruited their own deputies, collected taxes, and charged peasants to settle land and personal disputes. They also had the power to arrest and sentence people in their localities and to suppress civic or peasant organizations they considered subversive. In short, they exercised authoritarian control over their respective local populations and often ruled through extortion and terror. There is no doubt that abolishing the section chief system was one of the most important steps that the Aristide-Préval government could have taken to establish the rule of law in Haiti (AW/NCHR/CR 1991, 9; O'Neill 1993, 106).

Separating the police and the section chiefs from the army and placing them under the jurisdiction of the Ministry of Justice, as mandated by the 1987 Constitution, would reduce the army's role to one of protecting the nation against foreign threats. Yet, the modern Haitian Army (which was created during the U.S. occupation of 1915–34) had never fought a foreign war, and Haiti did not face any external threats. Historically, the army's primary function had been to preserve the status quo and suppress domestic opposition. The restructuring envisioned by Aristide's government, therefore, would disempower it. The army and its extended apparatuses stood to lose more than they would gain under the new order and, as expected, many within the army and the police, as well as the section chiefs, opposed the intended reforms.

A debate within the National Assembly over the structure of the new police force and the extension of civilian control beyond the Ministry of Justice to elected officials prevented the military reform bill introduced in the Assembly by the minister of justice in August 1991 from being enacted before the September coup. The 555-strong section chief force was placed under the control of the Ministry of Justice in April 1991 and ordered to turn in their weapons. Those found guilty of corruption or other violations were to be discharged, while others would be retired. These measures were not all successfully implemented. The section chiefs were renamed "communal police agents" and henceforth were supposed to report to local prosecutors. While some section chiefs were forced out, others managed to remain in the new positions and continued to operate as before. No new laws had been passed to specify their powers or the authority of the local prosecutors over them. Thus, peasants' demands for a thorough break with the old system and training a new rural police force remained largely unfulfilled (AW/NCHR/CR 1991, 9, 16; Gaillard 1991, 48).

In addition to separating the police and the section chiefs from the army, the reforms called for the creation of a small but highly trained presidential security service (SSP—Service de Sécurité Présidentielle). The proposal to train a personal security force to protect Aristide came initially from the U.S. State Department and the Central Intelligence Agency shortly after the December 1990 elections in order not to leave him "dangerously exposed" to a "restive military." The security team was to comprise three aides and fifteen soldiers. After accepting the offer, Aristide apparently became suspicious of the team and changed his mind. He turned, instead, to the French and Swiss governments to train the presidential security team (Marquis 1993). The suggestion of forming this security team immediately gave rise to speculation in the pages of the anti-Aristide weekly *Haiti Observateur* and other media sources that Aristide intended to pattern the security force after Duvalier's *Tontons Makout* and, like Duvalier, use that force to establish his lifetime dictatorship (*Haiti Observateur* 1991a, 1991b). These rumors persisted despite evidence that the SSP would not be larger than thirty men and that it would be placed under the command of an army officer. The chief of the Swiss police team who was sent to Haiti along with French police officers to train the presidential security force also gave assurances that the SSP was to serve as a personal security guard for the president and not as his private militia. Obviously, the rumors were purposefully aimed at fomenting discord between the army and Aristide to block the desired reforms (AW/NCHR/CR 1991, 18) and to create the "Tonton Makout syndrome," putting Aristide on the defensive and preventing him from taking any measures to assure his own security. Regardless of the real reasons for creating the security force, the army leadership interpreted this move as yet another indication that Aristide did not trust them and intended to dilute their power and influence as much as possible.

If Aristide's government did not succeed in fully implementing the military reforms, it made significant headway in combating corruption, contraband, drug trafficking, and human rights abuses within that institution. The government established an interministerial commission in February 1991 and a second independent commission in August to investigate and bring to justice those accused of crimes and massacres between 1986 and 1990, such as those at Jean-Rabel, Piatte, Danty, Labadie, and Saint Jean Bosco. Several former officers and government officials were arrested, and arrest warrants were issued for others. Aristide also replaced several "compromised" Supreme Court justices, along with many other judges in the countryside. Soldiers conducted raids against the makouts, disarming and arresting scores of them. With the exception of five young men killed in July 1991, human rights abuses committed by soldiers and the police no longer occurred with impunity and declined significantly during the seven months of the first Lavalas government. With the reestablishment of a relative climate of security, citizens no longer feared resuming nightly activities, and corpses would no longer be found on sidewalks at dawn (AW/NCHR/CR 1991; D'Adesky 1991; Wilentz 1991; Gaillard 1991; FBIS 1991h, 1991r).

Rather than consolidating the "marriage" between the army and the people Aristide had announced in his inaugural address, the measures pursued by his government antagonized relations between the army and the president during his short term in office. The provocative behavior and speeches of some of his supporters, instead of being persuasive and conciliatory, caused tremendous fear even among sectors of the bourgeoisie willing to cooperate with the government. Unrest within the army increased throughout the first six months, some targeted against Duvalierist officers whom soldiers wanted removed, but other disturbances against the government, including several government-preempted plots by civilians and soldiers to assassinate Aristide or overthrow him (Ives 1991; FBIS 1991p). On at least two occasions, U.S. Ambassador Alvin Adams, acting on CIA intelligence reports, warned Aristide of such assassination and coup attempts (Marquis 1993). Makouts also engaged in many actions designed to spread panic and destabilize the government. The most dramatic event occurred when some of them carried out their threat to burn the landmark Hyppolite Public Market in Port-au-Prince, which housed more than 2,000 mostly independent petty merchants and crafts workers, on April 16–17, 1991 (FBIS 1991o). Thus, by the time of the September coup, the makout camp and "rank-and-file soldiers had been whipped into an anti-Aristide frenzy" (Constable 1992–93).

The government also came under fire from several quarters for not doing enough to reduce the high cost of living and not moving fast enough to "uproot" the makout functionaries from the public enterprises, ministries, and agencies. Aristide and his ministers responded that the government was determined to implement the reforms during its allotted six-month period. They warned the impatient activists that reforming a state system in complete disarray and ridden with corruption necessarily required time and care to avoid arbitrary dismissals and keep in their posts those not implicated in criminal activities, whose competence and skills were needed to keep the public sector functioning (Caroit 1991; *Haiti Progrès* 1991a, 1991c). Nonetheless, the manner in which the government carried out its dismissals gave the impression that it was engaged in a witch-hunt, leading some of its ever watchful critics to charge that the government "confuses dismissals with reform" (FBIS 1991i).

In addition to removing the "old guard" who ran the public sector as their private prebend, the government sought to curb waste and corruption by closing some offices and agencies completely and by reducing the budget, the salaries of functionaries, and the size of the public sector. To set the example, in his inaugural address, Aristide asked the National Assembly to cut his $10,000 monthly salary, and he often donated his paycheck to nongovernmental organizations, such as UNICEF or citizens' groups, to help them prepare for the literacy campaign (FBIS 1991c, 1991dd). The government also took steps to reduce the size of the public sector and its Office of Management and Budget issued a report in May 1991 stating that at least 5,000 employees had lost their jobs in the public administration and public enterprises. By early September 1991, the number had risen to more than 8,000, thereby reducing the total of public-sector employees to 37,000 (*Haiti en Marche* 1991j; *Haiti Observateur* 1991d; Ives 1991).

Those measures began to pay off. The government took steps to collect the payment of arrears owed to it and to prevent tax evasion by the wealthy and fraud in the ministries and public enterprises. As a result, the *Direction Générale des Impôts* (Internal Revenue Administration) registered a historic increase in total revenues, thereby reversing the opposite tendency of previous governments. Two public monopolies that in the past served primarily as sources of graft and corruption for government officials showed dramatic improvements in their performance under Aristide. The *Minoterie d'Haiti*, the government's flour mill—hitherto always "in the red"—showed a profit in April, and *Ciment d'Haiti*, another bankrupt public enterprise, reduced its deficit by 60 percent between February and April 1991. Total monthly government expenditures were reduced from $32.9 million in November 1990 to $17 million in June 1991, recording for the first time in many years a budgetary surplus of $8.2 million (*Haiti Progrès* 1991b; Ives 1991).

The government also prevented importers from hoarding and inflating food prices by fixing the price of certain basic food items. It proposed to raise the daily minimum wage from 15 to 25 gourdes (from $3 to $5), primarily for urban workers who made up a relatively small proportion of the labor force. But after heavy opposition and lobbying by the private sector, the National Assembly set the minimum wage at 24 gourdes in March, officially $4.80 but in reality worth only $2.82 given the market exchange rate of 8.5 gourdes to $1 in 1991 (*Haiti en Marche* 1991f; *Haiti Observateur* 1991d).

In its short seven months in office, then, the government increased internal revenues and customs receipts, transformed hitherto inefficient and unprofitable state enterprises into efficient and profitable operations, brought government spending under control and reduced the internal financing of public sector deficit, increased the foreign exchange reserve by $20 million, and reduced the public debt by $127 million, from $874 to $747 million (Haiti 1994).

The Lavalas government went on the offensive on many fronts. Though it achieved mixed results with its attempted reforms in the military, public administration, magistracy, and public enterprises, there is no question that the measures it took struck at the heart of the power base of the old regime and intensified the antagonism between the pro-makout camp and the government. The makout camp and the prebendary military and public sector officialdom would be the biggest losers with the advent of democracy and a government bent on implementing sweeping reforms in these institutions. They had an interest in subverting the democratization process, and this could only be done by reverting to dictatorship. To avoid a collision between the makout or neo-Duvalierist forces and the Aristide government, the latter would have had to respect the status quo and do nothing. But to do so would have earned

Aristide the enmity of the popular democratic movement and of the 67 percent of the voters who had elected him to carry out the *déchoukaj* or "uprooting" of the Duvalierist and prebendary state system. Moreover, to capitulate to the makout camp would have meant abandoning all hopes for a democratic alternative, of whatever kind, since this would grant the forces in control of the army and the state apparatuses veto power over any reforms.

If the animosity between the Aristide government and the neo-Duvalierist forces was expected and inevitable, the friction with the bourgeoisie, as well as the altercations with the National Assembly that paralyzed the government and enticed popular violence, could have been minimized. Aristide needed the cooperation of the bourgeoisie and the National Assembly if his reforms and his government were to have any chance of survival. It was imperative for him to woo the bourgeoisie, as well as his supporters and opponents in the Assembly, by forming a broad coalition government that included representatives from these sectors. Aristide failed to do so not only because he was predisposed to pursue a "go-it-alone" strategy but also because the events of January 1991 which he did not provoke reinforced his conviction that he could not trust those who were not proven Lavalasians.

Aristide's contradictory messages and actions as president helped in souring relations with the bourgeoisie and the National Assembly. The Lavalas Project, Préval's general policies, and the Cadre de Politique Économique made it clear that the government intended to pursue an economic policy ostensibly acceptable to the IMF/World Bank, international aid donors, and the Haitian bourgeoisie. After nearly four months of negotiation, the government and the IMF signed a Stand-by Arrangement in September 1991 (*Haiti en Marche* 1991g; *Haiti Observateur* 1991f). President Aristide, who had once denounced the IMF as the "*Front de Misère Internationale*" (International Misery Front), tried to put the best face on the agreement. Addressing the mass organizations that had criticized him and his government for negotiating with the IMF, Aristide argued:

> The rules of the game have changed. The situation with the IMF is almost identical. The difference is that they are not here to give orders. They cannot give us orders. They can come to hold discussions with us and we will be willing to speak with them. They have recognized the good job we have been doing, and have said so. We are happy that they said so. They did not order us to do a good job. We are simply doing a good job. They recognize that, and will capitalize on it. In our negotiations with them, we continue doing a good job for best results. (FBIS 1991a)

Aristide could have sounded less defensive about his government's negotiations and could have deflected these criticisms by pointing out to his critics that structural adjustment in Haiti would not mean the same thing as in other Third World countries. For example, in Jamaica under Manley and Nicaragua under the Sandinistas, the governments were being asked to cut social spending and social services that targeted the working classes and the poorest sectors of society. In Haiti, by contrast, the government had never provided social services or subsidies to the poor or the working and peasant classes, and any reforms in the public sector would affect primarily the prebendary state officials, the clientelistic civil servants, and the extended makout network that siphoned off public resources for their benefit. As such, Aristide could have argued that the structural and other adjustments his government intended to implement were necessary if it were to reach the goal of dismantling the prebendary state system and substituting for it a modern liberal state that would for the first time provide essential services and subsidies to the poor majority.

As things stood, Aristide tried to dismiss the misguided and instinctive criticism of the government's structural adjustment agreements by invoking an equally misleading and defensive nationalist stance. Be that as it may, the "good job" that Aristide referred to simply meant that his government had adopted an economic program sufficiently compatible with the IMF and the World Bank for those institutions and other donor governments to pledge about $500 million in loans and foreign aid to Haiti (*Haiti en Marche* 1991d). The much-promised foreign aid had not materialized by the time of the September coup, but the United States, which had established cordial relations with and approved several aid packages for the Aristide government, did agree to cancel Haiti's $107 million debt to the United States as a result of the IMF agreement (FBIS 1991g; French 1991a; Tarr 1991b).

Despite the government's moderate economic policies, the Haitian bourgeoisie, especially the few powerful families that dominated the private sector and were most closely allied with the neo-Duvalierists, withheld its support from the government. If the Lavalas Project had been implemented, the bourgeoisie would have benefited and its influence as a class would have been strengthened. However, this would be in the long run, and the Haitian bourgeoisie usually pursued its short-term interests. For most of its history, the Haitian bourgeoisie has been a visionless, retrograde social class concerned primarily with safeguarding its immediate wealth and privileges. The monopolist faction of the bourgeoisie collaborated closely with the Duvalier dictatorships and their successors. It has been said that "if the Duvaliers did not exist, [the wealthy elite] would have invented them" (*Haiti en Marche* 1991h). Aristide understood this and, though a formidable task, it was imperative for him to try to persuade the bourgeoisie that it had more to gain under the new regime, even if that called for making concessions. Unfortunately for

Aristide, he attempted to persuade the bourgeoisie by threatening it, thereby dashing any hope for a rapprochement, improbable as the latter may have been in any case.

As expected, the business elite opposed the social-democratic and redistributive thrust of the Aristide government, particularly the reforms that targeted the loopholes and other prerogatives it had enjoyed under the old regimes. The business elite considered the law that raised the minimum daily wage by a mere $1.80 to be "antieconomic and antinational," arguing in a meeting with Aristide that its implementation would impact negatively on Haiti's competitiveness vis-à-vis its Caribbean neighbors, increase unemployment, and compel many investors to relocate to those countries where labor was cheaper (Daniel 1991; FBIS 1991f, 1991cc). USAID also opposed the proposed increase in the minimum daily wage on grounds similar to those offered by the Haitian business elite. The agency knew, however, that an increase as high as $0.75 an hour (or $6.00 a day), well above the wage level proposed by the Aristide government, would still keep Haitian labor cheaper than its Caribbean and Central American competitors, except for the Dominican Republic. The Haitian business elite and USAID wanted nothing other than the oppressive, but highly profitable, labor conditions that existed prior to February 1991 (National Labor Committee 1994, 144–45).

Above all, the bourgeoisie felt threatened by the policies of the new government, especially by what they saw as Aristide's encouragement of the increasing militancy of the grassroots organizations, student organizations, TKL community-based organizations, trade unions, peasant organizations, and vigilante groups. The bourgeoisie, in other words, feared the empowerment of the social classes whose abject exploitation and suppression the dictatorships had guaranteed.

The momentum created by the election of Aristide and the reformist thrust of his government opened a Pandora's box of pent-up grievances and demands. Hardly a month went by without demonstrations or other actions—some violent—by one or another group or mass organization in Port-au-Prince and other cities, towns, and villages throughout Haiti. Both organized and unorganized groups made various demands on the government: workers calling for higher wages, better working conditions, and management changes in enterprises; public sector employees for uprooting the administrative personnel from the old regime in the provinces as well as in Port-au-Prince; students for university reforms; peasants for land reform; consumers for lowering the high cost of living and ending food stockpiling by merchants to inflate retail prices; citizens for more jobs, health care, education, and a literacy campaign; others for reversing deforestation and the degradation of the environment; and some popular organizations for removing several government ministers accused of protecting the bourgeoisie's interests, against negotiations with the IMF, and against U.S. interference in Haiti's internal affairs (FBIS 1991l, 1991q, 1991t, 1991u, 1991x, 1991ee, 1991hh, 1991gg, 1991ii, 1991jj)

Besieged by these multiple and conflicting demands, the government devoted considerable time and energy responding to them. Aristide, Préval, and other ministers met with various groups to listen to them and discuss their grievances and, where they could, took prompt action to satisfy them. Aristide held unprecedented and open meetings at the National Palace with the press, trade union representatives, peasant delegations, thousands of unemployed people, youths, and leaders of popular organizations. When he spoke to them, Aristide tried to reassure and encourage them in their struggle. For example, Aristide told the trade union representatives to organize themselves better to become a stronger and more effective force. He told the peasant delegations that his government intended to take away state-owned lands from landowners and redistribute them to peasants in accordance with the constitution. To the unemployed, he said that "militants who worked in the field, who worked hard so the avalanche could overflow, should not have to go and ask for favors to get work, as if they do not have the right to work" (FBIS 1991a, 1991e, 1991u, 1991ii).

Yet, when he spoke to the private-sector bourgeoisie or to other groups about the bourgeoisie, Aristide often employed a more severe and even threatening tone. While he told the bourgeoisie that "without them it would be difficult to promote a productive society and reach a balanced economy," he also reminded them that "all private property has a social mortgage, and [that] to mortgage the sovereignty [of the State and of the president's power] is to reject dignity" (FBIS 1991d, 1991jj). He went even further, making a distinction between the "good" and "bad" bourgeois. The "patriotic" bourgeois was willing to make concessions, while the "selfish" bourgeois—the *bourgeoisie patripoche*—did not identify with the national interest, having collaborated with the dictatorships to safeguard its privileges. Basically, Aristide advanced a voluntaristic argument with a compulsory dimension. According to him, the bourgeoisie had to learn new human values, respect the society as a whole, and behave differently. It had to learn that it is in its interest to make concessions, to accept the hand offered by the lower classes, and to form an alliance between its capital and the "revolutionary capital of Lavalas" to create the new economic order. Should the bourgeoisie remain passive and selfish and refuse to cooperate with the new movement, the starving masses could be pushed to demand more radical measures. In Aristide's words, "The people who are sleeping like a log today could be roaring tomorrow" (Aristide 1992a, 162–64; FBIS 1991f).

Aristide's argument was premised on the threat of force as a determinant in the last instance. The bourgeoisie was left with a choice: either cooperate with the "Lavalas revolution" or risk pushing the Haitian masses to revolution (Aristide 1992a, 164). It is difficult to see why the bourgeoisie would accept such a proposition and why, under such a threat, it would believe Aristide when he said that he would respect its rights and property. The populist contradictions of the Lavalas Project were rearing their heads and placing the government in an untenable position.

The provocative and threatening actions of some of the groups and organizations that supported Aristide—with his encouragement of their behavior in several instances—further damaged his credibility with the bourgeoisie. One example occurred with the actions taken by Jean-Auguste Mesyeux, the leader of the *Centrale Autonome des Travailleurs Haitiens* (CATH, Autonomous Union of Haitian Workers) who launched *"Opération Vent-Tempête"* (Operation Storm Wind) in June 1991 (FBIS 1991s). In the name of "uprooting" makouts from the public administration, Mesyeux and his followers threatened to enter government offices, take employees hostage, and deliver them to the National Palace. On June 17 and 18, some 2,000–3,000 protesters demanded the dismissal of the prime minister, his cabinet, and even the president himself. The demonstrators also threatened Préval with *Père Lebrun*. On August 13, supporters of Aristide retaliated and burned down the CATH's headquarters (FBIS 1991v). Yet, later, Aristide received Mesyeux at the National Palace and offered him a job as an advisor in Préval's office, which Mesyeux refused (*Haiti en Marche* 1991c). This led some critics to charge that the government itself was implicated in Operation Storm Wind (FBIS 1991n). The government did nothing to repudiate this allegation. That event also made it clear that Aristide had not broken with the clientelistic system, his rhetoric to the contrary notwithstanding.

Another damaging incident for Aristide occurred with the trial of Lafontant and his accomplices in July 1991 for their attempted coup d'état in January. Unable to find lawyers willing to defend them for fear of popular reprisals, and refusing to accept court-appointed lawyers, Lafontant and fifteen of his accomplices were found guilty of plotting against the state. They received life imprisonment at forced labor, even though the law for such an offense provided for only fifteen to twenty years. Only four of the defendants received a lesser sentence of ten to fifteen years at forced labor (*Haiti en Marche* 1991e).

Several days before the trial, Aristide lashed out against the alleged maneuvering going on to delay the trial, denounced the corruption in the judicial administration, asked the population to remain vigilant and to follow the trial closely, and threatened to take action if the trial did not go on as scheduled

(*Haiti en Marche* 1991i). Speaking at a youth rally a few days after the trial, Aristide praised the people for their vigilance and their wise use of the threat of *Père Lebrun*:

> Was there Père Lebrun inside the courthouse? [Audience yells no.] Was there Père Lebrun in front of the courthouse? [Audience yells yes.] Did the people use Père Lebrun? [Audience yells no.] Did the people forget it? [Audience yells no.] Did they have a right to forget it? [Audience yells no.] Do not say that I said it. [Laughter.]
>
> In front of the courthouse, for 24 hours, Père Lebrun became a good firm bed. The people slept on it. Its springs bounced back. The Justice Ministry inside the courthouse had the law in its hands, the people had their cushion outside. The people had their little matches in their hands. They had gas nearby. Did they use it? [Audience yells no.] That means that the people respect [Audience yells "the constitution."] Does the Constitution tell the people to forget little Père Lebrun? [Audience yells no.]
>
> Therefore when those inside know what is going on outside, those inside had to tread carefully [literally, walk on thirteen so as not to break fourteen]. [The audience answers: "Fourteen is the masses of the people."] The masses have their own tool, their own secret way, their own wisdom.
>
> When they spoke of 15 years inside the courthouse, according to the law, outside the people began to clamor for Père Lebrun. . . . That's why the verdict came out as a life sentence. The people, who respect the law, who uphold the Constitution, when the people heard "life in prison," they forgot their little matches, little gasoline, and little Père Lebrun. Did the people use Père Lebrun that day? [Audience yells no.] But if it had not gone well, wouldn't the people have used Père Lebrun? [Audience yells yes.] That means that when you are in your literacy class you are learning to write "Père Lebrun," you are learning to think about "Père Lebrun," it's because you have to know when to use it, and where to use it. And you may never use it again in a state where law prevails (that's what I hope!) as long as they stop using deception and corruption. So, that's what they call real literacy. (cited in AW/NCHR/CR 1991; FBIS 1991y)

Aristide's motives may well have been to rally, educate, and shape the people into a credible force "capable of exerting legitimate pressure on the judicial system, but without threatening it, so that when the judge knows that the people are there, the judge can feel strengthened to render justice and not succumb to the weight of money or the pressures that will come upon him" (Danner 1993, 51). As with many of his other speeches, however, the above speech sent contradictory messages to different audiences. As Mark Danner observed, Aristide may have wanted his followers to hear that he still believed that only they could constitute the revolutionary force to change things in Haiti. At the same time, his speech frightened the moneyed and privileged classes, for whom the threat of deadly violence to change the system "did not seem at all reassuring coming from an elected President of the Republic, the man who was supposed to have responsibility to govern his people through the constitution and the established mechanisms of power" (Danner 1993, 51–52).

Aristide committed a fatal error here. He had chosen the electoral path to reform over the revolutionary or armed takeover of the state. Therefore, alluding to the use of deadly violence to change the status quo was an irresponsible act, as well as a violation of the constitution he was sworn to uphold. The trial posed no danger to his government, and he had everything to gain by using the opportunity offered by the trial to set an example and show that his administration would enforce the rule of law, respect the principle of separation of powers outlined in the 1987 Constitution, and allow the courts to exercise their functions without interference from the executive. The masses who assembled in front of the courthouse during the trial had the right to demand a life sentence for Lafontant and his collaborators, but not the right to threaten the justices for imposing a sentence in accordance with the law. Aristide overstepped his powers by encouraging them in that direction. As Moïse and Olivier observed, instead of using the trial to indict Duvalierism as a whole, the government preferred a

> botched job that left the troublesome impression that the courts were being used as an instrument to settle accounts with the *macoutes*. The general offensive of the Executive against a wanting judicial system, the indiscriminate accusations of corruption against the judges encouraged the popular pressure groups to intimidate judges in several regions. (1992, 167)

Another costly error on Aristide's part came when he failed to condemn the threat of *Père Lebrun* by his supporters against members of the National Assembly who opposed the government. The government became embroiled in a ceaseless conflict with the National Assembly over the interpretation of the "transitional" Article 295 of the constitution, the delays in approving government appointments, voting on the budget presented by the government, the separation of the police from the army, the law to create a Permanent Electoral Council, and a series of other government initiatives. It may be the case that, at bottom, the conflict between the executive and the legislative was about which of the two branches would exercise greater control over the government. Ironically, the unfolding power struggle pitted Aristide against the FNCD, the very coalition that made his candidacy and his election possible.

The FNCD began to feud openly with Aristide and accused him of having betrayed them when he referred to the FNCD as "just a legal hat that enabled him to run in the elections" and when he opted to form a cabinet excluding representatives from the FNCD and other political organizations that offered to form a broad left-of-center parliamentary majority in support of the government. Some of Aristide's supporters contend that the FNCD wanted Aristide to choose an FNCD member as prime minister. When Aristide refused, the FNCD began to oppose him, signaling that the newly formed National Assembly would become the locus of opposition to the Lavalas government. The president and prime minister furthered the rift by bypassing the FNCD and other parliamentary parties for administrative posts, reserving them instead for close Lavalas supporters. Aristide considered the political parties to be mere "talk shops" and believed that he and Lavalas alone truly represented the people. With the people behind him, he thought, he could govern without the National Assembly and the "give and take" of democratic politics (*Haiti en Marche* 1991a, 1991c, 1991d; French 1991b; FBIS 1991x; Tarr 1991a). Aristide, in short, made it clear that his government would serve the interests of the faction of the petite bourgeoisie that formed the cadres of the Lavalas movement and, through the traditional clientelistic practices, solidify support from his mass base by giving its leaders public-sector jobs whether or not they were qualified for them.

The conflict between the legislative and the executive reached its boiling point when the National Assembly summoned Préval to appear before it to account for his government's performance during the previous six months. When he failed to appear, the Assembly called for his resignation and threatened a vote of no confidence against him, which could have brought down the government. Reacting to these parliamentary maneuvers against the prime minister, and seeing them as attacks against Aristide himself, the ever-vigilant popular groups who had burned the CATH headquarters now attacked the homes of an FNCD senator and of KID leader and Port-au-Prince Mayor Evans Paul, and ransacked the latter's offices of the KID (a faction within the FNCD). Between 2,000 and 4,000 demonstrators descended on the National Assembly, threatened legislators with *Père Lebrun*, beat two of them, and trapped them along with the prime minister inside the Legislative Palace. The police finally intervened with tear gas to disperse the protesters and allow the legislators and prime minister to leave the premises (FBIS 1991v, 1991bb).

The government condemned and distanced itself from the actions of the demonstrators, called on the people to respect the rights of others, and expressed sympathy for the legislators and the victims of the violence. This communiqué was too little and too late, however. The message that Aristide sent to the dominant classes and his political opponents was unmistakable: he was building his own counterforce with the masses who supported him and was not at all reluctant to use that force to get his way. The National Assembly, bowing to popular threats, postponed the censuring debate, but subjected Préval to a six-hour public interrogation and criticism of his government's behavior. The Senate also unanimously denounced the popular acts of intimidation against members of the National Assembly and saw them as a threat against the burgeoning democracy. There is little doubt that the four major political blocs in the Chamber of Deputies, including the FNCD, would have voted in favor of the censure motion if it had been taken (FBIS 1991v, 1991ll, 1991mm; Tarr 1991a; French 1991e). By the time the coup d'état got under way in September, Aristide and the government of his prime minister had clearly lost the support of their former allies in the National Assembly.

It is in the context of the preceding events that one is to understand Aristide's (in)famous September 27, 1991, speech, the last impassioned speech he made before his overthrow three days later by the military. Aristide had just returned to Haiti from New York, where he had gone to address the United Nations on September 25, and the defiant tone of the September 27 speech was a reaction to the information that he received about the impending coup against him (AW/NCHR/CR 1991, 24; Danner 1993, 52). Aristide launched a direct attack against the makouts and the bourgeoisie patripoche. It is worth quoting from that speech at length. Talking to the bourgeoisie, he said:

That money which you have is not really yours. You earned it in thievery, through bad choices you've made, under an evil regime and system and in all other unsavory ways. Today, seven months after February 7, in this day ending with the numeral 7, I give you a chance, because you won't have two, nor three chances. It's only one chance that you'll have. Otherwise, things won't be so good for you!

If I speak to you in that way, it's because I've given you seven months to conform, and the seven months are up—to the day. . . .

[Turning to the masses, he said:] Now whenever you are hungry, turn your eyes in the direction of those people who aren't hungry. Whenever you are out of work, turn your eyes in the direction of those who can put people to work. Ask them why not? What are you waiting for?

Whenever you feel the heat of unemployment, whenever the heat of the pavement gets to you, whenever you feel revolt inside you, turn your eyes in the direction of those with the means. . . .

And if you catch a cat (the slang in the Creole language for thief), if you catch a sticky finger slob, if you catch a false *Lavalassien*, if you catch . . . (he stopped in the middle of the word), if you catch one who shouldn't be there, don't-he-si-ta-te-to-give-him-what-he-de-serves (staccato for effect and repeated twice).

Your tool in hand, your instrument in hand, your constitution in hand. Don't-he-si-ta-te-to-give-him-what-he-de-serves.

Your equipment in hand, your trowel in hand, your pencil in hand, your constitution in hand, don't-he-si-ta-te-to-give-him-what-he-de-serves.

The 291 . . . says: Macoute isn't in the game. Don't-he-si-ta-te-to-give-him-what-he-de-serves (repeated twice).

Everywhere, in the four corners, we are watching, we are praying . . . when you catch one, don't he-si-ta-te-to-give-him-what-he-de-serves.

What a beautiful tool! What a beautiful instrument! What a beautiful device! It's beautiful, yes it's beautiful, it's cute, it's pretty, it has a good smell, wherever you go you want to inhale it. Since the law of the country says Macoute isn't in the game, whatever happens to him he deserves, he came looking for trouble.

Again, under this flag of pride, under this flag of solidarity, hand in hand, one encouraging the other, one holding the other's hand, so that from this day forward, each one will pick up this message of respect that I share with you, this message of justice that I share with you, so that the word ceases to be the word and becomes action. With other actions in the economic field, I throw the ball to you, you dribble it, you shoot . . . on the goal adroitly, because if the people don't find this ball to hold it in the net, well, as I told you, it's not my fault, it's you who will find what-you-de-serve, according to what the Mother Law of the country declares.

Alone, we are weak! Together we are strong! Altogether we are *Lavalas*! (*Haiti Observateur* 1991e)

The September 27 speech was inflammatory insofar as it condoned popular violence against the recalcitrant bourgeoisie and the makouts. But this speech was also defensive and preemptive. Aristide knew of the impending coup, and he probably believed that, with the events of January 7 and 8 still fresh on everyone's mind, he could preempt the coup plotters by "brandishing what had always been his greatest strength and his most feared weapon—the Flood, the avalanche represented by the poor multitudes who were now cheering before him" (Danner 1993, 52). Aristide acknowledged this himself later in an interview when he said in response to a question about his speech that the text should be put in context. As he put it, "The coup had started. I was using words to answer the bullets," a vain effort to forestall the coup (Attinger and Kramer 1993, 28; Danner 1993, 52n). This time around, however, the army high command and the makout camp, with the support of the bourgeoisie and especially its wealthiest faction, were prepared to unleash the most brutal wave of repression, terror, and assassination against Aristide's supporters and the entire spectrum of the pro-democratic forces.

Three days after this speech, a unit of the army under the command of Chief of Police Michel François, then a major, launched the coup that toppled Aristide and his government (Danner 1993, 52; Moïse and Olivier 1992, 177). Thanks only to the intervention of the French, U.S., and Venezuelan ambassadors, the putschists spared Aristide's life and allowed him to flee into exile (Goshko 1991).

There are times in history when a leader is justified in calling on the people to rise up against their enemies and to use whatever means are necessary to repel them. Such a situation existed in Saint-Domingue in 1802 during the revolution when Napoleon Bonaparte sent an expedition to recapture the colony from Toussaint Louverture and restore the slave regime. As C. L. R. James argued, Louverture should have acted decisively once he learned of the expedition. He should have called the population to arms and given the French colonialists a clear choice: either leave the colony or accept the new order and defend it. The properties of all those who refused to side with the new regime, James maintained, should have been seized, and those French who showed any sign of treason should have been summarily executed. Moreover, rather than reassuring the whites that they and their properties were safe, Louverture should have spoken to the masses to explain to them what was happening and what had to be done. For it was what they thought that mattered then, not what the imperialists thought. James added, "If to make matters clear to them [the masses] Toussaint had to condone a massacre of the whites, so much the worse for the whites. He had done everything possible for them" (James 1963, 286–87).

Haiti under Aristide, however, was not in a revolutionary situation. Nor was his government seeking to expropriate the dominant classes and establish a new social order. Quite the contrary, his government preached class conciliation and proposed an economic program that depended for its success on the collaboration of the bourgeoisie. This does not mean that Aristide should have remained passive against threats to his government. He may have been justified, for example, in not condemning the violent reaction of his supporters to the stillborn coup d'état by Lafontant in January 1991 and in placing the blame for the violence squarely on the shoulders of the coup makers. He certainly had a right to call on his supporters to be vigilant and to defend his government on September 27 if a coup were to be launched against him. But, just as he was wrong to praise his popular supporters on August 4 with his reference to their "wise" understanding of when to use *Père Lebrun* during the trial of Lafontant and his accomplices, he was wrong to threaten popular violence against the bourgeoisie for the latter's recalcitrance and exercise of its property rights. Aristide himself, after all, had promised to respect the bourgeoisie's property and interests. In politics, it is always dangerous to threaten the use of force against one's opponent unless one is willing and able to carry out the threat. In a fragile transitional period, as was the case in Haiti, empty threats to opponents who are by class instincts predisposed to subvert the democratization process are disastrous. Aristide had never armed or formed a disciplined organization among his supporters and therefore had only veiled threats and an unpredictable populace to rely on. This combination is always deadly. Thus, rather than hollow threats, Aristide should have had his large crowd surround him and the National Palace to deter any coup attempt. The army, by contrast, had all the weapons, was organized (at least against Aristide's defenseless supporters), and was anxious to strike against the defiant priest.

As president, it was Aristide's ultimate responsibility to uphold the rule of law and human rights, "to refrain from any statement that could be understood to support *Père Lebrun*, and to speak out firmly and consistently against this barbaric practice" (AW/NCHR/CR 1991, 28). Aristide failed to do so because he became deluded by his own charismatic powers and believed that, with the masses behind him, he was invincible and that he could rule without respecting the law and without winning over the bourgeoisie, the parliament, or the army. This was his greatest mistake. The error that Aristide made in all these instances, where popular violence was used or threatened with his explicit or implicit encouragement, was political and not moral. It stemmed from his failure to distinguish between democratic rights and violent and illegal threats to democracy (and his presidency).

Aristide's erratic behavior and errors of judgment divided and confused his defenders and weakened them. But they reinforced the worst fears of the bourgeoisie, which came to believe that its fate lay in joining with the neo-Duvalierists to topple the Lavalas government and get rid of Aristide once and for all. By the time of the coup, the bourgeoisie—which from the start had wanted to topple Aristide—had found its excuse to act. Aided by Aristide's blunders, the bourgeoisie convinced itself that he was determined to carry out his "social revolution" and that there was no alternative but to overthrow him (Danner 1993, 52).

The makout forces in control of the armed forces, for their part, needed no justification to act, only the right moment. For them, the right moment came with Aristide's departure for New York to address the United Nations. Aristide's standing with the Haitian parliament had reached a low point, even among his own supporters. He was under attack by many popular organizations for his government's agreement with the IMF. He had completely alienated the bourgeoisie after the events of July and August. The military hierarchy was angered by Aristide's attacks against corruption and drug trafficking and was worried that the warming of relations between the Aristide government and the U.S. Embassy in Haiti would lead to even greater drug enforcement activities in the country. They were also restive about the formation of a presidential security force that would be loyal to Aristide, his intentions to disband the infamous Leopard Battalion, and Colonel Cédras's "interim" status as commander-in-chief of the army. The political climate seemed propitious and, if they did not act, they might well lose their chance to do so later, especially if Aristide returned from his intended visit with President George H. W. Bush with hundreds of millions of foreign aid dollars starting to flow into the country (Danner 1993, 52; Council on Hemispheric Affairs 1991).

It is quite wrong to say, as Aristide's detractors did, that this speech was "the straw that broke the camel's back . . . about the military rebellion that forced the Haitian president out of power" (*Haiti Observateur* 1991g). The coup had been plotted well before the September 27 speech, and the latter was a desperate attempt on Aristide's part to forestall it. And if the speech was not the immediate cause of the coup, neither was Aristide's alleged human rights record or violation of the constitution. Such arguments were used as ex post facto justifications by the putschists and their supporters in the U.S. government and media in an attempt to discredit Aristide and convince the Bush and Clinton administrations to find a solution to the Haitian crisis that did not involve the return of Aristide to power.

For all his political errors and even the abuse of his powers as president, the human rights record under the first Aristide government showed dramatic improvement, compared favorably with the record of any of his predecessors, and certainly paled in comparison with the reign of terror that followed his overthrow.[4] Whatever the human rights failings of the Aristide government, an Americas Watch report concluded, they "cannot be used to justify committing yet a further, serious human rights violation by depriving the Haitian people of the right to elect their government" (AW/NCHR/CR 1991). As Danner put it succinctly, "In the end human rights did not bring Aristide down, politics did" (1993, 52). The September 30 coup d'état resulted from a classic power struggle between, on the one hand, a reformist and populist (but unpredictable) president who lacked a well-organized and disciplined political base, a parliamentary majority, and control over the military and, on the other hand, economic and prebendary political-military elites who feared democracy and the masses, as well as losing their power and their privileges.

Aristide himself understood his overthrow in political terms and referred to the social forces lined up against him as the "gang of four": the army, the political class and the bourgeoisies, the Church hierarchy, and the United States. First, he argued, the army could not tolerate any reform that would affect it directly and weaken its powers and prerogatives. The creation of a constitutional order would take away from that institution its true vocation, that is, its expertise in coups d'état and ruling by terror. The army also feared losing control over its lucrative and illicit activities, particularly its participation in drug trafficking, which it shared with the makouts and the continental mafias.

Second, the bourgeoisie and the political class allied to the army also had an aversion to democracy and the creation of a government of laws. For the political class (that is, the functionaries of the public bureaucracy and public enterprises), total control over the state apparatuses and the prebendary practices that this made possible constituted the source of their power, wealth, and privileges. For the bourgeoisie, who held the uneducated popular classes in contempt, nothing was more frightening than the masses attaining the status of citizens. "Seven months of the 'Lavalasian nightmare,'" Aristide wrote, "excused and justified the reinforcement of the walls of class, their watchtowers lined with armed watchmen" (Aristide 1994b, 31–33).

Third, the Church hierarchy, which vehemently opposed the emergence and influence of the *ti-legliz* liberation theology movement, sided openly with the putschists and legitimized the coup by appointing a new papal nuncio to Port-au-Prince. The Vatican was the only foreign state to recognize the new regime diplomatically (Aristide 1994b, 34–35).

Fourth, there was the United States, which, after the fall of communism, sought to change its ugly image as the defender of dictatorship by promoting an "ersatz of democracy" in the poor countries. The problem for the United States in Haiti was how to compel its traditional allies—the bourgeoisie and the military establishment—to accept a minimal democracy, sever their ties with the system of corruption, and abandon their age-old practices of treating the masses like slaves, yet preserve Haiti as a source of cheap labor for the assembly industries and the multinational agribusinesses. The solution lay in electing a candidate who accepted the new game plan and who was supported by the local oligarchies and the United States. Unfortunately, the Haitian masses, which had been excluded from this new schema, spoiled it (in the opinion of the U.S. government) by voting for their own unexpected and unpredictable candidate (Aristide 1994b, 35–37).

Aristide succinctly summarized the underlying fears of his protagonists and the reasons they ousted him or supported his ouster from power. His musings, however, do not go far enough to consider the role that his behavior as president played in these actions. The creation of a liberal social-democratic state threatened the most fundamental interests of the prebendary Duvalierist state and military, and short of capitulating to them, there is little that Aristide could have done to win their support for democracy. They had vowed to oppose and topple Aristide and, for them, it was a matter of when, not whether, they would act.

While the "marriage" that Aristide called for between the army and the people may not have been possible since some of his closest associates were bragging about abolishing the army, he could have done much more to reassure the bourgeoisie and win it over to his side, improbable as that task was. In fact, the entire postelection conjuncture worked against this rapprochement. Even if Aristide had succeeded in wooing the bourgeoisie, it may still not have been sufficient to prevent the military from toppling him. The class imperatives of the military leadership, not those of the bourgeoisie, compelled it to act. But, the army would have acted alone and been left completely isolated and without influential and wealthy supporters within Haiti. As things stood, Aristide's contradictory behavior reinforced the bourgeoisie's distrust of him and encouraged it to side with the army and the makout camp against him.

On the one hand, Aristide preached class conciliation, and the entire social-democratic project of his government was based on forming a broad consensus and a class alliance among the bourgeoisie, the working class, and the peasants. On the other hand, he threatened to unleash popular violence against and expropriate the bourgeoisie when the latter refused to go along with his program. He preached respect for the constitution and the rule of law, yet he sanctioned the use of force if necessary to achieve his vision of justice, even when that contravened the law. He declared his adherence to the democratic process and the separation of powers, yet he disdained all established political parties, sought to bypass the National Assembly and the judiciary, and even encouraged his popular supporters to harass and intimidate parliamentarians and the justices who opposed him or sought to exercise their independent functions.

Aristide, therefore, sent quite contradictory messages to his supporters and opponents alike, and the confusion that this caused among all sectors of the population eroded confidence in him and weakened his defenders, while at the same time emboldening his enemies to act. In short, though the demise of Aristide's presidency stemmed from the unwillingness of the antidemocratic forces to accept any changes in the status quo, Aristide's confrontational and sometimes threatening behavior "added fuel to the fire" of class conflicts exacerbated by his election to the presidency. Aristide, in other words, failed to make the change from prophet to prince. He proved unable to abandon the radical rhetoric he employed as a charismatic opposition leader and adopt the compromising discourse and conciliatory behavior of a democratically elected president. Doing so was all the more important because he lacked a parliamentary majority and had no control over the army and its extended apparatuses and instruments of power. Under such conditions, the chances that his reformist program would succeed were slim at best.

Given the configuration of class interests and the balance of class forces in Haiti and globally after Aristide took office, the antidemocratic forces would have sought to overthrow him even if he had adopted a conciliatory and princely approach. By eschewing that approach, however, Aristide played into the hands of his zealous enemies and gave them the excuses they needed to topple him. Only a power bigger than the Haitian Army could have prevented the latter from being able to veto the democratic process. That power

did not reside with Aristide or his Lavalas movement that he failed to structure into a strong deterrent mass movement, but with the "cold country to the
North."

NOTES

1. The name "*Père Lebrun*" is a euphemism for "necklacing" and originates from
a well-known tire salesman in Port-au-Prince who used to advertise his tires by stick-
ing his head through them.

2. For a full discussion of the growth-with-equity model in the Caribbean, see my
Haiti in the New World Order (Dupuy 1997), 93–113.

3. Many of the arguments advanced in *La chance qui passe* (Opération Lavalas
1990b) were originally developed by Georges Anglade, especially in his *Espace et
liberté en Haïti* (1982).

4. For a thorough analysis of the human rights situation under Aristide's government, see AW/NCHR/CR 1991. For comparisons with the records of preceding governments, see AW/NCHR 1989 and 1990. For comparisons with the post-coup military regime, see Amnesty International 1992, AW/HRW/NCHR 1994, AW/NCHR
1993, and Coalition for Civilian Observers in Haiti 1993.

Chapter Five

The Prophet Checkmated:
The Political Opposition and the
Low-Intensity War against Aristide

THE ROOTS OF THE POLITICAL CRISIS

On May 21, 2000, Haiti held legislative, municipal, and local elections to fill approximately 7,500 offices throughout the country. This was the third polling at the national and local levels since the return of Aristide to office by a U.S.-led multinational force in October 1994. That intervention, approved by the UN Security Council, removed from power the military junta that had toppled Aristide three years earlier in a September 1991 coup d'état. As expected—because of the party's popularity—candidates for Aristide's Fanmi Lavalas (FL) party swept these elections, thereby granting the FL overwhelming control of government at the national and local levels. The day after the elections, the political opposition parties which had "cried 'foul' before, during, and immediately after May 21," issued a list of unsubstantiated charges of widespread fraud which they claimed rendered the elections null and void (Carey 2002). The very next day, fifteen of those opposition parties without any significant popular support came together to form the *Convergence Démocratique* (CD, Democratic Convergence) (Dupuy 2002, 5–6).

It is important to understand, however, that the rise of an organized opposition to Aristide and the political crisis it provoked after the May elections did not occur in 2000 but in 1995 and 1996. In 1995 the *Plateforme Politique Lavalas* (PPL, Lavalas Political Platform) coalition—within which Gérard Pierre-Charles's *Organisation Politique Lavalas* (OPL, Lavalas Political Organization) was dominant—won control of most local administrations and the majority of seats in parliament in elections that international monitors, including those from the United Nations, the Organization of American States (OAS), and the United States, considered to have been fraudulent. As a result, many of the parties and organizations that had formed the *Front National pour le Changement et la Démocratie* (FNCD, National Front for Democracy and Change) and had supported Aristide in 1990, but were now opposed to him and the Lavalas Political Platform, boycotted the second round of the elections. Nevertheless, that did not prevent the United States and the United Nations from accepting the elections as valid.

By 2000, however, the OPL had joined many of the parties that opposed it in 1995 to form the Democratic Convergence against Aristide's Lavalas party by charging the latter with using fraud to win control of parliament. The struggle for power is seldom governed by ethical principles. As expected, René Préval, Aristide's former prime minister in 1991, also won the December 1995 presidential election and assumed the presidency in February 1996 after the first peaceful transfer of power in Haiti's post-1915 occupation history.

Well before 2000, however, the PPL coalition that was in power in 1995 was in disarray. Tensions between the OPL and Aristide increased in 1995 over the question of whether or not Aristide should reclaim the three years he spent in exile and thus prolong his mandate. Responding to widespread calls by his supporters to do so, Aristide hinted that he might indeed reconsider his agreement with the United States to leave office in February 1996. A quick visit to Haiti by Anthony Lake, President Bill Clinton's national security advisor, got Aristide to back off and put the issue to rest definitively (Dupuy 1997, 172). Nonetheless, this issue alarmed many of his former allies, especially the cadres of OPL, who now saw him as a dangerous demagogue with dictatorial ambitions (Fatton 2002, 112–13).

The rift also occurred over the democratization of the Lavalas coalition. Always distrustful of organizations he could not control, Aristide resisted the transformation of the Lavalas movement into a structured party. Knowing that he still enjoyed strong popular support and that he could win elections without the cadres of the OPL, Aristide broke from the broad coalition in November and formed his own Fanmi Lavalas party. As Robert White put it:

[With] the creation of the new party . . . Aristide appears to have reverted to the ecclesiastical authoritarianism he once condemned. Confronted with a Lavalas movement escaping his personal control, he did not seek to build new coalitions within the party. Instead he excommunicated his longtime friends in the old Lavalas and created a new church, without doctrine or dogma except unquestioning loyalty to its leader (1997, 2–3; also in Fatton 2002, 113).

The formation of the FL party also signaled the demise of OPL as the majority party in parliament. Proof of that came in the April 1997 elections, which the OPL claimed were rigged in favor of Aristide's FL by the *Conseil*

Électoral Provisoire (CEP, Provisional Electoral Council). Though the Clinton administration initially declared the elections "free and fair," it soon changed its mind when it realized that the FL had fared well in the first round and was poised to win enough seats in the second round to have veto power in the Senate, thereby allowing it to block the implementation of the structural adjustment reforms supported by the OPL, President Préval, and his prime minister, Rosny Smarth. The OPL demanded the resignation of the CEP and boycotted the second round, which President Préval eventually canceled. Prime Minister Smarth resigned in June in protest over both the elections and the stalled privatization reforms. The OPL then severed its ties with the Lavalas movement altogether and changed its name to *Organisation du Peuple en Lutte* (Organization of the People in Struggle), thereby retaining its original acronym. The renamed OPL, which controlled the lower house of the National Assembly, blocked several attempts to replace Smarth with a new prime minister until Préval refused to renew parliament's term that ended in January 1999. That decision allowed him to form a new government and rule by decree until February 2001 when the new parliament and Aristide took office.

By 1996–97, then, it had become evident that Aristide's FL was unquestionably the dominant political force in Haiti. If unchecked, Lavalas could build a formidable political machine and clientelistic network that would ensure its continued electoral dominance and control of the government, with or without Aristide as president—that is, even after Aristide's anticipated second and final term as president. That realization also made clear the real nature of the political opposition to Aristide. The struggle for power between Aristide and his FL party and all the others, including the newly formed OPL, was essentially a struggle to determine which faction of the middle class would come to control the state and all its prebends. As Kern Delince put it so clearly, the primary concern of the members of the political class who for the most part come from the upper ranks of the middle class is

> to gain their place in the urban bourgeoisie that they have kept as a reference model. Political life offers them a means of social promotion, a trampoline for gaining access to a higher social status, a shortcut allowing them to cross the ditch separating them from various strata of Haitian society. (1993, 97)

Since his rise to power in 1991, however, Aristide had effectively shut out the coalition of parties—the FNCD—that had backed him in 1990. These parties were again marginalized when his Lavalas Political Platform swept the parliamentary elections of 1995. And the OPL, which was then the dominant bloc within the PPL thanks to its association with Aristide and the fraudulent elections of that year, was now destined for the same fate with the breakup of the PPL and the formation of Aristide's FL party. Aristide, in other words, deprived those sectors of the political middle class that had supported him a share in the spoils of power and sought to monopolize state power for his benefit and those who formed the cadres of FL. Thus, as Robert Fatton observed:

> Personal rivalries and jealousies nourished by the struggle for power fueled the divorce [between Aristide and his former allies] and threatened any attempt at national reconciliation. The cadres that had supported Aristide saw him as the vehicle that would facilitate their own political ascendancy, fully expecting to control him once he conquered the presidency. Things, however, unfolded very differently; Aristide had such massive popularity that he could ignore, alienate, and break free from these cadres and govern as he saw fit. The intellectuals, who had contributed to his rise and hoped to use him for their own strategic purposes, found themselves excluded from his circles and increasingly powerless. Aristide had proven more astute than they had ever imagined; instead of becoming their puppet, he emerged as the pivotal and dominant figure of Haitian politics. . . . This feeling of "being had" has generated among key members of the opposition a visceral personal dislike for Aristide. They resent his cleverness and are busy preparing the moment when they can savor their revenge. (2002, 113)

That moment came in 2000 when, after Lavalas's victory in the elections of May and Aristide's reelection in December, the OPL joined with the former members of the FNCD and others, including former Duvalierists, to form the Democratic Convergence whose sole objective was to wage a low-intensity war against his government and ultimately force him out of power. The charge of irregularities and other malpractices in the May elections made by the OAS's Electoral Observer Mission (EOM) provided the excuse the CD needed to launch its offensive against Aristide. The most serious problems cited in the mission's report prior to the elections were the acts of violence that resulted in the death of seven candidates or activists of political parties. Still, the EOM declared, the elections themselves were a major success: 60 percent of those eligible were able to cast their ballots on election day without major incidents. Most of the problems that ultimately shook confidence in the elections came afterward. Among the most important cited by the EOM were the intervention by armed groups in some electoral offices in parts of the country where they burned ballot boxes; the mishandling of vote-tally sheets that had been dumped on the streets of Port-au-Prince, Delmas, and Cap-Haitien but later recovered; the arbitrary arrest and subsequent release of several opposition candidates, and at least three deaths related to the elections; and the lack of transparency in compiling and publishing the results of the elections in several communes. Nonetheless, the EOM concluded that even though a series of irregularities may have affected the outcome in a number of local and municipal contests, the majority of the offices contested at those levels were not (OAS 2000, 2–3).

The most serious and uncorrected irregularities, however, occurred at the legislative level (the Senate and Chamber of Deputies), most notably in the senatorial elections. The OAS accepted the results for the Chamber of Deputies, where the FL won seventy-two out of eighty-two seats. At issue in the senatorial elections was the vote-counting method used by the Provisional Electoral Council, which was charged with presiding over and verifying the results of the elections. To be elected to on the first round, a candidate must receive an absolute majority (at least 50 percent plus one) of the valid votes cast; otherwise, that candidate must participate in a second round. The EOM found that the CEP used an unconstitutional method of calculation based on the votes cast for the top four candidates only, thereby granting them a majority in the first round and avoiding a second round. Based on this method, nineteen senate seats had been won in the first round, eighteen of which went to FL candidates. However, if the calculation had been based on the total number of votes cast, as required by law, then only eight of the eighteen FL candidates would have won an absolute majority in the first round.

The EOM, with the support of the Caribbean Community (CARICOM), asked the CEP to modify its calculation for the remaining ten FL candidates who should have had to compete in the second round. However, the CEP, which was controlled by both President Préval and Aristide's FL party, refused to reverse its decision and claimed that the method in question had been used in elections since 1990. This was clearly false and in contravention of Haiti's electoral law. Declaring that the CEP was preventing the votes of all candidates from being treated equally and, hence, disenfranchising millions of voters, the OAS withdrew its observer mission and refused to monitor the second-round elections in June or the presidential elections in November 2000 (OAS 2000, 4). The United States followed suit in July by suspending approximately $600 million in foreign aid and debt relief to Haiti. The European Union and international financial institutions (IFIs) such as the World Bank and the Inter-American Development Bank also suspended their aid (Council on Hemispheric Affairs 2001, 6–7).

One may ask why, given his and FL's popularity and greater name recognition, Aristide felt he needed to have the CEP engage in this illegal practice to ensure that his candidates won in the first round. That is, why was Aristide so afraid of a second round? One reason is that, as H. F. Carey put it, Aristide almost got away with cheating, because the OAS did not discover the flawed calculations until weeks after the results had been announced. Second, despite his enormous popularity, Aristide feared a second round because there are many examples from other elections where well-known candidates ended up losing to relatively unknown candidates in second-round voting. Aristide simply did not want to take the risk (Carey 2000).

Carey does not elaborate on his second point, but it is no doubt the most important reason for Aristide's refusal to go to a second round. Aristide's concern lay in his experience in 1990, when he was elected president by a landslide only to face a divided parliament that opposed and obstructed his initiatives. As tensions increased between Aristide and his opponents, including the military, the latter seized the moment to mount a coup against him in September 1991 with the full support of the Haitian bourgeoisie. Then in 1995, Aristide's successor and former prime minister, René Préval, was elected president, and he, too, faced a divided parliament that made it impossible for him to govern effectively (Dupuy 2002, 3–5). In light of these experiences, then, Aristide was determined to govern this time with his party in complete control of government, which required him and his party to win at least two-thirds of the seats in parliament. This would buffer Aristide and his prime minister from any possible censure or a vote of no confidence in parliament.[1]

As Fatton put it succinctly, in 2000 Aristide sought to establish

the terrain for an imperial presidency through the electoral omnipotence of Fanmi Lavalas. In this instance he will be able to rely on his parliamentary supermajority to have a prime minister of his own choosing. An unmitigated form of presidential monarchism could thus be restored through the ballot box.

A mere majority is simply insufficient, however, for the establishment of presidential monarchism. This is why fraud became necessary to ensure both the annihilation of the anti-Lavalasian parties and the two-thirds majority for Aristide. An overwhelming victory in the first round was thus the means to that end. (2002, 120)

As Fatton goes on to suggest, if in the first round FL had an "easy task since it faced a thoroughly divided opposition," things could have changed in the second round "because it would have had to contend against a single and possibly united anti-Aristide front. In these circumstances, the final outcome might have diluted the scope of Lavalas's victory, making the coveted two-thirds majority an impossibility" (120).

Despite the legitimate criticisms of the CEP's illegal counting method, the decision of the OAS to refuse to monitor subsequent elections and the continued suspension of financial assistance to Haiti by the United States and the European Union must be placed in context. There is great inconsistency in the international community's stance toward governments that violate human rights and commit electoral fraud. In the case of Haiti, financial and military aid was suspended by the United States, France and other European countries, and the IFIs between 1961 and 1966 after "Papa Doc" François Duvalier was "reelected" and declared himself president-for-life. They resumed their assistance to that government after 1966 and continued to do so during the fifteen-year rule of "Baby Doc" Jean-Claude Duvalier (1971–86), despite the fact that he "inherited" the presidency from his father, no credible elections were held, corruption was rampant, and his government had a deplorable human rights record. Foreign aid continued in 1986 after the military took over the government and was not suspended until after General Namphy stopped the elections of 1987 and the army and armed militia attached to the military killed dozens of voters and wounded scores of others. Even though the U.S. ambassador to Haiti sided with Namphy on the grounds that Gérard Gourgue, a human rights lawyer and presidential candidate, was a front man for the leftist opposition coalition, the U.S. Congress, along with other aid donors, canceled foreign aid to the military government.

The United States and other aid donors made the renewal of aid conditional on the holding of free and fair democratic elections, which Aristide won by a landslide in 1990. Aristide, however, lasted a mere seven months in office (February–September 1991) before he was overthrown by the military. Because of antipathy toward him, the foreign aid donors never released most of the aid promised to his government. Aid remained frozen during the three years of military rule after Aristide's overthrow. Despite the fact that the U.S. government had opposed Aristide, it could not deny the legitimacy of his election. This was also the post–Cold War era, and the United States could no longer justify its support of the military junta that toppled Aristide in the name of anticommunism (Dupuy 1997, 47–68, 115–34).

International aid resumed after Aristide was returned to office in 1994 and turned power over to his successor in 1995. Yet, as we just saw, international observers, including those from the United States, United Nations, and OAS, documented fraudulent practices in both the parliamentary and presidential elections of that year, yet still approved them. As Carey argued, the 1995 elections occurred nine months after the UN-sanctioned military intervention reluctantly returned Aristide to office, and he could not run again for president for another five years. There was then a willingness to support the redemocratization process (Carey 2002). International aid was again suspended after the fraudulent 1997 elections left a divided parliament, led to the resurgence of Aristide and his newly formed FL party, and caused a prime minister to resign and President Préval to suspend parliament and rule by decree until his term ended in February 2001.

There had also been fraudulent elections elsewhere in this hemisphere at the same time as the 2000 elections in Haiti. But unlike in Haiti, foreign aid was not suspended as a result. The most notorious instance was that of the Peruvian presidential elections of May 2000, where Alejandro Toledo, the opposition candidate, was denied an outright victory against incumbent President Alberto Fujimori due to widespread fraud by the latter. The OAS declared those elections to have been unfair, and, as in Haiti, withdrew its observer mission for the second round. Nonetheless, the OAS, with U.S. approval, validated Fujimori as the winner (Council on Hemispheric Affairs 2000, 1, 6).

The difference between Peru and Haiti was that the former had a president who was closely allied with the United States and committed to the latter's free trade policies and war on drugs. By contrast, the U.S. government distrusted Aristide. It always considered him a threat to "order" and "stability" in Haiti and the Caribbean region, meaning that Aristide could not be trusted to observe the "rules of the game" as dictated by Washington. This perception of Aristide was largely based on his past advocacy of liberation theology, his uncertain commitment to the free trade and free market reforms advocated by the United States, and his professed championing of the cause of Haiti's downtrodden masses. The administration of President George W. Bush signaled its displeasure with Aristide's reelection early on by not sending a delegation to his inauguration in February 2001. Moreover, Bush replaced the Clinton administration's Latin America policy team with staunch Cold War warriors and anti-Aristide ideologues, including Otto Reich as assistant secretary of state for Latin American affairs and Roger Noriega, a former aide to former North Carolina senator Jesse Helms (Dupuy 2002, 7). In the U.S. Congress as well, Aristide faced strong animosity from vocal and conservative Republicans like Rep. Peter Goss of Florida and Senator Helms, then chairman of the Senate Committee on Foreign Relations, who was instrumental in blocking the release of aid monies to Haiti after the elections (Council on Hemispheric Affairs 2001, 6–7; Blumenthal 2004).

Be that as it may, the hybrid nature of Aristide's presidency discussed in chapter 3 would show more of its authoritarian than its democratic tendencies at the same time that his radical liberation theology views of politics waned. At the first national congress of Fanmi Lavalas in December 1999, speaking before hundreds of members of the Haitian bourgeoisie, Aristide struck a moderate tone as he unveiled his party's platform, called the "White Paper of Fanmi Lavalas." He continued to criticize the inequities caused by globalization, neoliberal policies, and what he termed the "sanctity of the market," but he no longer equated capitalism with a mortal sin. Instead, he called for adding an "ethical dimension" to the imperatives of the market to attend to human needs such as access to health care, education, food, and housing, which he still considered basic human rights. He deplored the fact that 1 percent of the Haitian population owned 48 percent of the country's wealth, but he no longer argued that it was time for those who were under the table to come and sit at the table with the wealthy bourgeoisie. Gone was the provocative assertion that whether it liked it or not, the bourgeoisie would have to accept and accommodate the needs and interests of the poor. He called for building a "strategic and regulatory state" to promote human development and economic growth through a "partnership between the public and private sectors." The strategic and regulatory state, he argued, must also "democratize democracy," by which he meant including "those who have been excluded until now [and] demand full participation," rather than moving forward "without them, or against them" (Bauduy 1999; Aristide 1999, 2000, 2001).

This approach was a far cry from the original "option for the poor" of liberation theology. As previously explained, the "option" prioritized the needs and interests of the poor and saw democracy as being synonymous with the direct participation of the people in deciding the agenda, rather than having it dictated from above—that is, a state that responds to the imperatives of the market (meaning the interests of capital, foreign and domestic) but maintains an ethical dimension (meaning capitalism with a conscience, as Aristide was now suggesting).

By 2000, in short, Aristide had jettisoned his radical liberation theology views and accepted the reality of "globalization," but maintained nonetheless a rhetorical commitment to the poor and a left-of-center perspective that did not differ much from those of the other left-of-center social democratic parties that he was once allied with. The main difference, however, was that by 2000 all these parties and most of the intellectual cadres of Lavalas had broken with Aristide and had either left the movement altogether or, like Pierre-Charles's OPL, become the spearhead of the opposition against Aristide. For its part, the Haitian private-sector bourgeoisie, which despised Aristide and was angry at the Clinton administration for having returned him to Haiti in 1994, was not in the least interested in his conciliatory tone, instead throwing its support behind the CD in its effort to topple Aristide. Similarly, as already noted, the incoming Bush administration distrusted and disliked Aristide—essentially for not implementing fully the neoliberal policies he had agreed to in 1994, especially the privatization of all the public enterprises—and was instrumental in blocking the resumption of foreign aid to his government after the parliamentary elections and his reelection in 2000.

Aristide realized that he was once again shunned by the dominant classes and their international allies and believed he was left with little choice but to rely on his mass base, especially the gangs of *chimès*, for his support. That strategy would prove to be the Achilles' heel of his second term. In effect, I will argue, by relying on armed gangs rather than mobilizing his popular base as a counterforce to the opposition, as he tended to do in his first term,

Aristide would marginalize the latter. Henceforth, Lavalas would become equated with the chimès, and the entire popular movement associated with Lavalas that made possible the defeat of the neo-Duvalierists after 1987, the election of Aristide in 1990, the resistance against the military junta between 1991 and 1994, and the return of Aristide in 1994 would become discredited, demobilized, and demoralized.

It is important to note, however, that well before his reelection, Aristide and other Lavalas officials were using the chimès as a *force de frappe* against his opponents. Many acts of violence and a number of killings occurred between 1999 and the May 2000 elections, including the assassination in April 2000 of the renowned journalist Jean Dominique, a onetime supporter turned critic of Aristide. In March 1999 gangs of chimès used violence and demanded the dismissal of the electoral council over a dispute with President Préval on the dates for the new elections. Five people were reported killed in fights among criminal gangs. In April 2000 and on the day of Dominique's funeral, some chimès burned down the headquarters of the *Espace de Concertation* and threatened to kill Evans Paul, leader of the *Konfédérasyon Inité Démokratik* and former ally of Aristide in 1990. Chimès attacked the headquarters of the *Rassemblement des Citoyens Patriotes* (RCP, Rally of Patriotic Citizens), injuring one person and nearly killing another. In June, when the CEP was being pressured to annul the results of the first-round parliamentary elections, hundreds of pro–Fanmi Lavalas supporters erected barricades, burned tires, and effectively shut down Port-au-Prince in an attempt to intimidate the CEP. In all these incidents, the police failed to stop, investigate, or arrest and punish their perpetrators. But the police did arrest many opposition candidates and activists who had protested against the May elections, including Sen. Paul Denis of the OPL (Human Rights Watch 2001).

The creation of armed groups that would become the chimès, however, goes back to 1995 after Aristide had abolished the Haitian Army and a new Haitian National Police was created with help and training from the United States, France, and Canada. Aristide understood the need to control that force and placed trusted allies in its command. It was then that the link between Aristide and the chimès was formed. The director of the police, along with the minister of interior and the chief of presidential security, served as the liaison with the gangs, who received cash and weapons for their operations (Caroit 2003).

There is disagreement on Aristide's role in creating the chimès. Some, like Maurice Lemoine, maintain that it still remains to be proven whether Aristide personally created and directed them or simply left that task to others (Lemoine 2004, 16–17). In my view, however, it is immaterial whether or not Aristide had a direct role in creating and directing the chimès. As Clive

Thomas noted, authoritarian regimes and rulers have often made use of armed civilian groups to do the government's dirty work without giving these groups official sanction or status. This allows such governments or rulers to deny responsibility for the operations of these groups, thereby avoiding official investigations and allowing the groups to operate with impunity (Thomas 1984, 91). This is exactly how Aristide would use the chimès. He denied being connected to them, but would never condemn or declare them illegal, fight against them, or hold them accountable for their actions. The chimès, along with the police, would attack and kill members of the opposition, violently disrupt their demonstrations, burn their residences and headquarters, intimidate members of the media critical of the government, and engage in countless other human and civil rights violations with impunity. As Anne Fuller remarked, the "gangs [carried] out their criminal activities with impunity as long as they [helped] the police and political leaders" (Fuller 2003). Some leaders also became a force in their own right by forming criminal gangs that acted autonomously, turned their neighborhoods into wards under their control, engaged in drug trafficking and other criminal activities, and even requisitioned the government itself. But they could also switch allegiance, fall out of favor with the government, and be discarded or even killed when they outlived their usefulness or became a threat to government officials or the president himself (Caroit 2004; Regan 2003).

It is in the context of this history and pre-reelection violence, intimidation, distrust, and personal rivalries that the behavior of Aristide and the organized opposition is to be understood. Faced with a foreign-backed opposition whose stated goal was to remove him from power and strangled economically by the foreign aid donors and the IFIs, Aristide would increasingly emphasize the authoritarian face of his hybridity and rely on the chimès to intimidate the opposition while pursuing OAS-mediated negotiations with the CD that would prove fruitless. The goal of Aristide and the FL was to maintain power at all cost until the end of Aristide's second and final term as president. As we will see, the idea of amending the 1987 Constitution to remove the restriction on more than two nonconsecutive presidential terms surfaced in 2003 but got nowhere because of the growing opposition to Aristide. Be that as it may, the goal of Lavalas was to lay the groundwork for its continued dominance through the ballot box after Aristide.

Insofar as Fanmi Lavalas was not a disciplined or democratically structured political party, its leaders were not accountable to anyone. This inevitably would lead to the emergence of rival factions within the party, the use of power for personal gain, and corruption and cronyism becoming systematized as before. Similarly, insofar as the relationship between the leadership of Lavalas and the popular organizations that formed its base, and especially the chimès,

was also unstructured and unaccountable, the same processes of fractionalization, rivalries, and extortion would emerge among them as the climate of violence and insecurity escalated. As we will see, this was a recipe for disaster for
both Aristide and his party.

In any case, it is important to distinguish between Aristide and the dictators
who came and went before him. First, the unsubstantiated claims of the CD
notwithstanding, Aristide had been legitimately reelected in 2000, and the international community never disputed that fact. The controversy over his reelection was about the percentage of voters who cast their ballots, not that it
was fraudulent. Second, while there is no doubt that Aristide had authoritarian tendencies, he understood that his and his party's legitimacy depended on
winning elections—even if that meant manipulating them—rather than simply declaring his presidency-for-life as the Duvaliers did. Proof of that came
with Aristide's willingness to hold entirely new parliamentary elections in
2003, even if he agreed to do so reluctantly under international pressure, and
to contemplate amending the 1987 Constitution to allow him to run for more
than two terms. Constitutional amendments are the prerogatives of every legitimate government, even if in this case it was politically unwise and dangerous for Aristide to attempt to do so. And third, while Aristide undermined
his legitimacy by abusing his powers and engaging in egregious human rights
violations against his opponents and critics—all possible grounds for his
impeachment—he never attempted to annihilate the opposition physically as
the Duvaliers did or as happened under the three-year rule of the military
junta led by Gen. Raoul Cédras between 1991 and 1994. Under Aristide, in
both 1991 and 2000–04, the opposition not only continued to function despite
various forms of intimidation but eventually succeeded in forcing him out of
power.

There are three other reasons why Aristide could not transform himself into
an outright dictator even if he had wanted to. First, he didn't have the means
to do so. Having abolished the army, he also deprived himself of the ability
to monopolize the means of violence, assuming he could have brought the
army under his control in the first place. The National Police, which became
the legitimate armed force that replaced the army, was not sufficiently large,
well equipped, or well trained and thus did not have the mobility or the military means to impose and sustain a dictatorship. Second, the chimès were not
a substitute for the army or the police. They, too, were a relatively small force
of not more than a few thousand and were mostly concentrated in Port-au-
Prince and a few other large cities. But they neither had the firepower nor
were organized as a national military force under a centralized and hierarchical command as the *Tontons Makout* were. Thus they could not be relied upon
to impose a dictatorship as the *makouts* were able to in conjunction with the

army. Lastly, and equally as important, the international constraints on Aristide were sufficient to deter him. Unlike the Duvaliers who ruled with the support of the core powers—principally the United States—and the IFIs, those elements opposed Aristide, denied him financial assistance, and compelled him to negotiate with an opposition they supported and that ultimately forced him out of power.

Thus, it could be argued, Aristide may have observed two of the three critical dimensions of democracy—the rule of law and the right of public contestation, the third being inclusiveness or the universal enfranchisement of adult citizens (Hartlyn 1998, 10–11)—more in the breach, but it is precisely because he did so that he was held accountable and his legitimacy challenged. Moreover, even if the authoritarian temptation predominated in Aristide's second term, the opposition CD was not any more democratic. The CD may have appealed to democratic principles and the rule of law to criticize Aristide and his authoritarian practices, but it sought undemocratic means to oust him. Put another way, the political class in Haiti, which claims to favor democracy, fears the most important elements in a democracy: accountability and the checks and balances of government. Politics for the political class has always been a zero-sum game of mutual destruction. As we saw in chapter 2, as they expressed themselves in the context of Haiti, the imperatives of the prebendary state system demanded that the "opposition" deny the legitimacy of those in power so as to substitute itself for the incumbents. The aim of a political opposition was not so much to influence the orientation of the decision of those in power as it was to eliminate the very existence of those in power. Consequently the political class has never learned, or has refused to learn, the basic rules of political competition and cooperation necessary to form governments, and its members hence have never understood that even when they lose, they are better off under a democratic regime, even an imperfect or a hybrid one, than they would be under a dictatorship.

As noted, the CD was a coalition of parties of diverse and seemingly incompatible ideologies, ranging from neo-Duvalierist, centrist, and social democratic to former members of the Lavalas coalition and close allies of Aristide. They were united only in their opposition to, and personal dislike of, Aristide, and they did not propose a common platform or program that distinguished them ideologically from Lavalas. As an editorial in *Haiti en Marche* put it, "99 percent of the program of the opposition [consisted] of hating Aristide" (2005). The CD was supported by the Bush administration and especially by the International Republican Institute (IRI), which provided "financial as well as logistical assistance and timely access to strategic international outlets for the CD to present its case and grievances against Lavalas" (National Coalition for Haitian Rights 2003, 7). The social democratic European Socialist International also offered support to some of the organizations within the coalition (OPL, CONACOM, PANPRHA), and others (RDNP) were supported by Latin American Christian democratic parties.

There is little doubt, however, that the IRI spearheaded the international effort to undermine and eventually topple Aristide. According to Max Blumenthal, the IRI and especially Stanley Lucas, the IRI's (Haitian-born) leader in Haiti and a staunch Aristide opponent who came from a pro-Duvalier landowning family, "conducted a $3 million party-building program in Haiti, training Aristide's political opponents, uniting them into a single bloc and, according to a former U.S. ambassador there, encouraging them to reject internationally sanctioned power-sharing agreements in order to heighten Haiti's political crisis" (Blumenthal 2004).

Eager to oblige its foreign sponsors, the Democratic Convergence adopted such a strategy of noncooperation with the Aristide government aimed at blocking a resolution to the crisis. Its objective from the outset was to force Aristide from power by prolonging the political and economic crisis as long as necessary to make it impossible for Aristide to govern and thereby to erode public support for him. Despite its demand for completely new national and local elections, however, the CD was neither prepared to participate in nor in a position to win an electoral contest, whether legislative or presidential. Hence, as we will see, the CD had no intention of participating in elections with Aristide still in power. For their part, Aristide's supporters blamed the CD for the political impasse that aggravated the already grim economic conditions, and hence the chimès targeted its leaders for reprisals.

In addition to declaring the entire legislative and local elections invalid, the CD also withdrew from and boycotted the presidential elections, which Aristide won overwhelmingly. According to the CEP, 60.5 percent of those eligible voted, and 92 percent of those voted for Aristide. The CD, however, claimed that voter participation was between 5 and 10 percent, and it refused to recognize the legitimacy of Aristide's reelection (*Caribbean and Central America Report* 2000, 1). The CD proposed instead the creation of a three-member presidential council, of which Aristide would be a member, whose sole responsibility would be to organize fresh all-around elections in 2003. In the meantime, a prime minister chosen by the opposition would rule by decree. When, as expected, Aristide dismissed the offer, the CD adopted its "Option Zéro" (zero-option) strategy aimed at removing Aristide from office. It threatened to set up a "parallel administration" by declaring Gérard Gourgue as "provisional president" and conducted a parallel inauguration ceremony with Aristide's on February 7, 2001. During his "inaugural address," Gourgue changed his mind about the military government that had denied his legitimate election to the presidency in 1987 and had ousted Aristide in 1991, calling for the reincorporation of the armed forces that Aristide disbanded in 1994 and even the return to Haiti of the exiled leaders of the military junta (*Caribbean and Central America Report* 2001b, 3; Council on Hemispheric Affairs 2001, 6–7).

Such a defiant starting point foreshadowed the failure of the OAS and CARICOM to broker an agreement between the government and the opposition between 2001 and 2004 that could have led to a peaceful resolution of the political stalemate. Before it left office, the Clinton administration had negotiated an eight-point agreement with Aristide that, if implemented, could have led to the renewal of financial and other assistance to the government of Haiti. Two of the eight points dealt with resolving the disputes of the May 2000 legislative elections and the formation of a new provisional electoral council. The other six points dealt with issues of governance, including combating drug trafficking and money laundering, curbing human rights violations and reforming the judicial system, curbing illegal migration, pursuing economic reforms, and creating a more broad-based and inclusive government (Council on Hemispheric Affairs 2001, 6–7; White House 2000). When the Bush administration took over in January 2001, it accepted the eight-point agreement as a basis for resolving the conflict, but, in the words of then secretary of state Colin Powell, "We don't rule out that we might have other conditions or things we might want to add to that" (Council on Hemispheric Affairs 2001, 6–7). No one in Haiti misunderstood the message that Powell was sending to Aristide: either negotiate an agreement that satisfied the demands of the United States, the IFIs, and the CD or your government will continue to be denied legitimacy and financial assistance. Explicitly this meant that even though the anti-Lavalas parties in the CD had not won enough seats in the legislative elections to check Aristide's power within the legislature, the United States would ensure through its support that the CD would constitute a de facto, if extraparliamentarian, counterforce that Aristide would have to contend with. More to the point, however, as I will show below, while the official policy of the Bush administration was to pursue a negotiated resolution of the crisis, its unstated but real objective was to undermine and remove Aristide from power.

Aristide was thus brought once again to the realization that winning control of all branches of government was not synonymous with possessing or exercising power to achieve his ends. As such, he had no alternative but to enter into negotiations with the CD in 2001 under the auspices of the OAS and CARICOM even though both sides knew that they would be fruitless. Several OAS/CARICOM-mediated meetings during the year failed to yield a definitive agreement between the FL and CD. Nonetheless, the negotiations made clear that the main obstacle to a successful resolution to the conflict remained the CD, which at every turn either refused to endorse agreements that were arrived at in the negotiating process or issued new demands that it insisted had to be met before it could agree to endorse any proposed resolution. For example, under pressure to show some movement toward resolving the impasse, Aristide wrote a letter to the OAS outlining the steps he would agree to or had already taken. They included the resignation of seven FL senators whose elections had been contested in the May 2000 elections; reducing the terms of the senators elected in May 2000 and the terms of the entire Chamber of Deputies by two years; holding elections for those senators elected in May 2000 and for the entire Chamber of Deputies in November 2002; and reconstituting the CEP in line with OAS recommendations (see below). Aristide's letter was accepted by the OAS General Assembly on June 5, 2001, but summarily dismissed by the CD and the Haitian Catholic Church (*Caribbean and Central America Report* 2001a, 1; Council on Hemispheric Affairs 2002b). Further negotiations took place in June and July without agreement being reached, primarily because either the CD or the Civil Society Initiative Group introduced new demands that the FL could not accept without conceding, contrary to the OAS findings, that all the legislative and local elections of May 2000 were flawed.

Then, on July 27–28, 2001, armed members of the former Haitian Army attacked the Haitian National Police Academy and three other police stations, killing five police officers and wounding fourteen others. Dominican authorities arrested eleven former members of the Haitian armed forces who were allegedly connected to the incident. These events intensified the mistrust between the government and the opposition, as the former accused the latter of complicity in the attacks, and the opposition charged that the government was using them to crack down on its supporters (Dupuy 2002, 9; *Haiti en Marche* 2001).

In an attempt to bring the yearlong negotiations to a successful resolution, the OAS presented what it called "Elements of a Compromise Proposal," which reflected the concerns of the two sides and which the OAS believed to be the "basis of a fair deal that could work" (OAS 2002a). The OAS further recognized that the FL was willing to agree to legislative and local elections in March 2003, and on the status of local officials who engaged in abusive behavior once an agreement was signed. The OAS considered the Lavalas proposal to be "a serious offer" that could lead to a solution, but only "if the opposition showed greater flexibility" (ibid.).

The OAS proposal contained the following main points:

• The CD recognized and accepted the results of the presidential elections of November 2000.

- The FL agreed to new legislative and local elections in January 2003 at a time to be decided by the new CEP.
- The CEP would be comprised of nine members, three representing religious institutions and one each representing the FL, the CD, other political parties, the judiciary, employers' organizations, and human rights organizations.
- Either by presidential decree or by the next elected parliament, the tasks and acts performed by the officials elected in May 2001 would be ratified.
- In January 2003 the new CEP would organize elections for the entire Chamber of Deputies, two-thirds of the Senate, and municipal and local elections and would be empowered to reject any candidate for office it deemed unworthy of standing in the elections. Those who were elected to the legislature in May 2000 would remain in office until their elected successors assumed office.
- After signing the accord, a number of local officials agreed upon by the FL and CD would be removed from office for their abusive behavior and be replaced by appointed interim officials until new elected officials assumed the vacant offices. (OAS 2002a)

Matters stood at that point in early December 2001 when new acts of politically motivated violence rekindled the distrust between the CD and FL and gave the former new reasons to walk away from the negotiations and add new demands. On December 17, 2001, a group of armed men in former Haitian Army uniforms attacked the Presidential Palace in Port-au-Prince. The national police regained control of the palace after an exchange of gunfire with the assailants that left eight people dead, including five of the attackers. Soon after the attack, angry supporters of Aristide, blaming the CD and claiming the attack was an attempted coup d'état against him, took justice into their own hands and launched reprisals against the homes and offices of opposition leaders. Members of the press critical of the government also came under attack; forty or more went into hiding, and several others either sought refuge in various embassies in Port-au-Prince or fled Haiti to seek asylum in other countries.

For its part, the CD quickly accused Aristide of staging the coup to justify cracking down on the opposition, a view that seemed to be shared by some U.S. and Latin American diplomats despite a lack of evidence to substantiate the claim. As it turned out, the attack was carried out by former members of the Haitian armed forces, some of whom were also allegedly involved in the July attack against the National Police Academy. One of the alleged leaders of the attempted coup, former Haitian army sergeant Pierre Richardson, was apprehended by authorities in the Dominican Republic, and he, in turn, implicated other members of the defunct armed forces in the attack. One of them was Guy François, a former colonel in the Haitian Army, and another, Guy Philippe, also an ex-soldier and former Cap-Haitien police chief, had fled Haiti for the Dominican Republic. Dominican authorities refused to hand over Philippe to Haitian authorities because the two countries did not share an extradition treaty (Council on Hemispheric Affairs 2002a, 6; Maguire 2002). But they would not stop him from crossing over the border into Haiti in February 2004 along with other former soldiers of the army and members of the paramilitary death squad known as the *Front Révolutionnaire pour l'Avancement et le Progrès d'Haiti* (FRAPH, Revolutionary Front for the Advancement and Progress of Haiti) to topple Aristide for the second time.

The armed attack on the National Palace in December 2001 and the violence that followed gave the CD new reasons to break negotiations with Aristide. The United States, which believed, in the words of a State Department official, that "the events of December 17 demonstrated a failure of the Haitian government to protect its people from mob violence" (Council on Hemispheric Affairs 2002a, 6), pressured the OAS to invoke the Inter-American Democratic Charter in order to compel Aristide to reach a negotiated settlement with the CD. If invoked, the Inter-American Democratic Charter, adopted in Lima, Peru, on September 11, 2001, could have, under its Articles 20 and 21, suspended Haiti's right to participate in the OAS and taken "necessary diplomatic initiatives, including good offices, to foster the restoration of democracy" (OAS 2001). Basically, that would have meant sending foreign mediators to negotiate an agreement between Aristide's FL and the CD (Council on Hemispheric Affairs 2002a, 2002b). In the end, however, the OAS adopted a weaker version of the charter. The OAS noted that President Aristide condemned the violence of December 17 and thereafter, that the Haitian government had initiated an inquiry into the events, and that it had shown a willingness to work with the international community to resolve the political crisis. Consequently, the OAS called on the government and all political parties to condemn all forms of political violence and to work toward bringing an end to them (OAS 2002c).

The CD, however, insisted that no negotiations could take place until new security conditions spelled out in the OAS resolution of January 15 were met, a thorough investigation of the events of December 17 and after had subsequently been conducted, the culprits had been identified and punished, and the victims of the ensuing violence had been compensated (BBC Monitoring Service 2002b). To bolster its support from the Bush administration, the CD sent a delegation to Washington in late January 2002 to meet with Assistant Secretary of State for Western Hemispheric Affairs Otto Reich and other State Department officials. Paul Denis, a member of OPL and a spokesman for the

CD, declared the meeting with Reich and others a total success: "We have found the Americans very receptive to the views of the Convergence. They have also shown their understanding for the struggle we are waging for democracy" (Haiti Press Network 2002).

In February, an IRI delegation led by Georges Fauriol—a member of the Republican National Committee and the Center for Strategic and International Studies, a conservative Washington think tank—went to Haiti to meet with and offer its support to CD leaders. According to Hubert De Ronceray, leader of the *Parti de la Mobilisation pour le Développement National* (PMDN, Mobilization for National Development Party) and a member of the CD leadership, the IRI reaffirmed its support for the CD's continued opposition to Aristide, but it also wanted to see the CD go beyond resistance to become a viable alternative to Lavalas. That, De Ronceray acknowledged, was what they were working on becoming (BBC Monitoring Service 2002e). But Fauriol's admonition was more public posturing than a serious warning to the CD. Given the CD's confidence that it enjoyed the support of the Bush administration and of the IRI and that their shared objective was to remove Aristide from power rather than participating in new elections or share power with Aristide, it was more likely to insist that Aristide leave Haiti as a precondition to resolving the political crisis.

The CD's hardened attitude was revealed in its reaction to the meeting of the Caribbean heads of state in Belize on February 3–5, 2002, which issued a call for the international community to release the foreign aid that Haiti desperately needed. The CARICOM heads of state argued that the unblocking of the aid monies was justified because the Aristide government had taken concrete steps to move the political process forward and called on the opposition parties to respond positively to the government's initiatives. Another concern of CARICOM was that continuing to withhold foreign aid to Haiti was detrimental to its shattered economy, which could only compel more Haitian "boat people" to take to the high seas toward the Bahamas, either to settle there illegally or as a staging post to the United States (Caribbean Community 2002).

The United States, however, remained opposed to the renewal of foreign aid and blocked the release of some $200 million from the Inter-American Development Bank to Haiti. Taking a view opposed to CARICOM's, Secretary of State Powell maintained that Aristide had not done enough to resolve the political crisis and that "we would have to hold [him] and the Haitian government to higher standards of performance before we can simply allow the flow of funds into the country" (Wright 2002). Denis, the CD's spokesman, praised Powell's statement, which he saw as reflecting a "good understanding of the situation in Haiti" and as vindicating the position of the CD that "Aristide can draw the conclusion that he is unable to manage this country, that he has no legitimacy and should therefore decide to withdraw to allow the country to reach a consensus" (BBC Monitoring Service 2002a). Countering that Powell's argument was simply leading to a dead end, CARICOM secretary-general Edwin Carrington warned: "What you have is a situation where you never get what you call all parties agreeing. Now if the US is waiting for all parties agreeing, you might as well call it a day. It is not going to happen" (Saunders 2002). The CD, in short, was counting on the U.S. government's refusal to renew aid as the only means by which it could continue to oppose Aristide, block a resolution to the crisis, and contemplate his overthrow. Put differently, without direct or indirect external support, the CD would never have become a major political force in the 2000–04 conjuncture.

Pressure to end the foreign aid sanctions against Haiti, however, increased, as did the desire on the part of the OAS to move the political crisis toward a resolution. Representatives of the U.S. Congressional Black Caucus went to Haiti to meet with Aristide and joined CARICOM in urging the unblocking of the foreign aid monies, arguing that not doing so perpetuated an injustice against Haiti (*Haiti en Marche* 2002a).

Believing that the momentum was on his side, Aristide replaced Prime Minister Jean-Marie Chérestal with former Lavalas senator and Senate president Yvon Neptune. In presenting his program of government to parliament, Neptune pledged to make as one of his top priorities the resolution of the two-year-old political impasse. While Neptune was quickly approved by the FL-dominated parliament, many of the grassroots organizations that supported Aristide opposed his nomination and ratification on grounds that he was not a strong advocate for the poor. For its part, the CD also saw Neptune as a nonstarter, given the latter's past criticisms of the opposition and the international community whom he blamed for the current crisis (BBC Monitoring Service 2002c). These maneuvers proved to be once again merely strategic moves in the political chess game between Aristide and the foreign-backed opposition.

Then in July 2002, the OAS released its long-awaited report on the December 2001 palace attack. The report invalidated the government's claims that the attack was an attempted coup d'état against it and that Democratic Convergence leaders were behind it. At the same time, the report confirmed that former members of the Haitian Army had carried out the attack in complicity with some officers from different police units, in an apparent attempt to test the ability of other units to defend the government. This suggested that, as much as he may have tried to be, Aristide was not in complete control of the national police. It also suggested that another, more targeted attack could, and would, come later. That may explain why, despite his promise to do so, Aristide found it difficult to crack down seriously on the gangs of chimès that defended him.

Though the report did not make the point, I believe it is important to distinguish between chimès and popular organizations. Unlike popular organizations, some of which may be prone to violence and increasingly became chimès-like, the chimès were primarily hired thugs with no ideological commitment or political objectives and were willing to do anyone's bidding. Thus, they could and were used by both the government and the opposition, and they could and did switch allegiance whenever circumstances warranted. Gang leader Amiot (alias Cubain) Métayer's on-and-off support for Aristide illustrates this point.

The OAS report held the government responsible for the acts of violence committed against the opposition after the December 17 attack and ordered it to pay reparations to the victims of these acts, crack down on and disarm the chimès, bring those responsible for the acts of violence to justice, and ensure a climate of security conducive to the holding of new elections (OAS 2002b). Aristide quickly committed his government to doing so and began implementing some of these demands, such as paying reparations to victims of the post–palace attack violence, but stalled on others, especially arresting those responsible for the acts of violence, bringing them to justice, and disarming the chimès. Aristide's refusal to disarm, arrest, and prosecute the chimès revealed that they were the Achilles' heel of his politics. Put differently, Aristide showed that he was willing to make most of the concessions demanded of him by the international community concerning the holding of new parliamentary elections, which he believed his party could win, but was not certain of the loyalty of the police or of his closest supporters—which explains why he contracted with a San Francisco–based firm to provide his personal security, the first time a Haitian president has sought such service.

Unwilling to rely on the rule of law or even to mobilize his popular supporters to counter the threats of his opponents peacefully, Aristide chose instead to use the chimès to do that job. However, there were two main problems with that strategy. The first was that using repression as the means to his ends undermined his legitimacy and played into the hands of his enemies, who could portray him as a tyrant who abused his powers and discarded the rule of law. Second, the chimès were even less reliable than the police. Insofar as they were mercenaries without ideological convictions, their loyalty to Aristide and their willingness to do his dirty work depended principally on the monetary and other concrete benefits they derived from the government, such as jobs, as well as acting with impunity and being able to enhance their own power by becoming ward captains in the city slums where they lived. Therefore, any attempt by Aristide to crack down on them would lead them immediately to turn against him and threaten his hold on power. As Fatton put it, the "militarization [of the chimès] transformed them into armed gangs with increasingly independent interests and leaders. . . . The danger thus is that, having begun as a mere political instrument in the struggle for power, the *Chimères* have now become a power unto themselves" (2002, 148). As we will see, this is exactly what happened in 2003 and paved the way for Aristide's overthrow in February 2004.

To make this point another way, consider the difference between the chimès and the Tontons Makout under the Duvalier dictatorships. Unlike the chimès, the makouts were a formally structured and hierarchical military organization with direct links to the Haitian Army and the chief executive. The makouts, therefore, did not operate autonomously but were in fact accountable to a command structure and ultimately to the head of state. They acted as they did to terrorize the population with explicit official sanction. Their power, in other words, derived from the power of the state and those who controlled it. As such, it would have been unthinkable for local units of the makouts to challenge the authority of the command structure or the dictator, much less take up arms against them. Any such attempt would have been swiftly and immediately crushed. By contrast, the chimès had no official legal status and were accountable to no one, especially the head of state who denied his ties to them. To be sure, everyone knew the chimès were working for Aristide and others, including the opposition, but such links had to be proved. That is, the Duvaliers (father and son) were the commanders-in-chief of the Tontons Makout, but the same could not be said of Aristide vis-à-vis the chimès.

Now, one can argue, as I do, that the Duvalier regimes, and hence the Tontons Makout, were not legitimate because, *pace* Jürgen Habermas, they were not constituted through law, that is, recognized by a sovereign people who gave their *consent*, as opposed to only their *de facto* recognition, of the government(s) by exercising their autonomy as politically enfranchised citizens through their rights of communication and participation in the democratic process which alone can "justify the presumption of legitimate outcomes" (Habermas 2001, 114–15). By contrast, one could argue, as I do, that the Aristide government *was* legitimate, because it was formed with the consent of the people through the democratic exercise of their autonomy as enfranchised citizens. But Aristide undermined that legitimacy by using coercive means— the chimès or the police—that violated the rule of law. That is why human rights and other international organizations such as the OAS rightly accused him and his government of violating the human and civil rights of Haitian citizens, that is, the rights that guarantee the life and private liberty of citizens and "ground an inherently legitimate rule of law" (Habermas 2001, 116).

There was another consequence of relying on the chimès. It allowed the opposition and critics of Aristide to make Lavalas synonymous with chimès, thereby discrediting and marginalizing the popular organizations and even significant sectors of the population who continued to support Aristide for what he supposedly represented. Aristide, in other words, had "chimerized" Lavalas and betrayed his mass base while cynically continuing to cultivate his image as a defender of their interests against the wealthy elites and their allies who were determined to overthrow him.

Be that as it may, seeing that some progress was being made, the OAS in September 2002 adopted Resolution 822, which outlined the steps needed to resolve the political impasse and hopefully restore the rule of law. The central components of this resolution included the need:

1. To restore a climate of security by implementing a comprehensive disarmament program and bringing to justice all those who engaged in the acts of violence of December 21, 2001
2. To pay reparations to the individuals and organizations who were the victims of the violence of the December 2001 palace attack and its aftermath
3. To create a new CEP to be comprised of nine representatives from various sectors of Haitian society in accordance to the agreement reached in July 2001 in the Draft Initial Accord appended in the May 2001 report of the secretary-general on the situation in Haiti
4. For the new CEP to organize free and fair legislative and local elections in March 2003
5. To offer support and technical assistance to the government of Haiti, political parties, and civil society to facilitate the creation of the new CEP and to encourage all parties to participate in this process and in the elections organized by the CEP
6. To support the normalization of economic cooperation between the Haitian government and the international financial institutions (OAS 2002d)

The resolution set November 4, 2002, as the deadline for the formation of the new CEP. By mid-November, eight of the nine sectors had submitted the names of their representatives, though the Group of Five, representing the Catholic, Protestant, and Episcopal Churches, the Chamber of Commerce, and human rights groups, instructed its representatives not to assume their functions in the CEP until the government took concrete steps to ensure a climate of security conducive to elections.

Not surprisingly, the Democratic Convergence was the lone holdout. It justified its decision on the ground that the government had not fully implemented all the commitments it had agreed to in OAS Resolution 822. That resolution, however, did not make this a requirement for participation in the process and called instead on all parties to take consensus-building measures toward reaching a peaceful and democratic—that is, legitimate—solution. In a further attempt to sabotage the process, the CD instigated several antigovernment demonstrations in different parts of the country in mid-November. Those demonstrations gave yet another sign of the rapprochement between the Convergence and former members of the defunct army.

On November 17, CD leaders joined with ex-army colonel Himmler Rébu in a demonstration in which between 8,000 and 15,000 people participated, one of the largest anti-Aristide rallies since he took office in February 2001. In that demonstration, Rébu called on the nation to "rise up" against the government (Regan 2002; Deibert 2002b). Violence quickly escalated and spread to other cities. On November 21, thousands of high school students and their supporters took to the streets of the provincial city of Petit Goâve to denounce the police shooting of several students during a protest the day before. Calling Aristide a "criminal," the students demanded his removal from office. Echoes of this demand were also heard in Gonaïves and Port-au-Prince as several thousand high school and university students, respectively, protested in solidarity with the Petit Goâve students (Deibert 2002a; Norton 2002). The entry of students, especially university students, into the protests against Aristide marked a major turning point in the opposition against him, since it signaled that Aristide had lost the support not only of the dominant-class and middle-class political parties but also of the middle class and its future members as a whole.

Support for the CD was bolstered yet again with the formation in December 2002 of the Group of 184, so named because of the number of groups, organizations, and institutions represented in the coalition. Led by Andre (Andy) Apaid, a wealthy and prominent member of Haiti's business elite, and his brother-in-law Charles Henri Baker, also a wealthy businessman—who later left the Group to become a presidential candidate—the Group of 184 presented itself as apolitical and representing the voices of different sectors of Haitian society. In fact, however, the Group of 184 was an extension of the Civil Society Initiative, which, as previously mentioned, was also led by members of business and religious elite organizations that opposed Aristide. And, as with the CD before it, the IRI was instrumental in forming the Group of 184, which also received financial support from the European Union and the United States Agency for International Development (USAID) (Blumenthal 2004; Haiti Support Group 2003). Many of the organizations, groups, and individuals who joined the Group of 184 were either part of the CD or closely allied with it. The Group's leaders and principal spokesman, including Apaid and Baker, were well known for their anti-Aristide views (National Coalition for Haitian Rights 2003). According to Blumenthal, however, the leadership of the Group of 184 consisted of a so-called constitutionalist wing that emphasized protests and diplomacy as the path to forcing Aristide out, and a hard line faction quietly determined to oust Aristide by any means necessary. The constitutionalists were represented by Group of 184 spokesman . . . Andre Apaid Jr. The hard liners were led by Wendell Claude, a politician who was hell-bent on avenging the death of his brother Sylvio, a church minister burned to death by a pro-Aristide mob after the coup in 1991. (2004)

In its public pronouncements, the Group of 184 presented only its peaceful image, issuing a document that called for an end to all violence, a consensual and peaceful resolution of the crisis, and for the government to implement all the stipulations of OAS Resolution 822 (Group of 184 2002). The Group gave the government until January 15, 2003, to show that it was taking steps toward implementing the resolution. As expected, the government did not meet the Group's demands, and on January 16 the Group condemned the government for its contemptuous disregard of its earlier declaration and for its lack of goodwill. On January 20, the Group issued its second communiqué, which, while "not yet" calling for Aristide's resignation, nonetheless came to the same conclusion as the Convergence that it was not possible to put in place the structures and mechanisms to hold free, fair, and transparent elections under Aristide (Group of 184 2003).

This conclusion was as expected as it was disingenuous, since the CD and now the Group of 184, supported by the United States, had no intention of ever participating in elections with Aristide still in power and spurned any and all overtures made by Aristide to resolve the crisis peacefully. Another proof of this came on January 12 when the CD rejected an offer of a power-sharing arrangement Aristide made at a meeting with two CD leaders. Alluding to a failed attempt by President Préval to woo sectors of the opposition—the Espace de Concertation coalition that later joined the CD—for a power-sharing arrangement to resolve the impasse with parliament in 1999, the CD claimed that Aristide's offer was a similar ruse to use the opposition to slip out of the crisis he had created (Radio Métropole 2003a). The CD's rejection of this offer was not surprising since a month earlier on December 17, 2002, it had issued a resolution that called for Aristide to be replaced by a new provisional government (Convergence Démocratique 2002). If Aristide can be said to have undermined his legitimacy by violating the rule of law, the opposition, too, was just as willing to use undemocratic means to achieve its ends.

Aristide was not opposed from the Right only, however. Also in December, four progressive nongovernmental organizations (NGOs) linked to the popular movement since 1986 also called for Aristide's removal. They were the *Institut Cultural Karl Lévéque* (ICKL, Karl Lévéque Cultural Institute), *Institut de Technologie et d'Animation* (ITECA, Animation and Technology Institute),

Programme Alternatif de Justice (PAJ, Alternative Justice Program), and *Société d'Animation en Communication Sociale* (SACS, Society of Animation in Social Communication). They were joined by the *Coordination Nationale de Plaidoyer pour la Défense des Droits des Femmes* (CONAP, National Coordination for the Defense of Women's Rights)—a group of nine organizations involved in the women's movement—and the *Groupe de Réflexion et d'Action pour la Liberté de la Presse* (GRALIP, Action and Reflection Group for Press Freedom) to condemn the violence, intimidation, and threats against critics and opponents of Aristide, the criminalization of political life, and the corruption of his government. As the four NGOs—the ICKL, ITECA, PAJ, and SACS—put it most succinctly, Lavalas "has betrayed the masses and demobilized the popular movement . . . reestablished fear and repression in the heart of the popular movement . . . [and its] only compass is impunity and reconciliation with criminals, thieves, and drug traffickers" (Haiti Support Group 2002).

Indeed, since the return of Aristide to office in 2001, his government faced not only a political crisis but a crisis of governance as well. There is no doubt that this crisis of governance was exacerbated by the destabilizing strategy of the organized opposition and the foreign aid embargo against the government. But it also stemmed from the fractionalization, conflicts, and corruption within the ruling Lavalas party and at every level of government, as well as the inability of President Aristide to maintain control and exercise clear leadership over his party and government. Aristide may not have been directly responsible for all the politically motivated criminal acts committed by local officials, his grassroots supporters, or the police. But he also failed to take an unconditional stance against such acts, as we have seen.

Such a strategy inevitably opened the door to abuses of power and widespread corruption by government officials and facilitated the emergence of rival factions and power struggles within the governing party itself. Under such conditions, responsible, accountable, effective, and legitimate government was impossible. Thus, despite Aristide's promise to "democratize democracy" and to bring transparency, honesty, and an end to impunity, his government reverted to the practices of his predecessors. Internecine conflicts among rival factions of the ruling party and corruption made governing impossible. Prime Minister Chérestal, for example, was forced to resign in January 2002 after members of the ruling FL party in parliament accused him of using $1.7 million of public monies to buy an official residence. Drug traffickers paid off public officials to use the country to transship cocaine to the United States. Police officers and elected officials with close ties to Aristide were implicated in drug trafficking, kidnappings, and bank robberies. People arrested for drug trafficking, including alleged Colombian traffickers, were released without trial, but several people involved in drug trafficking and money laundering in Haiti were later convicted in U.S. courts. So far, however, Aristide has not been directly implicated in these activities (Associated Press 2005; United Press International 2005).

Vast sums allocated for microprojects or road construction, whether from domestic or foreign sources, were not used for those purposes or were unaccounted for. Elected and other government officials were implicated in a scandal involving the redistribution and sale of rice imported duty-free and exempted from consumer taxes that cost the government millions of dollars in revenue. Similarly, high-level government officials, including perhaps Aristide himself, were implicated in a cooperative investment scheme known as *Coeurs Unis* (United Hearts) that went bankrupt in 2002, taking with it the savings of poor and middle-class Haitians who had been lured to invest in the cooperative with the promise of high monthly interest rates. Members of the Chamber of Deputies allegedly embezzled money from that body's accounts. And mayors in towns throughout the country were accused of theft and mismanagement of their budgets.

A report issued in July 2005 by the *Unité Centrale de Recherches Économiques et Financières* (UCREF, Central Unit for Economic and Financial Investigation) of the post-Aristide interim government of Prime Minister Gérard Latortue, shed some light on the mafia-like corruption network set up under the second Aristide presidency. At the head of this network was the minister of finance, who set up a semipublic, semicommercial, autonomous bank run by a trusted appointee of the finance minister and who alone authorized all transactions. These individuals, in turn, answered directly to the president through his personal secretary. All transactions occurred through the autonomous bank, whether they involved issuing contracts, licenses, monopolies, subventions, gifts, loans, exemptions, and fiscal or financial privileges to the moneyed potentates of the country, and not just to Lavalas functionaries. This system also financed the charitable and social works of the president, such as his Aristide Foundation for Democracy, the Aristide University, his Lafanmi Sélavi orphanage, hospitals, a food-for-the poor program called *Sé Pa'n* (Our Own), and, not least, the base popular organizations and the gangs of chimès (*Haiti en Marche* 2005; Charles 2005).

The human rights situation also deteriorated significantly between 2001 and 2004. Local FL officials and members of the police persecuted, arbitrarily arrested, and physically abused members of the opposition or sometimes their family members. Supporters of Aristide and the police disrupted peaceful demonstrations by opponents of the government and ransacked or burned the offices and private residences of opposition leaders. And sometimes members or supporters of the opposition were killed. FL supporters also attacked and threatened members of several independent unions who had grievances against the government for violating workers' rights. In some of those crimes, either the police did not issue arrest warrants for those suspected of involvement or the government failed to bring to justice some of its local officials who were implicated.

Although radio stations and the press continued to criticize the government freely, FL officials and leaders of pro-Lavalas groups threatened members of the press who had been critical of the government. Consequently, many journalists and broadcasters suspended their commentaries or reporting, went into hiding, or fled the country for their safety. Several others were killed, such as Brignol Lindor in December 2001. The case of Lindor, as with that of Jean Dominique murder in April 2000, remained unsolved because the government dragged its feet and interfered with the judicial process. In the Lindor case, indictments were issued for ten men implicated in the murder, including members of a pro–Fanmi Lavalas organization. In the Dominique case, after the original investigating judge fled the country to escape death threats against him, the case was assigned to another judge, who issued several arrest warrants that were never enforced. The Senate also refused to lift the immunity of former FL senator Danny Toussaint, whom the judge named as a suspect in the case, for fear of reprisals against senators by Toussaint's supporters (U.S. Department of State 2002; Amnesty International 2002; National Coalition for Haitian Rights 2003; Reuters 2002; Radio Métropole 2003c; Associated Press 2005; United Press International 2005).

Similar processes of fractionalization and conflicts occurred among pro-Lavalas grassroots organizations that perpetrated violent criminal acts with impunity. In one such incident in June 2001, members of rival gangs in neighboring slums near Port-au-Prince engaged in a dispute over land, which left seventeen people dead, nineteen others injured, and more than 135 houses looted or burned. No one was arrested. Instead, Aristide held a meeting with the residents of the two slums in the National Palace to urge them to resolve their conflicts. The president held a similar meeting with representatives of several neighborhoods in another Port-au-Prince slum who had engaged in violent confrontations. Again, no arrests were made.

The level of insecurity even reached Aristide himself. Following the December 17, 2001, attack on the National Palace in which the palace guard offered little resistance to the attackers, and distrusting his own police force and fearing for his own personal safety, Aristide turned to a San Francisco–based security company to protect him. In short, as Michèle Montas, widow of slain journalist and once ardent defender of the Lavalas movement Jean Dominique, said in a radio editorial, the Lavalas government had been transformed into a "balkanized State where weapons make right, and where hunger for power and money [take] precedence over the general welfare, causing havoc on a party which, paradoxically, [controls] all the institutional levers of the country" (Montas 2002; see also *Economist* 2002; *Haiti Progrès* 2002; *Haiti en Marche* 2002b, 6–12 March 2002c; Haiti Press Network 2002; *Caribbean and Central America Report* 2002).

There was no doubt, then, that Aristide had failed to create the social and political conditions necessary for the consolidation of democracy in Haiti and that during his second presidency the tendency toward authoritarianism became predominant. As such, Aristide no longer represented the interests of the majority of Haitians but rather the interests of the Lavalas leadership, including himself, and those of their extended clientele, including among them the wealthy bourgeoisie, the network of armed gangs, and popular organizations through the practice of cronyism. Yet, for all that, the majority of the population had not seen a clear alternative to him. The population may have been disappointed with Aristide, but they distrusted the traditional political class, including the CD, even more; they believed Aristide, who made the point repeatedly that the opposition was responsible for the political crisis and the dire economic conditions of the country and was allied with and serving the interests of the wealthy and privileged elites.

In one of his most strident speeches, on February 9, 2002, marking the first anniversary of his second inauguration, Aristide cynically reminded the people how the bourgeoisie had despised them, shunned them, exploited them, and persecuted them for 200 years. As he put it:

> If they had not persecuted you for 200 years, would you still be in this misery? If they had not persecuted you for 200 years, would your children stay here, without going to school? If they had not persecuted you for 200 years, when your children are sick, wouldn't you be able to buy medicines for them? If they had not persecuted you for 200 years, would you have to walk in and breathe all that dust in the street?

And referring directly to the opposition, he continued:

> Unfortunately, during the last year, some of our brothers and sisters let themselves fall into the trap of hidden hands, which caused them to persecute other people with their mouths, with what they said, in the way they criticized and persecuted others with their mouths, and the way in which they perpetrated violence on people's ears with lies and disinformation.
>
> Do not let yourself be affected by provocation. The small group that is persecuting the peasants, that is persecuting the people when they either receive money from the white people to plot to overturn the car or when they accept money from the white people to tell lies about the people in order to discourage

the people, then today I come to tell them on behalf of all the Haitian people that I am also their president. My arms are open wide for you. (BBC Monitoring Service 2002d)

Aristide knew, of course, that such a speech would alienate even more the opposition, the bourgeoisie, and the United States by reinforcing their view that his allegiance to the masses, to "class warfare," and to upsetting the status quo had not changed and that he was untrustworthy. However, the speech was aimed not at them but to the masses whose support Aristide needed to bolster. And there is no doubt that despite all that had happened to erode that support, Aristide still resonated with a large sector of the Haitian population, especially the poor majority. This was shown, for example, in two unpublished opinion polls conducted by CID Gallup (a polling and consulting firm based in San Jose, Costa Rica) on behalf of USAID between March 1 and March 8, 2002. The polls confirmed that despite waning support for Fanmi Lavalas due to growing discontent with the government and the state of the economy, one-third of the adult population—especially outside of Port-au-Prince, among women, and with the less educated, that is, the poor—identified themselves with the FL. By contrast, only 8 percent—concentrated among young and well-educated respondents, that is, the middle class and elites of Haiti—supported the CD. And despite his lower job rating, 50 percent of the population still favored Aristide over any other public figure from the traditional political class and the CD (CID/Gallup 2002).

As the Miami-based weekly *Haiti en Marche* observed so poignantly, the question is worth asking why the majority of the population still remained faithful to Aristide despite all his failings and the evident degradation of the economy since 2000, no doubt made worse by the economic embargo against the government. The "secret," the paper pointed out,

is that this government, no doubt because of its origin, was able to impart to the people, the little people, who mathematically are the majority . . . the feeling that they also have a say in things . . . that they are not condemned to be perpetually neglected, the outsiders, the uncivilized, the big toes, who must hide even to watch the carnival procession on the Champs de Mars [as in the days of Baby Doc] while the sons of the well-to-do party to their heart's content on the macadam . . . [or] to flee timorously all their life the section chief or the police who fire on their cottages in Cité Soleil [a slum in Port-au-Prince] . . . as happened during the coup d'état of 1991, or under the Duvalier dictatorship and the reign of military despots that followed it. (*Haiti en Marche* 2003)

This awakening in the people of the belief that they had rights and deserved to be treated with respect and dignity is, more than anything else, the reason why the dominant classes feared and despised Aristide so much, even if he himself trampled on those rights and violated the people's trust. Despite the loss of considerable support, the polls confirmed that Aristide and his FL party would still likely win an electoral contest against the CD. That is why for the CD, negotiating any resolution to the crisis that kept Aristide in power and called for new elections in which his party would participate was unacceptable. Instead, the only negotiations its leaders were willing to entertain were, in the words of Evans Paul, a CD spokesman, "through which door [Aristide] leaves the palace, through the front door or the back door" (Council on Hemispheric Affairs 2004a). Thus, the only alternative was for the CD, with U.S. backing, to stick to its strategy of forcing Aristide out of power.

Evidence of planning for an eventual coup d'état surfaced on May 7, 2003, when Dominican authorities arrested five Haitians, among them Guy Philippe, at a meeting near the Dominican-Haitian border for allegedly planning to overthrow Aristide. The men were released the day after for "lack of evidence." But right after his release, Philippe declared that the time for negotiations with Aristide was over and that he would support a coup to remove him. Also on May 7, some twenty armed men attacked and disabled the main electrical plant in Peligre and killed two workers. The attack was considered yet another attempt to destabilize the government (Reeves 2003; Arthur 2003; Cala 2003). Philippe would emerge as one of the leaders of the armed attack by former soldiers of the defunct Haitian Army that toppled Aristide in February 2004.

In response to these perceived and real threats to his government, Aristide sought to suppress his opponents, and they also engaged in acts of violence against Aristide supporters. As a result, human rights abuses worsened, and the government became even more isolated. The fragility and volatility of the situation led the OAS to issue a report in May 2003 that, while identifying the inaction of the government as the "principal obstacle" to progress, also pressed the opposition and "civil society" groups to declare that they would participate in the new elections once the government acted (OAS 2003a).

Not surprisingly, rather than pressuring the CD to participate in the elections as the only peaceful and democratic way to resolve the three-year-old impasse, the U.S. Embassy in Port-au-Prince made it clear that it would not recognize the vote without the CD's participation—which the latter had no intention of doing (Regan and Lynch 2003). As the deadlock appeared to be nowhere near a resolution, violence and human rights abuses continued unabated between government supporters and opponents alike for the rest of the year. An Amnesty International report showed that the police and the pro-Lavalas gangs of chimès committed most of the violence and human rights violations, but the opposition, too, had its share of the sometimes deadly violence, as well as that committed by former soldiers of the defunct army against supporters of Aristide and government officials (Amnesty International 2003). While the CD denied ties to the killings committed by former army soldiers, it is also clear that those acts served its interests, and it must be remembered that it was the CD that called for a return of the army in Gourgue's shadow "inaugural address" in February 2001.

It is in this context that the significance of the uprising of a gang of chimès formerly allied with Aristide in September 2003 is to be understood. That uprising not only revealed the Janus-faced character of the chimès and their relationship with Aristide but was also the opening salvo that led to the second overthrow of Aristide. On September 22, 2003, Amiot Métayer was found murdered an hour away from the seaside slum of Raboteau in the northwestern city of Gonaïves, where he was a strongman and pro-Aristide militant who gave out jobs at the port authority that he and his brother Buter controlled. As Jane Regan put it, the "story behind Métayer's murder and Raboteau's revolt offers a glimpse at an ugly underbelly of Lavalas politics, a fragile formula where gangs rule the streets" (2003).

Métayer was a Lavalas activist since the post-coup period of 1991. Forced into exile after the Raboteau massacre of 1994 by the FRAPH, he returned to Haiti in late 1994 and became a staunch Aristide supporter until 2002. Arrested in August 2002 after intense international pressure on the government, he was subsequently broken out of prison by members of his "*Armée Cannibale*" (Cannibal Army). Despite renewed pressure from the United States, OAS, and human rights groups to rearrest Métayer, who had been accused of lynching an opposition party member on December 17, 2001, after the attack on the National Palace, the government refused. He left his stronghold of Raboteau on September 21 with a well-known former government employee, and when his bullet-ridden body and mutilated face were found the next day, violent protests and clashes with the police erupted in Raboteau. Buter Métayer charged Aristide with the murder, calling it "treason." The reason for Amiot's assassination, Buter and Winter Etienne, a spokesman for the Cannibal Army, maintained, was that he knew too much about the inner workings of the National Palace and was about to reveal some facts about the assassination of Jean Dominique. Buter Métayer and his followers vowed not to stop the uprising by their "army" until Aristide was overthrown (Regan 2003; Caroit 2003).

As if this escalation of violence was not enough, Fanmi Lavalas legislators committed another important political blunder that same month by proposing to amend the 1987 Constitution to allow a president to be reelected for more than two terms. The constitution stipulated that all proposed amendments must be introduced during the last session of the legislature, that all amendments would be effective only with the beginning of the new Parliament, and that the sitting president cannot benefit from such amendments. But these safeguards were not sufficient to allay the fears of the opposition that Aristide was planning to prolong his hold on power indefinitely. Before he left Haiti as U.S. ambassador, Brian Dean Curran warned the government against any attempt to amend the constitution's bar against a lifetime presidency. As he put it, "To change the clauses of the constitution particularly through the acts of a parliament elected under dubious circumstances would be, in my view, fundamentally destabilizing and incoherent and could even call in question the legitimacy of the government" (2003). There was opposition to the proposal even from within the ranks of the FL and among Aristide supporters. For example, Father William Smarth, one of the founders of the Lavalas Movement, called on the population to mobilize to resist against the proposed amendment, and former senator Samuel Madistin argued that the legislators could not tamper with Article 143.3 of the constitution, which places a limit of two presidential terms with a five-year interval between terms, without plunging the country into an unprecedented crisis (Radio Métropole 2003b).

But the FL legislators would never be given the time to introduce their proposed amendments. With the negotiations with the opposition at an impasse, there was no hope of holding new parliamentary elections at the end of the year, and the mandate of the 2000 parliament would expire in January 2004. In the meantime, the month-long and deadly clashes in Gonaïves spread to other parts of the country, and the "Cannibal Army" changed its name to the *Front de Résistance des Gonaïves pour le Renversement de Jean-Bertrand Aristide* (Gonaïves Resistance Front for the Overthrow of Jean-Bertrand Aristide). Another group, the *Rassemblement des Militants Conséquents de Saint-Marc* (RAMICOS, Union of the Important Militants of Saint-Marc), rose in support of the Gonaïves Front. The uprisings spread to the northeast and central regions, including Cap Haitien, Haiti's second largest city (north of Port-au-Prince), Hinche (northeast of Port-au-Prince), and Port-de-Paix (northwest of Port-au-Prince). Equally as significant in the mounting opposition to Aristide and the demand for his resignation was the part played by students from the State University of Haiti and women's organizations, such as the CONAP, which represented important middle-class constituents, in condemning the government's abuse of power, its violence against opponents, its human rights violations, and its impunity.

Even though Aristide supporters and the police responded to these developments with even more violence, it became clear for the first time since 2001 that the government had lost the support of significant sectors of the population and that the momentum had swung decisively in favor of the opposition. In response to a pro-government attack against university students in early December 2003, tens of thousands of demonstrators took to the streets of Port-au-Prince to demand Aristide's ouster. Haitian and international human rights groups, as well as the OAS, condemned the violence against the students and the government for not stopping it. Even some prominent members of Fanmi Lavalas took part in the demonstrations against the government, and other members of the government resigned in protest (Arthur 2003; Vital 2003; CONAP 2003; Regan and Ottey 2003; OAS 2003b, 2003c; Sérant 2003). The violence between supporters and opponents of the government resulted in the deaths of nearly fifty people and injury to many more between December 2003 and February 2004.

All these events played right into the hands of the CD and the hard-liners of the Group of 184, who, as Blumenthal put it, were hatching "plans for a coup" while the constitutionalists were busy mounting "a series of protests through late 2003, provoking increasing unrest" (2004). The hard-liners, Blumenthal claimed, "tapped Guy Philippe . . . to lead a band of insurgents consisting almost entirely of exiled members of the FRAPH death squads and former soldiers of the Haitian army" (2004). In early February, Philippe and his band of some 200 insurgents crossed the border into Haiti from their refuge in the Dominican Republic, and they would immediately supplant the anti-Lavalas gangs that had sparked the rebellion to become the principal force against Aristide. As the new rebel forces gained control of several major cities in the north and northwest of the capital and made their advance toward Port-au-Prince, they forced Aristide to leave Haiti on February 29, 2004 (Blumenthal 2004; Norton 2004; Christie 2004a, 2004b; Sutton 2004; Loney and Scrutton 2004). I will analyze the diplomatic process that convinced Aristide to resign his office and leave Haiti in the next chapter.

Aristide's second term in office, then, was disastrous on all fronts—political, economic, and social. Three years of unrelenting power struggles between Aristide and his organized opposition had brought the country on the brink of chaos. It is clear that Aristide, as well as his Fanmi Lavalas party in power, relied on intimidation, violence, and corruption to maintain themselves in power, had become discredited, no longer represented the interests of the majority of Haitians who brought them to power, and were a major obstacle to the democratization of Haiti. But if Aristide and the FL subverted democracy, so too did the organized opposition, the Haitian bourgeoisie, and their foreign allies. The Democratic Convergence, made up of a motley group of individuals and political parties who were devoid of principles, did not share a common ideology, had no alternative program or vision to offer the citizenry, and gained no significant popular support. Its only raison d'être was to overthrow Aristide, and the unconditional support it received from the Bush administration and the IRI in particular gave it a veto power over the negotiations with Aristide. Similarly, the Civil Society Group and the Group of 184, who represented the interests of the Haitian bourgeoisie and saw Aristide and the FL as unpredictable partners with whom to form a pact of domination, threw their support to the CD and the former members of the military and right-wing militias to topple Aristide once again and dismantle the Lavalasian juggernaut.

In the end, mutatis mutandis, in February 2004 Aristide confronted the reality he faced in September 1991. That reality was that in a peripheral society in the capitalist world system, gaining control of the state is not synonymous with having real and effective power. In 1991, Aristide came to power with an immense popular mandate, and he also had the support of a significant sector of the anti-Duvalierist political middle class. But fearing for their interests, the neo-Duvalierists and the Haitian bourgeoisie, with the tacit support of the United States, constituted a greater power than Aristide and toppled him in a coup d'état. In 2000 Aristide, drawing the lessons of 1991, sought to monopolize state power while trying to enter into a power-sharing arrangement with the middle-class opposition parties to form a pact of domination with the bourgeoisie and foreign capital. But distrusting Aristide, who had shown his ability to outmaneuver and outfox them before, these latter three interests formed a pact of their own to force him out of power once and for all. Thus, it could be argued, Aristide was overthrown a second time not because he had been illegitimately reelected or because his government was corrupt or used violence to intimidate his opponents, but because he thought he could play the game of politics according to his rules rather than those of the bourgeoisie and the core powers, principally those of the United States as formulated in the post–Cold War Washington Consensus.

There was yet another major difference between 1991 and 2004. When Aristide was overthrown in 1991, he had the people behind him because they could clearly see who his enemies were and why his opponents hated him. So they resisted the coup, as they had done before in January 1991 when Roger Lafontant attempted his, and made possible Aristide's return in 1994. In 2004, by contrast, the people did not resist the chimès who started the rebellion or the former soldiers who came over from the Dominican Republic to topple Aristide once more. The people may not have embraced the opposition and rebel forces that ousted Aristide, but many of them did not believe that he was worth rescuing either—not because they no longer believed in what he once stood for, but because they could see that he had betrayed their trust and their interests to serve his own and those of his cronies.

That experience also allows us to draw another conclusion about charismatic leadership. As I argued in chapter 3, an individual may have the ability to become a charismatic leader, but that potential can be realized only through his or her deeds in specific social contexts and historical conjunctures. So it was that the conjuncture of 1986–90, characterized by the struggles of the people against the reconsolidation of dictatorship and for democracy, created the conditions for the emergence of Aristide as a charismatic leader who articulated their needs and interests and in whom the vast majority placed their trust and expectations. By contrast, the conjuncture of 2000–04 was such that Aristide could not manifest his qualities as a charismatic leader because by then the people whose trust and interests he had betrayed were no longer willing to surrender their faith to "the extraordinary and unheard of, to what is alien to all regulation and tradition and therefore viewed as divine," as Max Weber put it (1978, 2:1114–1115). By then, the prophet had lost his garb, and the people could see him for who he was: an all-too-ordinary and traditional president who, like all the others who came before him, was using state power for his and his allies' personal gains. In 2004, then, Aristide the Prophet succumbed along with the political demise of Aristide the ordinary and hybrid president.

NOTES

1. According to Article 129.2 of the 1987 Constitution, any member of parliament from either chamber has the right to question or challenge a member of the government or the entire government. Such a challenge requires the support of at least five members of the chamber from which it emerges, and if it then receives a majority vote in that chamber, it becomes a vote of no confidence or a vote of censure (Art. 129.3). When the challenge that results in a vote of no confidence concerns the program of government or a general policy of the government, then the prime minister must submit his and his government's resignation to the president (Art. 129.4). The president must then accept that resignation and nominate a new prime minister (Art. 129.5).

Chapter Six

The Prophet Banished:
The Second Overthrow of
Aristide and the Pacification of Haiti

THE SECOND OVERTHROW OF ARISTIDE

By June 2003 it had become evident to me that if the three-year-old political crisis between the Aristide government and the organized political opposition forced him to leave office before the end of his term in February 2006, only a foreign military intervention could prevent the country from descending into a full-fledged civil war (Dupuy 2003, 6–7). At the time, I thought, such an intervention could be led either by the United States or a joint force from the United States and the Dominican Republic. The intervening forces could then install a provisional government headed by leaders of the opposition or others allied with it. The primary task of that provisional government would be to restore order and security in the country and organize new elections. Before elections could be held, I maintained, the new government would have to crack down on Aristide's supporters and his Lavalas Family party to lessen the latter's chances of winning again as it did in 2000 (Dupuy 2003, 8). Except for some of the actors involved, subsequent events confirmed my general prognosis (see also Dupuy 2005a, 186–90).

On February 29, 2004, Jean-Bertrand Aristide fled Haiti for the Central African Republic aboard an aircraft chartered by the United States and escorted by U.S. military personnel and his own personal security. He left the Central African Republic for Jamaica on March 15 and remained there until the end of May, when he flew to South Africa for an indefinite exile (Associated Press 2004b). As happened when he was overthrown by the Haitian military in September 1991, seven months into his first term, Aristide's departure in February 2004 cut short his second five-year mandate by two years.

171

Aristide was coerced into leaving Haiti after an armed insurgency erupted in the port city of Gonaïves in early February 2004 and quickly spread to other parts of the country. The rebellion was first led by a gang of *chimès*, the so-called Artibonite Resistance Front, formerly known as the Cannibal Army and led by Buter Métayer, which was once allied with Aristide but turned against him. But the rebellion was soon taken over by a group of some 200 former members of the defunct Haitian Army, former rural police section chiefs, and members of the death squad *Front Révolutionnaire pour l'Avancement et le Progrès d'Haiti* (FRAPH, Revolutionary Front for the Advancement and Progress of Haiti). As the rebel forces gained control over large portions of the country and advanced toward Port-au-Prince, they threatened to storm the city to remove or even kill Aristide. Aristide made the situation worse for himself by unleashing the chimès who went on a rampage in the days preceding his departure, thereby reinforcing his enemies' claims that that the country would be plunged into a bloodbath unless Aristide was removed (Amnesty International 2004a).

It was then that James Foley, the U.S. ambassador to Haiti, made it clear to Aristide that the United States would not protect him and that he was on his own. The U.S. State Department also prevented the San Francisco–based firm under contract to provide private security for Aristide from sending additional personnel as Aristide had requested. Aristide realized then that he faced the choice of staying and being killed or leaving the country. Perhaps believing he could be brought back to power, as in 1994, he made his final decision late on February 28 after Ambassador Foley informed him that the Bush administration had decided that staying was no longer an option and that it was time for him to go.

Immediately after Aristide's departure, the United Nations authorized the deployment of a Multinational Interim Force (MIF) comprised of troops from the United States, France, Canada, and Chile. In June 2004, the MIF was replaced by the United Nations Stabilization Mission in Haiti (MINUSTAH, from the French version of the name), which was led by Brazil but included troop contributions from a number of other countries (Dodds 2004b, 2004c; Davies 2004; Slevin and Allen 2004; Caroit 2004; Weiner 2004; Williams 2004).

With Aristide gone, a U.S.-approved "Council of the Wise" "chose" Gérard Latortue, a retired UN technocrat, business consultant, talk-show host, and former minister of foreign affairs under the brief government of Leslie Manigat (February–June 1988), to serve as prime minister of an interim government and Boniface Alexandre, a Supreme Court justice as the interim president. Alexandre was mostly a figurehead, and the real authority rested with Latortue, who, on March 17, formed a cabinet government of thirteen ministers and five secretaries of state. The interim government initially had an eight-month mandate to organize new elections and transfer power to a democratically elected government. However, immediately after his installation, Latortue signaled that the process of restoring order would take longer. (Semple 2004; Wilentz 2004; Reuters 2005; Delva 2005a). Originally scheduled to be held in November 2005, the elections were postponed four times and finally held on February 7, 2006. René Préval, who served as president from 1996 to 2001, was reelected for a second five-year term.

Controversy surrounded Aristide's departure. The United States denied the charge made by the exiled president that he had been kidnapped and forced to leave Haiti by a U.S.-backed coup d'état. The United States maintained that Aristide agreed to leave voluntarily and made public his letter of resignation. At the same time, the United States and France blocked an investigation by the United Nations into the circumstances of Aristide's departure requested by the Caribbean Community (CARICOM), Venezuela, and fifty-three African Union countries (Kramer 2004).

CARICOM remained the only block of member countries of the Organization of American States (OAS) that refused to recognize the interim Alexandre-Latortue government, on grounds of its unconstitutionality and its human rights record. CARICOM also succeeded in June 2004 in getting the OAS General Assembly to approve Resolution 2058, which expressed concern over the "abrupt departure of the democratically elected President of Haiti," the "subsequent questions surrounding his resignation," and the request by CARICOM for "the Permanent Council to undertake a collective assessment of the situation in Haiti" (OAS 2004a). As Kirstin Kramer noted, Resolution 2058 was the "first clear sign of concern from a major international organization that the democratically-elected president was overthrown in Haiti with the possible complicity of the United States" (2004). The OAS never carried out the requested inquiry, though, as the United Nations had failed to do previously.

The OAS not only failed to carry out the investigation but, now that Aristide was gone, it was sidelined by the United Nations, which assumed a peacekeeping rather than a mediating role. The UN's main mission was to work with the Haitian National Police (HNP) to pacify Haiti rather than to negotiate a peaceful resolution of a conflict between a government in power and a foreign-backed opposition.

Whether or not Aristide's allegations that he was kidnapped are true, it is clear that the administration of President George W. Bush forced him out. In late January 2004, the leaders of CARICOM proposed a power-sharing plan between Aristide and the opposition that called for allowing Aristide to complete his term as president; creating a broad-based cabinet with a new, neutral, and independent prime minister; disarming the armed gangs who supported Aristide, as well as the rebel forces; reforming the HNP and placing it under the control of the prime minister; allowing the opposition to protest freely; and establishing conditions for new parliamentary elections. Aristide accepted the plan immediately, but the opposition did not. The United States, France, and Canada initially supported the plan and maintained they were not seeking to force Aristide out and would not tolerate an armed overthrow of a democratically elected president. Yet they refused to authorize the deployment of a peacekeeping force to stop the armed insurgency until a political settlement had been reached (Helps 2004; OAS 2004b; BBC News 2004; Reuters 2004; John 2004; Hudson 2004; Ljunggren 2004; Craig 2004). That decision simply meant that, all the public pronouncements notwithstanding, the three powers simply let the rebel forces do their work and give them the excuse they needed to compel Aristide to leave.

As the violence escalated and the rebel forces gained ground and were poised to enter Port-au-Prince by the end of the month, the Bush administration sent Roger Noriega (Assistant Secretary of State for Western Hemispheric Affairs, 2003–2005) to Haiti on February 21 to negotiate the power-sharing plan with Aristide, who reiterated his acceptance of it. As expected, the opposition refused on the ground that Aristide could not be trusted, and Noriega did not pressure them. This last-minute effort by the Bush administration was transparent in its insincerity, for Noriega already knew that given the opposition's recalcitrance during the past two years—with his own and the Bush administration's unwavering encouragement—it was not about to change course now that the balance of forces had clearly shifted in its favor and that Aristide was in his last days as president.

Indeed, several months before the rebels crossed over the border to begin their attack against Aristide, Luigi Einaudi, the assistant secretary-general of the OAS who had been trying to broker an agreement between Aristide and the *Convergence Démocratique* (CD, Democratic Convergence) since 2001, made one last effort to bring the two sides together at the home of Foley, the new U.S. ambassador to Haiti replacing Brian Dean Curran who had left in August 2003. While Aristide was "prepared to give up much of his power," Einaudi reportedly said, "American officials 'pulled the rug out,' abruptly canceling the meeting without consulting him" (Bogdanich and Nordberg 2006). For Einaudi, canceling that meeting in effect killed "what was in fact my last move" (ibid.). And, according to Noriega, who had by then replaced Otto Reich at the State Department, the Bush administration canceled the meeting after talking to the opposition when it became clear that it was "going to be a failure for us and wreck our credibility" (ibid.).

Once the opposition made it clear it would not accept any compromise with Aristide, France and the United States made their move. On February 25,

French foreign minister Dominique de Villepin publicly blamed Aristide for the crisis and called on him to resign, echoed by U.S. secretary of state Colin Powell. By week's end,

> Bush's foreign policy principals—including Powell, [National Security Advisor Condoleezza] Rice, Defense Secretary Donald H. Rumsfeld and Vice President Cheney—held a teleconference Saturday morning, [and] agreed to press harder for Aristide's departure. They worked out a statement largely blaming him for the crisis. It went out under the White House Seal. (Slevin and Allen 2004)

As Peter Slevin and Mike Allen noted further:

> [President] Bush is rarely awakened by his staff, even for an international crisis, but at 1:30 a.m., Rice called Bush from her nearby cabin at the Camp David presidential retreat to let him know Aristide was leaving. Bush called Rumsfeld and authorized a deployment of Marines. (2004)

Though it came to power undemocratically, the new government formed by Prime Minister Latortue had the full backing of the United States, France, Canada, and the international financial institutions (IFIs) that had denied support (political and economic) to the democratically elected Aristide government. The foreign aid donors pledged some $1.3 billion to the Latortue government, although these funds were not likely to be delivered (*Economist* 2004). Nonetheless, this show of support made it clear once again that, for these governments and international organizations, the issue has never been whether a government is democratically elected but whether that government is willing to conform to their interests, especially those of the United States as the dominant power among them. Despite its claim of being a "government of national unity," the main task at hand was to pacify Haiti by ridding the country of Aristide's armed supporters and weakening what remained of his already fragmented and discredited Fanmi Lavalas (FL) party to ensure that candidates from that party would not gain control of the presidency or parliament in the next round of elections.

Most appointed members of the interim government have been depicted as "technocrats" who were not active in the coalition that opposed Aristide or other political parties. But several interim ministers, including those for foreign affairs, justice, social affairs, and commerce and tourism, as well as the secretary of state for education and culture, were ideologically close to the CD and the Group of 184. The foreign minister (formerly interior and national defense minister) was a retired general who had called on Aristide to resign and wanted to reconstitute the repressive and corrupt Armed Forces of Haiti that Aristide disbanded in 1995. Not surprisingly, no members of former President Aristide's FL party were included in the new government, but that was not enough to satisfy some leaders of the opposition who complained of having been excluded also, thereby depriving them of their rightful share of the spoils of power for their role in ousting Aristide.

In February 2005, Latortue reshuffled his cabinet, but the change of guards did not signal a change in the government's priority or objective. The middle-class parties, intellectuals, and bourgeoisie as a whole accepted Latortue and the members of his interim government because they came from the same social class and shared similar interests. Nonetheless, many members of the elite believed Latortue was incompetent and not doing enough to crack down on Aristide supporters, especially the chimès. The government's main objective was to pacify the country, by which was meant cracking down on Aristide supporters, especially but not exclusively the chimès; to prepare new elections that hopefully would bring to power a government that would respect the rules of the political game according to the dictates of the Washington; and to restore the balance of power between the bourgeoisie and the state rulers through the traditional pact of domination favorable to the former (Semple 2004; Agence France Presse 2004; Christie and Villelabeitia 2004; Dodds 2004a; Associated Press 2004a; Wilentz 2004; Radio Métropole 2005).

Latortue had made his anti-Aristide views known and had been preparing himself for the post he now filled long before Aristide's overthrow in February 2004. As a talk-show host in South Florida where he lived before going back to Haiti, Latortue used that platform to criticize Aristide, develop his own political and economic views, and launch his campaign for prime minister. As Michel Laguerre asserted, a full year before he assumed the post of interim prime minister, Latortue had launched his campaign by visiting the Haitian Chamber of Commerce and Industry in Port-au-Prince, giving interviews, and lecturing on the political and economic development of Haiti in Washington, D.C. As Laguerre put it:

> The Haiti visit was aimed at reconnecting him with the bourgeoisie, and he discussed things of common interest in an effort to appease their fears, while the Washington visit served to present and justify his plan of government before the Bush government and representatives of international organizations. From February 2003 to February 2004, his politics evolved from the goal of serving as prime minister with an independent agenda under President Aristide to advocating the departure of Aristide as the only viable solution to the political stalemate and the success of his future administration. (2005, 211)

Laguerre's analysis reinforces my own view that in fact planning for Aristide's overthrow was under way long before February 2004 and that the

United States and its allies already had identified those it would call upon to form an interim government after Aristide was removed. Indeed, then U.S. ambassador to Haiti Curran had hinted as much when he stated in a speech on July 9, 2003, to the Haitian American Chamber of Commerce that instead of looking to the past, Haitians should

> seek new leaders, preferably among your incredibly qualified young professionals educated at Harvard, Columbia, Stanford, Georgetown and other American universities, at the Sorbonne or the HEC, at McGill or Laval, for a new generation of political leaders, tested in the crucible of modern ideas, but now in Haiti, preparing a better future for Haiti. (Curran 2003; also cited in Sérant 2003 and Laguerre 2005, 213)

From this, Laguerre concluded, "Without the US embassy preparing the way, the choice of a diasporan as prime minister would not have happened" (2005, 213).

From the standpoint of the United States, it made sense to install Latortue and his government of "qualified professionals" rather than a government drawn from the anti-Aristide coalition. The United States backed the CD when it needed an opposition to Aristide, and the CD had served that purpose well. The coalition has since disintegrated, and its former members went their separate ways to form new alliances, on the right and left of center, to contest the new elections. But if the CD outlived its usefulness, that was not the case in the 2000–04 period. As I have shown in the previous chapter, though it was clear to the United States that the U.S.-backed CD could never win an electoral contest against Aristide or his FL party, it nonetheless served the United States'—as well as its own and the economic elites'—objective of undermining Aristide's second term in office. Without denying that Aristide had been legitimately reelected president in November 2000, the United States nonetheless portrayed the CD as a legitimate opposition to Aristide and insisted that it would not accept any resolution to the political crisis generated in the aftermath of the May 2000 parliamentary elections without the participation of the CD.

From that point on, the CD declared its zero-option strategy that consisted of rejecting the results of all the elections and demanding nothing less than the resignation (voluntarily or forcefully) of the reelected president. For the next three years, the CD refused all offers of negotiation by Aristide and his party and discarded all efforts by the OAS to negotiate a settlement to the crisis that Aristide had endorsed, even if reluctantly—including a power-sharing arrangement with the CD, creating a new independent *Conseil Électoral Provisoire* (CEP, Provisional Electoral Council), and holding entirely new parliamentary elections.

The Bush administration, especially with Roger Noriega as its permanent representative to the OAS (and later assistant secretary of state for Western Hemispheric affairs), encouraged the intransigence of the CD by blaming Aristide for the failure to reach agreement at every turn in the negotiating process. As Ron Howell pointed out, Noriega started his political ascent with his ties to North Carolina Republican senator Jesse Helms, who was by far the most archconservative foe of Aristide in the Senate until his retirement in 2002. Since then, Noriega's "influence over US policy toward Haiti has increased as he climbed the diplomatic ladder in Washington," and he never wavered from his determination to oust Aristide from power (Howell 2004).

The Bush administration, then, was from the outset complicit in the strategy to overthrow Aristide, and it granted its proxy to the CD to have veto power over the OAS-CARICOM mediations with Aristide. In this sense, it is legitimate to conclude, as did Amy Wilentz, that by refusing all meaningful negotiations with Aristide, the so-called democratic opposition "was being used to foment and mask what was essentially a coup against democracy by the island's elite, in concert with right-wing elements of the Republican Party" (Wilentz 2004).

None of this is to say, however, that Aristide did not undermine his legitimacy by his own actions or was not also responsible for creating the conditions that ultimately led to his downfall. True, the Haitian elite despised him, a U.S.-backed coalition of middle-class political parties challenged his reelection and demanded his removal, former army soldiers and paramilitaries attacked his government, and the United States and the IFIs imposed a foreign aid embargo on his government. In light of such obvious threats to his government, Aristide was determined to prevent a repeat of 1991 when he was ousted by a coup seven months into his first term and the military junta went on to kill an estimated 4,000 to 5,000 of his supporters.

But none of that justified the ultimate course that Aristide took to deal with the crisis or the threat to his government. As I have shown in the previous chapter, the government went on the offensive and, in the process, abused its powers and increasingly took on an authoritarian character. Instead of mobilizing his supporters to protect his government against his enemies through peaceful means, the government relied on its armed gangs to intimidate, and even kill, members of the press and of the opposition. Aristide and the ruling FL party also used the institutions of government to further their goals of monopolizing political power and promoting their individual and class ambitions through corruption and cronyism; in short, they perpetuated the prebendary and repressive practices of the state. In the end, it could be said, Aristide became the victim of his own politics. If the Haitian bourgeoisie and the foreign-backed opposition encouraged Aristide's authoritarian tendencies by threatening him, Aristide obliged them and by so doing undermined his and his government's legitimacy.

THE LATORTUE GOVERNMENT AND THE PACIFICATION OF HAITI

One of the purported priorities of the interim Latortue government was to pacify the country by disarming all those who possessed weapons illegally, including armed supporters of the deposed president and the rebel forces of the defunct military and FRAPH, and to end impunity and human rights abuses by bringing all those involved in or accused of crimes to justice. The MINUSTAH was also to "support the Transitional Government to ensure a secure and stable environment within which the constitutional and political process in Haiti can take place" (United Nations 2004). There is no doubt that a comprehensive program of disarmament—termed by the UN "disarmament, demobilization, and reintegration"—was essential and that all those accused of or involved in criminal activities, including politically motivated criminal acts, had to be brought to justice if a climate of security was to be restored. Without a sense of personal security, citizens cannot exercise their rights, participate freely and autonomously in the political process, and ground the legitimacy of government through their consent. Thus, one could argue that even if it came to power illegally and lacked legitimacy, the interim Latortue government could have quickly earned the support and even the recognition of the people if it had demonstrated its commitment to impartiality in the application of justice, to ending impunity, and to the rule of law. Moreover, as mentioned above, CARICOM was willing to reconsider its initial decision to withhold recognition of the Latortue government on such grounds.

From the outset, however, the Latortue government made it clear through its actions that justice was political and partisan and would be administered in the pursuit of objectives that corresponded to the class and political interests of those in power and their foreign backers. Essentially, the approach of the Latortue government and its domestic and foreign supporters, including the United Nations, was to use a military solution to what is fundamentally a social problem rooted in the profound social, economic, political, and cultural inequalities between a small wealthy and powerful dominant class, a middle class whose precarious standard of living had been made even more so by the degradation of the economy during the past ten years, and the vast majority of the population crushed by the most extreme poverty and denied the most elemental human rights and human dignity. As the Brussels-based International Crisis Group (ICG) put it, "Underlying much of the violence is the chronic failure to tackle the poverty, social deprivation and exclusion that endanger most of the population" (2005b, i). The ICG pointed out further that

> Haitian society is an atomized agglomeration of contradictory and antagonistic interests, relying on violence as the ultimate way to resolve conflicts. The economic model is one of the underlying obstacles to political as well as economic progress. Its main goal has been to maintain the power, interests and advantages of a few families that monopolise most of its sectors. A powerful segment of the private sector resists change and lacks any strategic vision for the people of Haiti. (2005b, 2)

As Camille Chalmers, leader of the Haitian *Platfòm Aysien Plédé Dévlopmen Altènatif* (PAPDA, Platform for the Defense of an Alternative Development), characterized it, the Latortue government was "composed of total lackeys to the United States [with] no social programme, and no interest in the peasantry or listening to the people in the poor neighborhoods" (Haiti Support Group 2005a, 2–3). As such, Latortue and his cabinet wasted little time in showing their true priority, which was to make an alliance with the former soldiers who toppled Aristide and then use them and the police to crush Aristide's supporters, whether they were chimès, members of grassroots popular organizations, or Lavalas party leaders. Latortue, then, did not differ from Aristide in believing that violence was the way to deal with one's opponents. The major difference between the two was that Latortue would have much greater firepower at his disposal and the full backing of the international community to accomplish his task. He therefore could get away with violating the law and human rights, whereas Aristide could not. Neither did the interim government differ from its predecessor in terms of its integrity and probity. As the ICG report noted, "More than a year after its establishment, allegations [were] increasing of widespread corruption in state institutions, reaching into the offices of the prime minister and presidency themselves" (2005b, 3). However, here, too, Latortue would get away with these practices because—unlike his predecessor—he enjoyed the support of the principal actors in the international community who put him in power.

Amid talk of reconstituting the Haitian Army by Interior and National Defense Minister (and former general) Hérard Abraham—a key demand of the rebel forces—Prime Minister Latortue hailed the rebels who had toppled Aristide as "freedom fighters." Among those embraced by Latortue were many who were accused or convicted of grave human rights violations, including killing Aristide supporters, as well as drug trafficking. Latortue also announced that one of the top priorities of his government would be to "neutralize" the pro-Lavalas chimès and other Lavalas partisans who had committed crimes, before focusing on those who perpetrated crimes against Aristide supporters and associates, either after the coup d'état of 1991 or since (Amnesty International 2004a).

The government's actions, however, belied its feigned commitment to justice, even at some future time, for the criminals it called "freedom fighters." To prove the point, on August 17, 2004, the government acquitted Louis-Jodel Chamblain, a former FRAPH leader, and former military police captain Jackson Joanis of crimes they had committed after the 1991 coup against Aristide. Chamblain, along with thirteen other members of the military, had been convicted in absentia for the 1993 murder of Antoine Izméry, a businessman and pro-Aristide activist, and for his involvement in a massacre in Raboteau in 1994. Joanis was also convicted in absentia for the murder of Izméry. Both he and Chamblain were sentenced to life imprisonment at forced labor. Chamblain had fled to the Dominican Republic, where he stayed until he returned to Haiti in February 2004 to lead the rebellion against Aristide. Joanis, who had been deported to Haiti from the United States in 2002 to serve his sentence, escaped from prison during the February rebellion against Aristide, but like Chamblain had turned himself in to the police after Aristide left Haiti, presumably knowing that they eventually would be freed and exculpated by the interim government.

According to Haitian law, both Chamblain and Joanis had the right to a retrial because they had been convicted in absentia. But a government-arranged and -rigged trial acquitted them one day after it began (Amnesty International 2004b; National Coalition for Haitian Rights 2004).[1] Many international human rights organizations and media, and some Haitian ones, roundly condemned this trial as a travesty of justice, and even the U.S. State Department saw the need to express its "deep concern" over the acquittal. But the Latortue government was unperturbed by such criticisms, especially since former justice minister Bernard Gousse had indicated previously that the government might pardon Chamblain because of "his great service to the nation" (*New York Times* 2004). What's more, on April 21, 2005, Haiti's Supreme Court threw out the conviction of fifteen former military and paramilitary members for their roles in the murder of Aristide supporters in Raboteau in 1994, a decision that Amnesty International considered a violation of the Haitian constitution. Seen as a landmark in the fight against impunity, the trial by jury held at the Criminal Tribunal of Gonaïves in November 2000 (under the Préval government) had been observed by national and international monitors, including the United Nations International Civilian Support Mission in Haiti

(Amnesty International 2005c). Latortue denied being involved in the high court's decision, but as the ICG noted, "It is unlikely such an important decision would have been taken independently by the Court given the judiciary's submissiveness to the executive" (2005b, 6).

The message the Latortue government sent through the April 2004 trial, the April 2005 Supreme Court decision, and many other acts was clear: no one would be prosecuted in Haiti for killing or abusing Aristide supporters, past or present. The real—as opposed to the ostensible—priority of Latortue, after all, was to "neutralize" the chimès, but the way in which the government defined them allowed it to pursue an indiscriminate persecution of Lavalas supporters and the population residing in the shantytowns of Port-au-Prince believed to be Aristide strongholds. Essentially the approach adopted by the government, the HNP, and the mainstream media has been to define all chimès or armed gangs as "Lavalas chimès." As we saw in the previous chapter, the repressive practices of the Aristide government had already led to the "chimerization" of Lavalas, but whereas not all chimès were Lavalas chimès—as the example of the breakaway gang of Amiot Métayer showed—that distinction disappeared under Latortue. A further reduction occurred by equating the "Lavalas chimès" with "bandits" and by responding to the mounting criticism of human rights violations by the police by either denying that the incidents ever occurred or referring to the victims as bandits killed in self-defense by the police (ICG 2005b, 12). As the ICG put it:

> The HNP seems to be criminalising many of the urban poor through indiscriminate declarations by senior officers and indiscriminate repressive operations in the slums. This same pattern appears in the media, which systematically associates residents of poor neighbourhoods with "chimères" or, more commonly, "chimères Lavalas". Members of the business elite have fueled this campaign, demanding a tougher stance towards "chimères Lavalas", ignoring the fact that many other gangs also are engaged in criminal, violent and destabilising acts. Repeated killings during pro-Lavalas demonstrations have been a consequence. Unfortunately, most Haitian human rights NGOs have not been [speaking] out about these abuses. (2005b, 11)

So blatant was the practice of denying human rights violations and characterizing all accusations of human rights violations by the government as mere pro-Aristide propaganda that the UN Security Council's Mission to Haiti April 13–16, 2005, noted in its report, "The mission was struck by statements by interim authorities that no human rights violations in the country were committed by the State." The Mission immediately contradicted the government by pointing out that it received reports that a culture of impunity remained pervasive, marked by arbitrary arrest, wrongful detention, inhumane prison conditions, excessive use of force, and extrajudicial executions. As a result, the population continues to view the national police with fear and lack of respect. (United Nations 2005c, para. 42)

Similarly, the June 2005 report of the Inter-American Commission on Human Rights noted, "Police officers have . . . been implicated in disappearances, summary arrests and executions, torture, rape, and drug trafficking, among other crimes and atrocities" (OAS 2005, para. 30). It continued, "Among the serious effects of longstanding deficiencies in the Haitian justice system has been the perpetuation of impunity for present and past human rights violations, as well as deterioration of public confidence in the system" (para. 41), and moreover, "there does not appear to be any clear or comprehensive government policy or plan to address accountability for past human rights violations, and nongovernmental groups in Haiti have claimed that the government lacks the political will to effectively address the issue" (para. 45).

Likewise, the U.S. State Department concluded in its 2005 "Country Reports on Human Rights Practices" that although "systematic state-orchestrated abuses [had] stopped," the "government's human rights record remained poor." It cited "arbitrary killings and disappearances committed by the HNP," "prolonged pretrial detention and legal impunity," "use of excessive—and sometimes deadly—force in making arrests or controlling demonstrations, often with impunity," "widespread corruption in all branches of government," and "violence and societal discrimination against women" (U.S. Department of State 2005).

As noted, however, all the evidence against it notwithstanding, the Latortue government was not alone in denying it was committing or tolerating widespread human rights violations. Some Haitian human rights organizations, the mainstream media, and the middle-class intellectuals who railed against Aristide's violations have also been complicit in this practice. Brian Concannon Jr., director of the U.S.-based Institute for Justice and Democracy in Haiti, pointed out: "When 20 to 30 people were getting killed a year there was a cascade of condemnation pouring down on the Aristide government. Now that as many as 20 to 30 [were] getting killed in a day, there [was] silence. . . . It is an obvious double standard" (cited in Lindsay 2004; see also Arthur 2004). Concannon misses the point, however, if he is arguing that because more people were killed under Latortue than under Aristide, the former should have been condemned even more. Both deserved to be condemned and be held responsible for the human rights violations that occurred under their governments, regardless of how many people were killed. I agree with Concannon, however, if his point is to reveal the partisanship and moral selectivity of some of the human rights organizations, the mainstream media, and the

middle-class intellectuals who relentlessly condemned Aristide but not Latortue. Likewise, the same principle holds for those on the Left who are now
criticizing Latortue for his abuses but were silent about Aristide's. The most
well-known example of this selective silencing on the Left would be the New
York–based weekly *Haiti Progrès*.

The double standard Concannon referred to on the part of the mainstream
media and anti-Aristide middle-class parties and intellectuals should not be
surprising. There are at least two reasons for it. First, as previously suggested,
reducing all gangs to "Lavalas chimès," whether or not they were pro- or anti-
Aristide, and not distinguishing between chimès (or "bandits") and grassroots
supporters of Aristide allowed media and human rights organizations to portray the violence in the slums especially as "settlement of accounts" rather
than as human rights violations committed by agents of the state or tolerated
by the state. One consequence of this was that many Aristide supporters refused to report their cases to those human rights organizations because they
perceived them as hostile (Amnesty International 2004a).

The second reason for the double standard, linked to the first, pertains to
the class interests of the supporters of the Latortue government, for whom
justice is not a neutral concept. Essentially, and as can be seen in the editori-
als of the mainstream newspapers or heard on mainstream radio stations, the
strategy of the defenders of the Latortue government consisted of blaming the
Lavalas chimès for all the violence and insecurity and criticizing those human
rights organizations or reporters who documented the abuses committed by
the government as being pro-Aristide. For example, in an editorial in the influential and anti-Aristide Port-au-Prince daily *Le Matin*, Sabine Manigat
characterized the June 2005 report from Amnesty International on the human
rights abuses of the government as "scandalous," "unprofessional," "seething
with allegations, counter truths and amalgams," "slanting the evidence and
propagandistic," and, for the coup de grâce, "hardly concealing a persistent
pro-Lavalas bias" (2005).

The above point can be made in yet another way. The same human rights
organizations, members of the media, and intellectuals who were active in
documenting and condemning human rights violations under Aristide fell
silent on the abuses of the Latortue government. They did so because the social class of the victims of the violence was different in the two cases. In the
case of Aristide, his chimès and the police targeted mostly leaders or activists
of the political opposition, members of the media, and eventually university
students, most of whom were members (or future members) of the middle and
dominant classes. For the most part, then, the victims of Aristide's repression
were *known* members of the *gens de valeur* (the important people), the "cul-
tured" and "civilized" members of the dominant and middle classes. Thus, it

was the entire middle class and bourgeoisie that felt threatened by Aristide, and his crimes against their members could not go unnoticed or uncondemned. By contrast, most of the victims of the Latortue repression were members of the *moun pèp*, the *moun endéyo,* or the *gwo zòtèy*. They were therefore unknown and socially invisible, and since they lived in the same slums as the "bandit" Lavalas chimès, the crimes committed against them could be denied, dismissed as pro-Aristide propaganda, or, if acknowledged, attributed to "settling their accounts" among themselves or retaliation by the police in self-defense.

All this, then, allowed the Latortue government to pursue its objectives with the support of those who were the spearhead of the opposition against Aristide: the business elites, the political middle class, the human rights organizations, media, and intellectuals, as well as the foreign governments, including the United Nations and the OAS, who supported the interim government. The Council on Hemispheric Affairs called the government's strategy a "scorch earth [*sic*] policy towards [Aristide's] supporters" (2004b). One side of the strategy was to round up prominent Lavalas party officials, former elected and appointed members of government, and well-known party activists under the guise of hunting for "terrorists"—defined as anyone "thinking, planning or somehow linked to others thinking of violence." Among those arbitrarily arrested were Father Gérard Jean-Juste, a renown pro-Lavalas radical populist and advocate of nonviolence; former prime minister Yvon Néptune; and other Lavalas legislators and party members (ibid.).

In the case of Néptune, who had been incarcerated since June 2004 when he turned himself in to the police, Amnesty International considered his detention to be politically motivated and hence declared that he was a "political prisoner of the interim government" (2005a). Even former U.S. ambassador James Foley weighed in on the issue and lent support to Amnesty International's classification by also calling Néptune's detention a human rights violation. Ambassador Foley made his charge on the same day that Louis-Jodel Chamblain was released from jail, calling it a "scandal." As Foley put it, "We know that he [Chamblain] is a man who had been found guilty on several occasions of horrible crimes. . . . Imagine, one moment, the tarnished image of Haiti today, with Chamblain being released and a former prime minister who continues to stagnate in prison" (Delva 2005d).

Foley could have said the same thing for Father Jean-Juste. Arrested once before, Jean-Juste was rearrested in July 2005 in connection with the murder of the well-known journalist Jacques Roche, though he was in Miami at the time of the murder. Considering the allegations against him to be transparently fabricated, Amnesty International declared Jean-Juste a "prisoner of conscience" and ascribed his detention to the fact that "he has been critical of the government and expressed his political beliefs freely and openly" (*De-mocracy Now* 2005; Montesquiou 2005). Responding to these criticisms, and to the arrest of Father Jean-Juste in particular, the Haitian human rights organization *Réseau National Haitien de Défense des Droits Humains* (RNDDH, Haitian National Network for the Defense of Human Rights) declared, "There are no political prisoners in Haiti, but people accused of common law crimes" (*AlterPresse* 2005a).[2] Jean-Juste, it must be noted, had not been formally charged with Roche's murder. Responding to strong international pressure from U.S. lawmakers and human rights organizations, the Latortue government released Jean-Juste from jail in late January 2006 to seek medical treatment for leukemia in the United States (Delva 2006a).

The other side of the "scorch earth" policy consisted, as we saw, of indiscriminate attacks against the population in the areas considered Aristide strongholds under the guise of combating the chimès or bandits. It should come as no surprise, then, that most of the victims of the violence and abuses were Aristide supporters or residents of the poorer areas, especially in Port-au-Prince (Council on Hemispheric Affairs 2004a, 2004b; Amnesty International 2004a).

There is no question, however, that in addition to the human rights violations and violence perpetrated by the HNP, violence by armed gangs—including kidnappings, carjackings, and rapes and other abuses against women and children—spread and seriously aggravated the climate of security and human rights violations. Groups that were illegally armed included pro- and anti-Aristide gangs, some of the latter with ties to members of the business elite; former soldiers regrouped under the *Front de Résistance du Nord* (FRN, Northern Resistance Front) led by Chamblain and Guy Philippe; and gangs tied to drug traffickers and arms dealers (OAS 2005, paras. 12–13; Amnesty International 2005a). As the ICG put it, many of what it called "spoilers" had

> much to gain from fomenting violence, insecurity and political instability. Out of a desire to seek, keep or maximize power, income, authority, or position, these individuals and groups [did] not want the transition to succeed. They [wanted] to prolong a status quo that suits their interests. (2005b, i)

It is important, however, to distinguish among the different interests and objectives of these "spoiler groups." Although the violence of the pro-Aristide gangs may have in part been due to intergang conflicts or in reaction to the crackdown of the police and the former soldiers and paramilitaries against them, they nonetheless had much to lose in a successful transfer of power to a new government that might not tolerate their continued activities or enter into clientelistic or patronage relations with them as did the Aristide government. The anti-Aristide gangs were also mercenaries who shifted allegiance depending on who was paying the bill and empowering them. As with the pro-Aristide gangs, these anti-Aristide groups would also be disempowered if an elected government came to power, disarmed them, and deprived them of their source of income. Some had ties to the police and to members of the business elite. The latter especially feared any change in the status quo that could threaten their privileges. Indeed, as the ICG pointed out, some sectors of the traditional business community wished for the return of the Duvalier era "when the armed forces acted as the enforcer of the status quo" (2005b, 3). Consequently, "talk [was] rife" among the economic elite "of delaying the vote and possibly replacing Latortue as interim prime minister so a new government could take 'tougher' action against the Aristide-aligned gangs" (ICG 2005b, 5). For their part, the former soldiers and paramilitaries sought the reestablishment of the army that was the source of their power and income, including corruption, and they believed this was more likely to happen under the transitional government and the climate of insecurity than under an elected government they may not be able to influence. As for the drug traffickers, arms dealers, and those involved in contraband who were behind much of the violence, their interest was to survive under any government by buying off public officials and the police as they had done in the past (ICG 2005b, 3–4).

Despite the various groups with an interest in destabilizing the country, it is remarkable the extent to which there was a concerted effort on the part of the Latortue government and its supporters to blame primarily the pro-Airstide gangs for the violence and insecurity. Seeking to justify lifting the fourteen-year embargo on selling weapons to the HNP to help it restore order before the new elections, the U.S. government contributed to this disinformation campaign by blaming pro-Aristide gangs for being behind much of the crime and unrest in the country (BBC News 2005).

It is in this context, then, that one can best understand the alliances, direct or tacit, between some of these groups and the Latortue government. Since the government had as its primary objective the destruction of the pro-Aristide gangs or supporters and the Lavalas infrastructure as much as possible, it was in its interest to allow the anti-Aristide gangs to do part of that work. The government also made an alliance with the former "freedom fighter" soldiers and paramilitaries to supplement the police force, which—understaffed (3,000–5,000 officers for a population of more than eight million), ill-equipped, ill-trained, and corrupt as it was—could not accomplish the task at hand alone. Reflecting on that part of his strategy since he came to power, Latortue complained publicly that, had the international community given him "a little more freedom to work with the ex-military, so that they could participate in the struggle against the armed groups," he could have accomplished his mission much sooner (*Haiti Info* 2005).

Insofar as armed gangs, of whatever political stripe, were engaged in violence against the civilian population or the police, the latter had an obligation to arrest the perpetrators of such violence and even the right to use deadly force, but only in response to "imminent threat of death or serious injury and only when all other measures [had] been exhausted" (Amnesty International 2005a). As Amnesty International and other human rights reports showed, however, the problem was that the Haitian police rarely observed these standards in using lethal force. It is true that the police were poorly trained and equipped and often confronted heavily armed gangs. But the police also engaged in widespread and serious human rights violations against residents of the poor neighborhoods of Port-au-Prince, especially young males who were gang members (or were suspected of being gang members), but also including women and children. At the same time, "little [had] been done by authorities to condemn or investigate these violations, and victims and witnesses [lacked] effective protection or remedies and [were] afraid of coming forward" (OAS 2005, para. 53). In addition to these groups, trade union activists were arbitrarily arrested, searched, and threatened, and, especially in the early months after Aristide's departure, radio stations and journalists who were sympathetic to him were also threatened, attacked, and forced into hiding. As the Committee to Protect Journalists noted, many of the "private radio stations, which plunged into the political arena by openly promoting the opposition's agenda during the Aristide administration, have ignored attacks against pro-Lavalas journalists and rarely criticized Latortue's government" for these acts (2004).

When conducting their raids, the police often wore balaclavas to hide their face and no other forms of identification than sometimes the police logo. Sometimes, the special riot police unit known as the *Compagnie d'Intervention et de Maintien de l'Ordre* (CIMO—Company for Intervention and Maintenance of Order) was also allegedly involved, wearing desert camouflage uniforms to hide their identity and thereby allowing them, or the government, to deny the violence they committed (Amnesty International 2005a; ICG 2005b, 11–12). In one example of this type of violence, several people who allegedly wielded machetes distributed by the police were also reportedly accompanied by the police when they lynched and hacked to death at least fifteen people in the slums of Bel-Air and Solino. While the spokesperson for the HNP declined to comment on the reported incident, a UN spokesman in Port-au-Prince said: "We can never tolerate a popular justice like that. We cannot tolerate people lynching people like that" (Delva 2005b; Hunter 2005a).

But the police were not the only force acting against actual or alleged Aristide supporters. Former members of the Haitian Army, former "section chiefs," and the paramilitaries (former FRAPH members) also engaged in arbitrary killings, arrest, and holding of prisoners, either in cooperation with the police or on their own in those parts of the country where the police force was either absent or insufficient to conduct the operations (OAS 2005; Amnesty International 2005a). In short, different reports estimated that between March 2004 and the beginning of 2006, about 1,500 people had been killed (Amnesty International 2005b; OAS 2005; Quigley 2005; Haiti Support Group 2005a). According to the RNDDH, this number included eighty police officers, nine MINUSTAH troops, four journalists, and 1,407 other civilians, including men, women, and children. Those responsible for these killings included armed supporters of Aristide, active and inactive police officers, members of the Front for National Reconstruction (FRN, formerly known as the Cannibal Army) that helped overthrow Aristide, former members of the military, people close to the interim government, MINUSTAH soldiers, and other armed gangs (RNDDH 2006). These killings occurred, Amnesty International remarked, "despite the presence of the nearly 7,000 UN contingent mandated to secure the country and protect the population" (2005a).

The number of people killed and injured, in addition to those who were victims of rape and other physical abuse, was undoubtedly higher than reported, since the government took no steps to investigate abuses, extrajudicial killings, or other human rights violations. Regardless of the actual number of people killed, injured, or abused after the Latortue government came to power, the vast majority of them were civilians, most residing in the poor ghettos of Port-au-Prince and other cities. And, as many human rights reports made clear, the police and their affiliates were responsible for the majority of the killings.

This last point is particularly important since it goes to the heart of my argument about the objectives of the Latortue government. Focusing on the police alone will not allow us to understand the nature of the Latortue government and why it did not observe the rule of law, on the one hand, or the political forces and contradictory interests at play since February 2004, on the other. To be sure, under the Latortue government, no less than under Aristide's, the police were corrupt, understaffed, ill-trained, and ill-equipped. But this no more explains the failure of the Latortue government to end impunity and human rights abuses than it can be used to justify Aristide's. The answer instead is political. Just as Aristide had done, Latortue opted to use the police, gangs, former soldiers, and paramilitaries, as well as the judicial system, to achieve its political ends. That is why the UN Security Council's mission found "the unified commitment of the Transitional Government to a comprehensive approach to disarmament, demobilization and reintegration questionable"

(United Nations 2005c, para. 27) and the Inter-American Commission on Human Rights also found that the government had not undertaken any "systematic or comprehensive disarmament initiative" (OAS 2005, para. 17).

As mentioned, the Latortue government aligned itself with former army soldiers and paramilitaries to help the police carry out its campaign of repression against Aristide gangs and key Lavalas leaders. Foreign Affairs Minister Abraham (formerly the interior and national defense minister) integrated former high-level officers from the Haitian Army into his staff and ex-soldiers into the national police. But many of the rebel leaders and rank-and-file soldiers still insisted that the army be reinstated—and given ten years' back pay. Accusing the government of betraying them, they even threatened to overthrow the government unless their demands were met. To placate the former soldiers and buy time, the government started to pay back the soldiers, intending to do so for all the 6,000 members of the former army at an estimated cost of $29 million, even though many of those who received checks were not in the army when it was dismantled (Haiti Support Group 2004; Delva 2004; Bracken 31 December 2004).[3]

Those measures were not enough, however. Since February 2004 the power of the rebel soldiers, whose strength was estimated to be between 3,000 and 5,000, increased significantly through their control of several port and provincial cities and towns, which they have used to expand their finances through smuggling and to recruit and rearm hundreds of new fighters (Kramber 2005). The power of these groups, however, could last only as long as it was not matched by a larger and more powerful force, such as MINUSTAH. As a UN peacekeeping force, however, MINUSTAH did not act independently, but followed orders that were essentially political. MINUSTAH confirmed as much when it told Amnesty International that "the mission [lacked] the executive power to undertake independent policing activity and to comply fully with specific provisions of its mandate, particularly to protect civilians under imminent threat" (Amnesty International 2005a). That is why the criticism by many that MINUSTAH failed to intervene to prevent human rights abuses by the Haitian police or former soldiers and paramilitaries missed the point: it acted only on decisions made by politicians, in Haiti and at the UN Security Council.

The situation changed, however, after MINUSTAH had reached significant strength levels by March 2005 and its troops came under direct attack and incurred some losses. That month, MINUSTAH retook control of the cities of Petit Goâve and Terre Rouge that had been held by former military soldiers (United Nations 2005c, para. 16). Rémissainthe Ravix and Joseph Jean-Baptiste, self-appointed leaders of the former soldiers, threatened revenge and a guerrilla war to drive MINUSTAH out of Haiti (United Nations 2005b, para. 14; ICG 2005b, 8–9). Believing he could really carry out his threat against the government and MINUSTAH, Ravix was killed in April in a confrontation between some of his troops and a joint operation by UN and Haitian police in an industrial area of Port-au-Prince. Another person killed in the clash was René-Jean Anthony, alias Grenn Sonnen (Ringing Bells), once a former police officer under Aristide who turned gang leader after Aristide left and collaborated with Ravix in fighting the police (United Nations 2005b, paras. 15–16; Weissenstein 2005; Haiti Support Group 2005b).

These events, however, did not signal the beginning of a comprehensive campaign to disarm the former soldiers, section chiefs, and paramilitaries who still controlled parts of the country, despite the declaration of a MINUSTAH official that the threat posed by the former soldiers had been solved (Sérant 2005). As the report of the UN secretary-general on MINUSTAH observed, other than the symbolic turning in of a number of weapons by 227 former soldiers in March 2005, "generally . . . the weapons being seized or surrendered [were] few in number and often inadequate." More important, however, was that the transitional government did not link its commitment to pay indemnities and pensions to the former soldiers to "disarmament and the national disarmament, demobilization and reintegration programme, thus hampering efforts to carry out immediate disarmament in a number of cases." And more worrisome still for the UN Security Council was that the government "made promises that led to voluntary disarmament, promises it has not fulfilled, thus increasing the risk that individuals will rejoin illegal armed groups." Moreover, "many former soldiers [refused] to disarm unless they [received] full benefits or [were] absorbed into the national police force or other public sector positions" (United Nations 2005b, paras. 20–21). In short, the report confirmed what was already known, namely, that the Latortue government had no intention of pushing for a comprehensive disarmament of the former soldiers and their affiliates because it needed them to maintain control of those parts of the country where state authority and the police were absent. And as long as the former soldiers didn't get the idea that they could overthrow the government or attack MINUSTAH forces, as Ravix did, then they could continue to "reap dividends" over the provincial areas under their control (Haiti Support Group 2005b).

MINUSTAH, then, had been made to accept a peaceful coexistence with the former soldiers and paramilitaries, no doubt on order of the UN Security Council in support of the Latortue government. And some of the former soldiers, like Guy Philippe, along with Buter Métayer, leader of the Gonaïves Resistance Front who started the rebellion against Aristide, have "been allowed to re-invent themselves as the [Resistance] Front for National Reconstruction (FRN) political party." Not only did the FRN control most of the city but the government also put Winter Etienne, a former leader of the

Gonaïves Front, in charge of the Gonaïves port, and Métayer in charge of security for the government regional delegate (Haiti Support Group 2005b). For his part, Philippe ran for president in the February 2006 elections.

The government's, and consequently MINUSTAH's, approach in dealing with the pro-Aristide gangs and the population in the ghettos of Port-au-Prince was altogether different, however. As the ICG remarked, such as it was, the "disarmament, demobilisation and reintegration (DDR) programs [were] offered only to the former army and those who were paid to spearhead the cross-border attack that helped bring about the ouster of Aristide in 2004" (ICG 2005a, 8). For the urban gangs, on the other hand, it was open warfare with the explicit objective of eliminating them. UN officials vowed to get tough with "those who [wanted] to foil the electoral process and those who believed they [could] achieve their goals only through violence. . . . The will of MINUSTAH to confront the violence [was] there and [would] be there until those armed groups that have launched organized violence have been eliminated" (Delva 2005c). This tough stance also coincided with the U.S. State Department's call for a "focused and robust response by MINUSTHA [as] the key to security in Haiti [to] lay the groundwork for successful elections and economic growth" (San Martin 2005).

Nancy Soderberg, a former ambassador who supervised UN peacekeeping for the U.S. mission to the UN but was now a vice president of the International Crisis Group, has argued that this willingness to use considerable force against armed groups they saw as a threat to peacekeeping was a shift from the mid-1990s when the UN seemed to be doing everything it could to avoid combat (*Washington Post* 2005). As we have seen, however, the renewed toughness of the United Nations applied only to the pro-Aristide gangs of primarily Port-au-Prince and not to all illegally armed groups, such as the former soldiers and their affiliates who also posed a threat, or for that matter, the police who used violence, committed serious human rights violations, and threatened peace and security, and with whom the UN collaborated. Put differently, political interests are always behind the designation of who is a threat and with whom to get tough.

Political as it may have been, there was no doubt that gang-related violence in Port-au-Prince (and elsewhere in the country) threatened security, though it was doubtful that using force would in fact "eliminate" them as UN, U.S., and Latortue government officials believed. As Guyler Delva, head of the Haitian Journalists' Association and a reporter for Reuters, put it, the "solution to violence [was] not a military one. . . . You could have 20,000 [peacekeeping troops], but there [was] still no way they could be present in every corner of this city, let alone the whole country" (Haiti Support Group 2005a). Or as PAPDA's Chalmers added, there was not a "military problem. . . . Violence [happened] with or without MINUSTAH, and sometimes they even helped the police attack people. . . . Insecurity [was] worse today [in July 2005] than it was one year ago" (ibid.).

Be that as it may, MINUSTAH launched its "Operation Iron Fist" in early August against the pro-Aristide gang led by Emmanuel "Dread" Wilme in Cité Soleil, a shantytown where 250,000 people lived. This raid followed an earlier one carried out in Bel-Air, another Port-au-Prince slum and Aristide stronghold. In the Cité Soleil raid, however, the MINUSTAH forces succeeded in killing Wilme and several other gang members, but in the process allegedly killed or wounded more than twenty unarmed people, including women and children. At first the United Nations said its forces killed or wounded several gang members but denied the claim of unarmed civilian casualties. The UN later acknowledged that that may have happened and said it would investigate the matter. No one could rule out, however, that gang members may have killed or wounded some of the civilians after the UN troops left in retaliation for their collaboration with the UN (Rizvi 2005; Hunter 2005b).

Raids such as those carried out in Bel-Air and Cité Soleil by MINUSTAH and the Haitian police against armed gang members may have inflicted more casualties on the latter and reduced their numbers but also caused considerable "collateral damage" among unarmed civilians, thereby increasing the resentment and anger of the population of these areas against both the UN and the government. Moreover, these military means neither "eliminated" the gangs nor stopped the violence, as previously noted. The United Nations itself admitted as much when one of its top officials in Port-au-Prince conceded that "the area remains under gang control. Security forces are still unable to enter into the inner areas of Cité Soleil or conduct foot patrols" (quoted in *Washington Post* 2005). But even if the military operations achieved more, drove the armed gangs underground, forced them to operate clandestinely, and reduced the level of violence, as the UN suggested (United Nations 2005a), they would not solve the underlying causes of violence, criminality, and popular discontent. These, as I have suggested throughout this book, have their roots in the social, cultural, political, and economic inequalities between a wealthy, privileged, and powerful minority and an impoverished, excluded, and powerless majority that all governments have perpetuated through their prebendary practices and misguided policies.

There are in fact two different types of criminality and violence: that committed by the state and its armed forces and the economic elite against the impoverished majority to preserve the status quo, and that committed by elements from the subordinate classes, usually from the most marginalized among the poor, condemned to live in wretched conditions in some of the most densely populated and squalid ghettos in the world, for whom violence and criminality are a source of income, whether as hired guns for those in power or seeking power or for those with powerful connections involved in drug trafficking or contraband. It could be said, in fact, that criminality and violence are the sine qua non of the prebendary state system writ large. The difference between criminality and violence from above and from below, however, is that those who perpetrate the former are usually connected to powerful domestic and external actors with whom they wheel and deal, and they become part of the global network of elites and "respectable people" referred to in Haiti as the *gens de valeur* (important people), albeit at the lowest rung in the hierarchy of wealth and power of the capitalist world system. Only when, for whatever reason, they fall out of favor with their more powerful cohorts from the core countries—the United States especially, in the case of Haiti—are they considered criminals, human rights violators, or "most repugnant elites" and are they dealt with accordingly. At the same time, not all those who commit crimes and violence from below are considered as such. In some circumstances they even become heroes, freedom fighters, and presidential candidates who, if things work out for them, may become members of the respectable global elite network of criminality and violence.

THE FEBRUARY 2006 ELECTION AND THE FUTURE OF HAITI WITHOUT ARISTIDE

The crackdown on the Lavalas strongholds and gangs was justified on the grounds that they threatened the presidential and parliamentary elections held on February 2006 after four postponements. The real objective, however, was to ensure that when the elections *were* held, Lavalas was in no position either to win the presidency or to gain control of parliament. The United States, Canada, and France desperately wanted the elections because they saw them as a means to justify their role in the overthrow of Aristide post facto and as essential to restoring legitimacy to the government, stability, and renewed economic growth. What these powers and international organizations wanted above all was to make Haiti safe for the Washington Consensus by restoring the traditional pact of domination between the Haitian economic elite and the state. They believed that by removing Aristide, vilifying him, persecuting Lavalas's loyal and most "radical" leadership, and crushing his chimès, they could pave the way for non- or anti-Lavalas parties to win the presidency and gain control of parliament at the next elections.

On February 7, 2006, Haitians went to the polls and, despite many technical and other logistical difficulties, voted to reelect René Préval for a second (and final) five-year term as president. Contrary to the government's self-serving predictions that Aristide supporters would disrupt the elections, the voting proceeded freely and peacefully throughout the country. Préval's re-election represented a major victory for what could be called the popular sector, and an equally major defeat for those Haitian elite- and foreign-backed forces that coalesced in the Democratic Convergence and the Group of 184 to oppose and ultimately overthrow Aristide in 2004 with the help of the former army and paramilitary rebels. These forces had hoped that, with Aristide gone, one of their own could win the presidency. Once again, the Haitian voters demonstrated that the candidates who were part of the coalitions and the former army and paramilitary rebel forces that toppled Aristide had no significant popular support or legitimacy, and, like Latortue, could come to power only through nondemocratic means. Together these ten candidates received a combined 32.4 percent of the approximately 2.2 million votes cast, and their individual percentages revealed even more starkly their lack of support among the population.[4] By contrast, from a pool of thirty-three candidates, Préval received 51.21 percent of the votes, thereby clinching his victory in the first round. Voter turnout was estimated at around 63 percent (Haiti/Conseil Electoral Provisoire 2006b).

As we saw above, the main objective of the Latortue government was to pacify the country by cracking down on Aristide's supporters, especially but not exclusively the armed gangs of chimès in the Lavalas strongholds in the ghettos of Port-au-Prince, and to prepare new elections that hopefully would bring to power a candidate from the bourgeoisie or the middle class that was hostile to Aristide and what he represented symbolically, if not in practice: the empowerment of the impoverished majority and the creation of a democracy that defended their interests. To increase the probability of such an outcome, Aristide's Lavalas party could not be allowed to field a presidential candidate who either had been endorsed by Aristide or had a strong popular base of his own to pose a serious threat on election day. The jailing of Father Jean-Juste, who was very popular among the poor and represented the "radical wing" of Lavalas, excluded him as a possibility. Marc Bazin, Aristide's former foe turned ally and the planning minister in Aristide's second government, ran instead under the Lavalas banner. But Bazin had no popular support and hence was no threat to the Latortue–ruling class–international community strategy. He received less than 1 percent of the votes.

Elections, however, especially when they are allowed to unfold freely, are unpredictable, and the people have a way of spoiling the best plans laid out by the dominant classes. And so they did on February 7, 2006. To the consternation of the anti-Aristide bourgeoisie and middle class, the people voted for Préval, despite a widespread campaign of defamation against him by those who depicted him as a continuation of "Aristidism without Aristide" because of his past links with Aristide and the Lavalas movement. Préval, however, had skillfully distanced himself from the discredited Aristide and ran under his own Lespwa (Hope) Platform[5] and not the Lavalas Family banner. Nonetheless, even though he built his reputation on his record as president from 1996 to 2001 and drew wide support throughout the country and even from sectors of the middle class hostile to Aristide, there is no doubt that Préval owed a significant part of his victory to the massive turnout of voters from the poor neighborhoods and Aristide strongholds in Port-au-Prince and its surrounding areas. For example, in the West Department, the most populated of Haiti's ten departments, in which the capital city of Port-au-Prince is located, Préval received about 63 percent of the votes. In Port-au-Prince alone, which accounted for 42 percent of all voters, Préval won nearly 70 percent of the votes. But he also fared well in the wealthier suburb of Pétion-Ville, where much of the bourgeoisie and middle class live, capturing about 64 percent of the votes (Haiti/Conseil Electoral Provisoire 2006b). Thus, while there is no doubt that the poorest sectors of Haitian society, both in the large cities and in the rural areas, constituted Préval's main base of support, he could not have won in the first round without some significant crossover from sectors of the bourgeoisie and middle class (*Haiti en Marche* 24 February 2006b).

Préval's victory, however, was not without controversy and could still prove troublesome for him. Leading early in the balloting, and projected by international organizations such as the National Democratic Institute and the Organization of American States to win in the first round with more than 51 percent of the votes, Préval saw his percentage drop to around 49 percent by Sunday, February 12. Believing that those who wanted to prevent him from winning in the first round were manipulating the vote count and engaging in extensive fraud, his supporters took to the streets in massive and sometimes violent protests that paralyzed Port-au-Prince and other cities throughout Haiti on Monday, February 13. Seeking to diffuse this potentially explosive situation that could not only derail the elections but plunge the country into chaotic civil unrest, foreign diplomats and interim government officials pressured Préval to call off the demonstrators. Préval answered by making his own public accusation of massive fraud, for which he claimed he had proof, and declared that he would contest the results of the election if the Provisional Electoral Council insisted on making them official as tabulated. At least two officials from the CEP—where Préval's Lespwa party had no representative —made similar charges. Rather than calling on his supporters to end the protests, Préval urged them to continue to do so peacefully and to respect the law, the rights, and the property of others. The goal of peaceful protests, Préval told his supporters, was to increase the capital of the Lespwa platform rather than to weaken it (Mozingo 2006a, 2006b; Williams 2006; *Haiti en Marche* 2006c). Préval made it clear that he and his supporters would not back down and let his opponents deprive him of the victory he believed he earned legitimately.

Such a strategy, however, has its costs. There is no doubt that without the massive show of popular support for Préval and the pressure it put on government and CEP officials to resolve the imbroglio, those responsible for perpetrating the fraud that was designed to force him into a second round might have succeeded. But relying on popular mobilization to deal with difficult political problems, justifiable as that may have been in this instance, also plays into the hands of Préval's opponents, both domestic and foreign, who can liken him to Aristide's use of mob rule rather than the rule of law to achieve political ends. That these same opponents have themselves relied on other nondemocratic means, including violence, coups d'état, and economic strangulation, to achieve their objectives is beside the point. Préval's opponents are concerned about power, not political or ethical principles. As the Haitian PAPDA put it, the vote tally manipulation was an expression of the political struggles wherein sectors "of the dominant classes refuse to accept the presence of the popular classes on the political scene and are prepared to do all they can to preserve an archaic apartheid political system that is in tatters and needs to be buried definitively" (Chalmers 2006).

As evidence of fraud surfaced, the attitude of UN, OAS, Haitian government, and CEP officials, who had previously denied such charges and even suggested that Préval supporters might have planted them to justify their claim, changed and was instrumental in the decision to declare Préval the winner. The discovery of some 85,000–90,000 blank ballots—where voters expressed no choice for a candidate—which represented more than 4 percent of total votes cast, raised suspicion among CEP officials. Knowing that Haitians have not cast blank ballots in past elections, the CEP doubted that such large numbers of voters would have walked for miles and waited in line for hours this time around only to cast blank or protest votes; furthermore, they appeared to have been stuffed in ballot boxes in a fraudulent manner. As Max Mathurin, the CEP's president, acknowledged, such ballots, which reduced the percentage of the votes for all candidates, amounted to one-quarter of the votes in some polling stations and a third of the votes in some others. In addition to the blank ballots, the CEP declared about 155,000 votes (7 percent of the total) invalid. This high number also raised suspicion, since the decision to nullify them was made by local election officials appointed by the CEP. In the more closely monitored polling stations, such as in the West Department, 5 percent of the votes were so designated, whereas in more remote and less well monitored areas, such as in the Nippes Department, about 14 percent were thrown out. Moreover, in some polling stations, the number of ballots counted was less than the number of people who had voted. Approximately 4 percent of total votes cast nationwide could not be found. On February 14, thousands of marked ballots, many for Préval, were discovered half-burned in a garbage dump outside Port-au-Prince (Delva 2006d; Selsky 2006; Thompson 2006b; Arthur 2006a).

At that point, ambassadors from the United States, Canada, and France—who initially insisted that the CEP continue counting the votes that would have forced a second round—reluctantly agreed to join with their counterparts from Brazil and Chile, and meet with UN, interim government, and CEP officials to come up with an acceptable and legal solution that would grant Préval a first-round victory. The solution was found in the so-called Belgian Option suggested by Brazilian and Chilean diplomats. According to Article 185 of the Haitian electoral decree,[6] blank ballots must be included as part of the total votes cast, but it does not stipulate *how* the votes must be counted. That ambiguity allowed the CEP to use the Belgian Option: distributing the blank votes proportionally to each candidate rather than simply adding them to the denominator. While that solution raised every candidate's percentage, it also put Préval over the 50-percent-plus-one-vote he needed to win in the first round. In the early morning hours of February 16, eight of the nine members of the CEP signed the agreement that declared Préval the winner (Mozingo 2006b; Williams 2006).

As Brian Concannon Jr. observed, based on exit polls and unofficial projections, a complete and accurate vote count would have given Préval a first-round victory, and while the solution the CEP agreed to yielded "the same result . . . it [did] so by changing the rules instead of correcting the violations of the rules" (2006). Moreover, at the same time that the deal let the Latortue government off the hook on the charges of vote-counting manipulation and discarding ballots to defraud Préval of his victory, it "provides leverage for those seeking to delegitimize Préval's presidency and block the progressive social and economic policies that he was elected to implement" (ibid.).

Concannon is undoubtedly correct, and Préval himself seems well aware of the potential pitfalls of the Belgian Option. As one of his closest advisors acknowledged, this may not have been the best solution, because it leaves the question of the role of fraud in the election unanswered. But, as he put it, "What else can you do? You have a population about to erupt. It may come out later what this was all about, but for the time being, there aren't any other options. Let's look forward now" (Klarreich 2006).

As Concannon anticipated, Préval's opponents wasted no time in denouncing the deal that gave him the victory and questioning his legitimacy. Leslie

Manigat, leader of the Christian democratic Gathering of Progressive National Democrats (RDNP), and Charles Baker, a wealthy member of the business class, former leader of the Group of 184, and leader of the right-wing party RESPECT, came in second and third with 12.4 and 8.2 percent, respectively, thereby trailing Préval by a wide margin. Rather than condemning the obvious attempt to defraud Préval of his victory in the first round, both men instead criticized the CEP for caving in to the pressure from Préval supporters, foreign diplomats, and the government to find a solution to the vote-count entanglement.

Manigat had served briefly as president between January and June 1988 under military domination. Handpicked by the military rulers who came to power after Jean-Claude Duvalier was overthrown and exiled in 1986, Manigat was "elected" president in an election controlled by the military, in which less than 10 percent of eligible voters participated, and all independent Haitian and foreign observers agreed were fraudulent (see chapter 3). As Marie Frantz Joachim put it so well, "Even if the intellectuals who supported Manigat rarely recalled how he arrived at the presidency in 1988, the population was not completely amnesic" (2006). Trounced by Préval in the current election, which was seen by all independent observers as free and democratic, Manigat shamelessly categorized the CEP's Belgian Option as an "electoral coup d'état" that "confiscated [his] right to a second round" (Bernard 2006; *AlterPresse* 2006b).

Manigat's anger can be better understood if we look at it not as an expression of a long-standing adherence to democratic principles but as frustration over a failed strategy. As soon as Préval declared his candidacy for the presidency in September 2005, it became clear that he would be the man to beat because it was assumed that with Father Jean-Juste in jail and the Lavalas Family party in disarray, Préval would win the support of the poor majority. In early November 2005 a group of thirty prominent intellectuals issued a call to rally around a single candidate to face Préval who, in the words of Micha Gaillard, a spokesman for the FUSION coalition and former member of the Democratic Convergence, "symbolized a return to the [Aristidean] past" (Caroit 2005). To that end, and supported by the Group of 184, nine political parties that were part of the Democratic Convergence, signed "A Political Agreement for Democracy and Modernity" on November 28, 2005.[7] Rather than fielding a single candidate for the presidency, the parties to the Agreement committed themselves to form a government of national unity should any one of their candidates win in the first round and to share positions in the government, in the public administration, or other public posts among themselves. In case a candidate of one of the parties acceded to the second round, if necessary, all the other parties agreed to form a bloc to support him. And at the level of the legislature, the members of the parties agreed to form a coalition to obtain a comfortable parliamentary majority (Entente 2005; *Alter-Presse* 2005b).

Manigat's and Baker's anger, then, was that under pressure from the masses who refused to be disenfranchised, foreign diplomats and the government compelled the CEP to use a different method of tabulating the blank votes rather than overlooking the fraudulent practices that would have forced Préval into the hoped-for second round. But if Manigat especially was angry at what he called the "betrayal" of the CEP, he must have been even more so at the signatories of the Agreement who failed to rally behind him. With no sign that the United States and its allies intended to deny the legitimacy of Préval's victory and oppose him as they did Aristide in 2000, several participants in the Agreement broke from the alliance to recognize Préval as the winner (Delva and Loney 2006). To save face, Manigat issued a call to the members of his party running for parliament to withdraw from the second round scheduled for April 23; only his wife Mirlande, who came second in the senate race in the West Department, heeded the call.

The Haitian business class also issued public statements recognizing Préval as president-elect, though only after the United States, the European Union, and Canada had done so. Also, like Tim Carney, the acting U.S. ambassador in Haiti, who issued a statement that Préval's opponents could use the dispute over the blank ballots to weaken his government "if he does not perform" (Jacobs 2006), the business class warned Préval that the CEP's use of a nonconsensual political formula rather than respecting the prescriptions of the electoral law has tarnished his legitimacy and represents a handicap that he will need to overcome. To do that, the Private Business Sector group and the Group of 184 cautioned in simultaneous press releases that Préval must respect the "rules of the game," reject the use of "street pressure" to resolve problems, and behave as the president of all Haitians and not only of that half of the population that voted for him (Secteur Privé des Affaires 2006; Group of 184 2006). The hypocrisy of the Haitian ruling class is boundless, but it also understands its class interests and will use any means at its disposal to defend them.

For his part, Préval knows he will walk a tightrope. As the purported champion of the poor majority who voted for him, but beholden to the members of the business class who bankrolled his campaign and whose investments he will need along with those of foreign capital, he embodies the classic contradictions of a populist politician. In a country where nearly 70 percent of the population is unemployed and annual per capita income is less than $400, Préval realizes that the people who voted for him expect him to prioritize their need for access to jobs, food, health care, housing, education, and secu-

rity. Popular organizations who felt betrayed by Aristide and opposed the Latortue government are already mobilizing to press those demands, which also
include, among other measures, a more comprehensive agrarian reform than
the limited one he (Préval) undertook during his first term and a break with
the so-called *Cadre de Coopération International* (CCI, International Framework for Cooperation)—the neoliberal structural adjustment program the interim government signed with the international financial institutions that ex-
pires in September 2007. Préval may seek to revise the CCI by working with
the Economic Commission for Latin America and the Caribbean (ECLAC) to
devise a global development strategy for Haiti (Pierre 2006; Kovac 2006; Cajuste 2006), but there is no doubt that the United States and the IFIs will pressure him to adhere to the neoliberal reforms of the Washington Consensus as
he had agreed to do during his first term.

Préval has also been busy wooing the business class and foreign investors
by promising to prioritize private-sector investments (Thompson 2006a).
Both will require him to preserve the extant capital–labor relations and hence
preserve poverty wages and Haiti's status as the cheapest source of labor in
the Western Hemisphere. Aware of the contradictory interests that are confronting him, Préval has warned against expecting too much from his second
presidency by saying during his campaign that Haiti's intractable problems
cannot be solved quickly (Roig-Franzia 2006). Though he argued that the
"gap is too big" between the "rich [who] are cloistered in their walled villas
and the poor [who] are crammed into slums and own nothing" (Renois
2006)—that is, between the 4 percent of the population who possess 66 percent of all assets in the country and the 65 percent who live in absolute
poverty—Préval also knows that those same rich Haitians and their foreign
allies will do everything they can to prevent any significant tampering with
the status quo. As Marc-Arthur Fils-Aimé put it so succinctly, herein lies the
source of the potential conflict between the new government and the dominant classes:

> If the [popular vote] meant the rejection of the traditional political class and its
> historical allies of large land owners, bankers and the big commercial and in-
> dustrial firms, it expects [from Préval] a real, non-demagogic improvement in
> its standard of living in the short term. The fifty-fifth president of the Republic
> of Haiti will not be able to continue to straddle simultaneously the popular camp
> and that of the bourgeoisie. (2006)

Préval also understands that he must deal with the thorny issues of disarmament and security, including the pro-Aristide armed gangs who control the
slums of Port-au-Prince, the armed members of the former Haitian Army,
and the gangs involved in other criminal activities such as drug dealing and

kidnappings. There has been a marked decrease in gang- and police-related violence since the elections. And, in what could be a hopeful sign, an influential gang leader who supported Aristide vowed that if Préval became president, the gangs would voluntarily disarm because they would no longer be fighting against an illegal government that tried to use military force to suppress them (Delva 2006c). Indeed, much of the criticism of the failure of the UN's MINUSTAH force of some 9,000 troops and police was that it pursued its disarmament mission through a military solution in collaboration with the Haitian National Police that resulted in increasing violence and widespread human rights violations (Council on Hemispheric Affairs 2006).

Préval also has as a priority a comprehensive disarmament program and argues for the need to keep the UN peacekeeping force for a while to achieve that goal (but with its mission redefined to reduce the number of military personnel), to increase the number of police, and to help build an independent and more effective judiciary (Renois 2006). Convinced that much of the violence of the past years stemmed from the profound misery of a population whose "hopes for a better life have been deceived," Préval believes that priority must be given to social and economic development. To that end, Préval intends to push for a constitutional amendment to abolish the Haitian armed forces permanently and to replace them instead with a specialized force that could "intervene in natural disasters, guard Haiti's ports and borders, while the police would serve as an auxiliary to justice" (Radio Kiskeya 2006b). Recalling the army's history as a repressive institution that might well not have allowed him to complete his first five-year term in office had it not been dissolved by Aristide in 1994, Préval maintained that public spending must be geared toward "education, health care, and infrastructure development rather than invested in an unnecessary and 'budget-guzzling' army" (ibid.). Such a move could also prove troublesome for Préval in light of the clamor on the part of the former soldiers, many of whom are still armed, and their supporters among the neo-Duvalierist forces and sectors of the bourgeoisie to reinstate the armed forces.

Last, but not least, Préval will have to confront the troublesome issue of Aristide's possible return to Haiti. As Kathie Klarreich observed, while Préval has maintained that Aristide is welcome to return as a private citizen, it would seem "counterintuitive for [him] to encourage such a move if he's trying to create a new image as an independent leader" (2006). There are at least three potentially destabilizing issues for Préval if Aristide returns. First, it could sour relations with the Bush administration, given the role the United States played in Aristide's overthrow in 2004. Second, it could jeopardize the pact Préval is seeking with the Haitian bourgeoisie and middle class, some of whom voted for him but remain weary of his past ties to the former president they despise. And third, it could undermine Préval's ability to deal effectively with the pro-Aristide and other armed gangs to restore peace and stability. That said, it is also clear that, while he could cause some difficulties for Préval if he were to return to Haiti, Aristide can no longer be a major player in Haitian politics. Aristide remains persona non grata with Washington, Ottawa, and Paris, and it is unlikely they would allow him to return to Haiti. He also no longer enjoys the support he once did from countries like Cuba, Venezuela, or even CARICOM, all of which, along with Brazil, Chile, and the other countries of Latin America, have embraced Préval (*Haiti en Marche* 2006a; Radio Kiskeya 2006a). To be effective, Aristide would have to resuscitate his shattered Lavalas party. But having held all the power once and no longer being eligible to hold office, he would have no interest in doing so since that would mean other leaders would benefit at his expense. For all these reasons, it is not likely that Aristide will return to Haiti anytime soon.

Nonetheless, how Préval tackles these intractable issues remains to be seen. Since no single party won a majority of the seats in both houses of parliament but Préval's Lespwa party captured a plurality (eleven of thirty seats in the Senate, and twenty of sixty seats in the Chamber of Deputies), Préval was able to choose a prime minister from his own party. He went with his trusted friend Jacques Edouard Alexis, who had held that post previously in the last two years of Préval's first term (1999–2001). Eager to show that they were committed to reengaging the traditional pact of domination that was suspended under Aristide, Préval and Alexis formed a government of "national unity" that gave five of eighteen cabinet posts to the leading parties that had opposed Aristide and one to Aristide's Lavalas party, including two women. The other twelve cabinet posts—and all the key ones—went to members of Préval's Lespwa party, several of whom had also served during his first term. In his address to parliament outlining his general government program, Alexis stressed that his priority would be on rebuilding and modernizing state institutions, expanding access to social services for Haiti's impoverished majority, and attracting private investments (Radio Kiskeya 2006c; *AlterPresse* 2006a). It is difficult to know how long the new government will be able to maintain and carry out its balancing act, but there is little doubt that its room to maneuver will be limited by those domestic and international forces whose power to shape events does not depend on the ballot box.

Be that as it may, the reelection of Préval signals the beginning of a new phase in the tumultuous transition to democracy in Haiti, temporarily derailed by both Aristide and his enemies. Even if for now that means a transition to a minimalist democracy compatible with the rule of capital, foreign and domestic, it nonetheless opens new possibilities for the majority to struggle to expand that democracy to include them and their interests and ensure they are not betrayed once again by false prophets.

NOTES

1. The trial was conducted without a proper investigation, without using evidence contained in government documents, and with one witness for the prosecution stating he had no idea why he had been called to the stand (Amnesty International 2004b; National Coalition for Haitian Rights 2004).

2. The RNDDH, formerly known as the National Coalition for Haitian Rights–Haiti (NCHR-Haiti) was linked to and formed by the New York–based National Coalition for Haitian Rights (NCHR) in 1992. After the overthrow of Aristide and the establishment of the transitional government, however, relations between the two organizations soured, and in March 2005 the NCHR publicly declared its break with NCHR-Haiti when the latter protested the decision by UN and Haitian authorities to place former prime minister Néptune under guard at a UN-operated medical facility in late February 2005 to receive emergency medical treatment. Noting that the handling of the case by Haitian government authorities amounted to a "travesty of justice," the NCHR declared that its onetime affiliate in Haiti was placing "itself in the dangerous position of defending a dysfunctional Haitian judicial system which delivers little other than injustice" (National Coalition for Haitian Rights 2005). In May 2005, NCHR-Haiti changed its name to the RNDDH.

3. The Latortue government did not deliver on its promise, however, since on March 6, 2006, a group of former soldiers threatened violent protests to force the newly elected, but not yet installed, government of René Préval to pay the arrears they believe they are still owed (Delva 2006b).

4. The candidates who were part of the Democratic Convergence (CD) coalition were, in descending order of their vote percentage: Leslie Manigat of the Gathering of Progressive National Democrats (RDNP), 12.4%; Luc Mesadieu of the Christian Movement for a New Haiti (MOCHRENHA), 3.35%; Serge Gilles of the Haitian Progressive Nationalist Party (PANPRHA), who ran under the banner of FUSION (a coalition of social democratic parties), 2.62%; Paul Denis of the Organization of the People in Struggle (OPL), 2.62%; Evans Paul of the Democratic Unity Confederation (KID), who ran under the banner of ALYANS (another coalition), 2.5%; Hubert De Ronceray of the National Development Movement (MDN), who ran under the *Grand Front Centre Droit* (GFCD, a coalition of right-wing neo-Duvalierist parties), 0.95%; and Reynolds Georges of the Alliance for the Liberation of Haiti (ALAH), 0.15%. Charles Henri Baker, the favored candidate of the Haitian business class and coleader of the Group of 184—another coalition allied with the CD to opposed Aristide—ran under the banner of RESPECT (RESPE in Creole) and received 8.24%. Guy Philippe, former army officer and rebel leader against Aristide, ran under his National Liberation Front (FLN), receiving 1.9%. Himmler Rébu, also a former army officer and rebel leader, ran under his Great Gathering for the Evolution of Haiti (GREH) and received 0.2%.

5. The Lespwa Platform is a coalition of three parties: the PLB (Open Gate Party), the Effort and Solidarity to Build a National Popular Alternative/*Grande Anse Resis-*

tance Coordination ESKANP/KOREGA), and the People's Cause, a peasant organization from the Artibonite. The PLB was part of the Lavalas Political Platform (PPL) in 1995, and it became an anti-neoliberal bloc in parliament after the PPL dissolved and joined with the ESKANP/KOREGA coalition. People's Cause was not allied with Lavalas and suffered persecution during Aristide's second term (Arthur 2006b).

6. Article 185 of the 2005 Electoral Decree states: "Are valid and counted the ballots marked with an 'X' or any other signature indicating unequivocally the intention of the voter to vote in the space (circle, photo, emblem) reserved for the candidate; Are also valid and counted all ballots that do not include any choice; Are declared null the ballots on which the [communal electoral] Bureau cannot recognize the intention or the political will of the voter" (Haiti/Conseil Electoral Provisoire 2006a, my translation).

7. The nine parties and their leaders were: Serges Gilles, FUSION; Leslie Manigat, RDNP; Chavannes Jeune, UNION; Luc Mesadieu, MOCHRENA; Hubert De Ronceray, GFCD; Paul Denis, OPL; Jean-André Victor, PLH; Evans Paul, ALYANS; and Charles Henri Baker/Chavannes Jean-Baptiste, PAIN/KOMBA (Entente 2005).

References

Agence France Presse. 2004. Haiti swears in new government, gangs hand in weapons. 18 March.

AlterPresse (www.alterpresse.org). 2005a. Lavalas donne son verdict sur le jugement du Père Gérard Jean-Juste. 6 September.

———. 2005b. Stratégie unitaire . . . contre toute menace à la démocratie, Port-au-Prince. 28 November.

———. 2006a. Haïti: Le nouveau gouvernement prône le dialogue et la réconciliation nationale. 6 June.

———. 2006b. Haiti—Elections: A la veille des premières déclarations de Préval, Port-au-Prince. 21 February.

Amnesty International (www.amnestyusa.org). 1992. *Haiti: Human rights held ransom*. New York: Amnesty International.

———. 2002. Update on the Jean Dominique investigation and the situation of journalists. 14 November.

———. 2003. Abuse of human rights: Political violence as the 200th anniversary of independence approaches. 7 October.

———. 2004a. Haiti: Breaking the cycle of violence; A last chance for Haiti. AMR 36/038/2004. 21 June.

———. 2004b. Haiti: Chamblain and Joanis overnight trials are an insult to justice. AMR 36/053/2004. 16 August.

———. 2005a. Haiti: Disarmament delayed, justice denied. AMR 36/005/2005. 28 July.

———. 2005b. Haiti: National Police must be held accountable in killings of civilians. AMR 36/002/2005. 29 April.

———. 2005c. Haiti: Obliterating justice, overturning of sentences for Raboteau massacre by Supreme Court is a huge step backwards. AMR 36/006/2005. 26 May.

Anglade, Georges. 1982. *Espace et liberté en Haïti*. Montreal: Groupe d'Études et de Recherches Critiques d'Espace, et Centre de Recherches Caraïbes, Université de Montréal.

Aristide, Jean-Bertrand. 1990. *In the parish of the poor: Writings from Haiti*. Translated and edited by Amy Wilentz. Maryknoll, N.Y.: Orbis.

———. 1992a. *Théologie et politique*. Montreal: Éditions du CIDIHCA.

———. 1992b. *Tout moun sé moun/Tout homme est un homme*. With Christophe Wargny. Paris: Éditions du Seuil.

———. 1994a. Aristide's talk: "Yes to Reconciliation." *New York Times*, 5 October.

———. 1994b. *Névrose vétéro-testamentaire*. Montreal: Éditions du CIDIHCA.

———. 1999. Investing in people, introduction to *The White Paper of Fanmi Lavalas*. Port-au-Prince: Fanmi Lavalas, December (English translation, Spring 2000). http://www.webster.edu/~corbetre/haiti-archive/msg06444.html.

———. 2000. *Eyes of the heart: Seeking a path for the poor in the age of globalization*. Monroe, Maine: Common Courage Press.

———. 2001. Discours du Président Jean-Bertrand Aristide à l'occasion de son investiture. *Haiti Online* (Miami), 7 February.

Arrighi, Giovanni. 1991. Marxist century, American century. In Robin Blackburn, ed., *After the fall: The failure of communism and the future of socialism*. London: Verso.

Arthur, Charles. 2003. Tens of thousands take to the streets of Port-au-Prince to demand the departure of President Aristide. Haiti Support Group.

———. 2004. Haiti's army turns back the clock. *Red Pepper*, 1 April.

———. 2006a. Open letter to Juan Gabriel Valdes, United Nations special envoy to Haiti. E-mail correspondence from ttnhm@aol.com, 16 February.

———. 2006b. Some background on LESPWA. Haiti Support Group.

Associated Press. 2004a. New Haitian cabinet draws criticisms. 17 March.

———. 2004b. S. Africa hails Aristide to live in exile. 31 May.

———. 2005. Haitian who ran a cocaine smuggling operation was sentenced to nearly 20 years. 9 February.

Attinger, Joelle, and Michael Kramer. 1993. It's not if I go back, but when. *Time*, 1 November.

AW/HRW/NCHR (Americas Watch, Human Rights Watch, and National Coalition for Haitian Refugees). 1994. *Terror prevails in Haiti: Human rights violations and failed diplomacy*. New York: AW/HRW/NCHR.

AW/NCHR (Americas Watch and National Coalition for Haitian Refugees). 1989. *Human rights in Haiti: One year under Prosper Avril*. New York: AW/NCHR.

———. 1990. *In the army's hands: Human rights in Haiti on the eve of the elections*. New York: AW/NCHR.

———. 1993. *Silencing a people: The destruction of civil society in Haiti*. New York: HRW/NCHR.

AW/NCHR/CR (Americas Watch, National Coalition for Haitian Refugees, and Caribbean Rights). 1991. *The Aristide government's human rights record*. New York: AW/NCHR; St. Michael, Barbados: CR.

Barros, Jacques. 1984. *Haïti de 1804 à nos jours*. 2 vols. Paris: Éditions l'Harmattan.

Barry, Tom, Beth Wood, and Deb Preusch. 1984. *The other side of paradise: Foreign control in the Caribbean*. New York: Grove Press.

Bauduy, Jennifer. 1999. Haiti's Aristide unveils party program. Reuters, 15 December.

BBC Monitoring Service. 2002a. Haiti: Convergence urges Aristide to withdraw so as to let country move forward. Source: Signal FM Radio, Port-au-Prince, in Creole 1230 GMT, 8 February.

——. 2002b. Haiti: FL, Convergence suggest subjects, conditions for negotiations, 1 February. Source: Radio Métropole, Port-au-Prince, in French 1145 GMT, 31 January.

——. 2002c. Haiti: Highlights of Radio Metropole News, 14 March. Source: Radio Métropole, Port-au-Prince, in French 1145 GMT, 14 March.

——. 2002d. Haiti: President Aristide calls for end to international aid sanctions, 9 February. Source: Radio Métropole, Port-au-Prince, in Creole 1400 GMT, 8 February.

——. 2002e. International Republican Institute officials meet Haitian opposition leaders, 19 February. Source: Radio Métropole, Port-au-Prince, in French 1145 GMT, 19 February.

BBC News. 2004. Haiti power-sharing plan rejected. 25 February. http://news.bbc.co.uk/2/hi/americas/3517837.stm.

——. 2005. US aims to lift Haiti gun embargo. 9 June. http://news.bbc.co.uk/2/hi/americas/4075520.stm.

Bernard, Robenson. 2006. Le droit au second tour confisqué. *Le Nouvelliste*, 16 February.

Blumenthal, Max. 2004. The other regime change: Did the Bush administration allow a network of right-wing Republicans to foment a violent coup in Haiti? *Salon.com*, 16 July, http://www.salon.com/news/feature/2004/07/16/haiti_coup.

Boff, Leonardo, and Clovis Boff. 1990. *Introducing liberation theology*. Translated by Paul Burns. Maryknoll, N.Y.: Orbis.

Bogdanich, Walt, and Jenny Nordberg. 2006. Mixed U.S. signals helped tilt Haiti toward chaos. *New York Times*, 29 January.

Bracken, Amy. 2004. "Haiti's interim prime minister met with former soldiers." *Associated Press*, 31 December.

Brzezinski, Zbigniew. 1997. *The grand chessboard: American primacy and its geographic imperatives*. New York: Basic Books.

Cajuste, Pierre Richard. 2006. Haiti: Le momentum de la lutte contre la pauvreté. *AlterPresse*, 10 March.

Cala, Andres. 2003. Former Haitian police chief and four others suspected of plotting against Hatiti's government released. Associated Press, 8 May.

Carey, Henry F. 2002. "Foreign Aid, Democratization and Haiti's Provisional Electoral Council, 1987–2002." *Wadabagei: A Journal on the Caribbean and Its Diaspora* 5, no. 2 (Summer): 1–47.

Caribbean and Central America Report (www.latinnews.com). 1988. Haiti: Manigat ousted in clash with Namphy. RC-88-06. 21 July.

——. 2000. Aristide wins by a landslide, but doubts remain over legitimacy of elections. RC-00-10. 5 December.

——. 2001a. Aristide and OAS reach agreement on proposal for fresh elections. RC-01-05. 12 June.

——. 2001b. Haiti: Parallel presidents jockey for power. RC-01-02. 20 February.

——. 2002. Haiti: PM resigns amidst corruption scandal. RC-02-02. 19 February.

Caribbean Community. 2002. Communiqué issued at the conclusion of the 13th Inter-Sessional Meeting of the Conference of Heads of Government of the Caribbean

Community, Belize City, 3–5 February. 6 February. http://www.caricom.org/jsp/pressreleases/pres23_02.htm.

Caribbean Conference of Churches. 1987. *Official report of a CCC goodwill and fact-finding mission to Haiti.* Bridgetown, Barbados: Caribbean Conference of Churches.

Caroit, Jean-Michel. 1991. Interview avec le Président Aristide: Bilan et perspectives. *Haiti en Marche*, 8–14 May.

———. 2003. Haiti, la loi des milices. *Le Monde*, 5 November.

———. 2004. Comment Jean-Bertrand Aristide a été poussé par les Etats Unis à quitter le pouvoir en Haiti. *Le Monde*, 6 March.

———. 2005. Les anciens opposants craignent un retour au passé. *Le Monde*, 22 November.

Castells, Manuel. 1996. *The rise of the network society.* Vol. 1, *The information age: Economy, society and culture.* Malden, Mass.: Blackwell.

Castor, Suzy. 1991. L'expérience démocratique haitienne. In Castor et al. 1991.

Castor, Suzy, Micha Gaillard, Paul Laraque, and Gérard Pierre-Charles. 1991. *Haiti: À l'aube du changement.* Port-au-Prince: Centre de Recherche et de Formation Économique et Sociale pour le Développement.

Chalmers, Camille. 2006. Position de la PAPDA sur la crise politique actuelle. E-mail correspondence from ttnhm@aol.com, 21 February.

Chamberlain, Greg. 1987. "Up by the Roots." *NACLA Report on the Americas* 21, no. 3 (May–June): 15–23.

———. 1988. Manigat wants to bring democracy. *Caribbean Contact*, March.

———. 1990a. The Duvalierists return. *Caribbean Contact*, July.

———. 1990b. As Pascal-Trouillot fumbles. *Caribbean Contact*, September–October.

Charles, Jacqueline. 2005. Report: Aristide diverted millions. *Miami Herald*, 4 August.

Charlier, André. 1990. Titid, les yeux grands ouverts. *Haiti en Marche*, 7–13 November.

Christie, Michael. 2004a. Aristide foes seek control of more Haitian cities. Reuters, 8 February.

———. 2004b. Rebels attack police station in central Haiti. Reuters, 16 February.

Christie, Michael, and Ibon Villelabeitia. 2004. Haiti's new government sworn in. Reuters, 17 March.

CID Gallup (http://www.cidgallup.com). 2002. Haiti public opinion poll, March 2002: Final report. March.

Coalition for Civilian Observers in Haiti. 1993. *Internal exile in Haiti: A country held hostage by its own army.* Washington, D.C.: Washington Office on Haiti.

Coll, Alberto R. 1992. America as grand facilitator. *Foreign Policy*, no. 87 (Summer): 47–65.

Collectif Paroles. 1981. Le FMI, l'Association des Industriels d'Haïti et le gouvernement haïtien: Nouvelle roulette russe pour 1981? June–July: 7–8.

Committee to Protect Journalists. 2004. Attacks on the press, 2004: Haiti. http://www.cpj.org/attacks04/americas04/haiti.html.

CONAP (Coordination Nationale de Plaidoyer pour les Droits des Femmes). 2003. Prise de position relative à l'attaque sanglante perpétrée par les "chimères/mercenaires" du pouvoir Lavalas contre les étudiants/étudiantes, Port-au-Prince, 5 December. E-mail correspondence to mailing list haiti@lists.webster.edu.

Concannon, Brian, Jr. 2006. Haiti elections: Right result, for the wrong reason. Institute for Justice and Democracy in Haiti (www.ijdh.org).

Constable, Pamela. 1992–93. Dateline Haiti: Caribbean stalemate. *Foreign Policy*, no. 89 (Winter): 175–90.

Convergence Démocratique. 2002. Le texte de la résolution de l'opposition haitienne, Port-au-Prince, 17 December. E-mail correspondence to mailing list MaxBlanchet@worldnet.att.net.

Council on Hemispheric Affairs (www.coha.org). 1991. The coup that is destined to fail. Press release no. 91.35, 2 October.

———. 2000. Fujimori yields power just in time. *Washington Report on the Hemisphere* 20, no. 29 (29 November).

———. 2001. Haiti needs help, Washington declines. *Washington Report on the Hemisphere* 21, no. 5 (11 April).

———. 2002a. Haiti: Political situation worsens. *Washington Report on the Hemisphere* 22, no. 3 (4 February).

———. 2002b. Hypocrisy at the OAS as Lima Declaration may be applied. 15 January.

———. 2004a. Aiding oppression in Haiti: Kofi Annan and General Heleno's complicity in Latortue's jackal regime. 16 December.

———. 2004b. Haiti: A brutal regime shows its colors. 12 November.

———. 2006. Botched job: The UN and the Haitian elections. Press release, 3 February.

Craig, Dan. 2004. Aristide leaves Haiti, U.S. administration official says; Multinational force likely to be sent, State Department official says. CNN, 29 February.

Curran, Brian Dean. 2003. Discours de l'Ambassadeur des États Unis Brian Dean Curran lors de la soirée organisée par la HAMCHAM le 9 juillet 2003, Port-au-Prince, 9 July. E-mail correspondence to Haiti mailing list MaxBlanchet@worldnet.att.net.

D'Adesky, Anne-Christine. 1991. Reform-minded priest is now Haiti's president. *San Francisco Examiner*, 7 February.

Dahomay, Jacky. 2001. La tentation tyrannique haïtienne. *Chemins Critiques* 5, no. 1 (January): 11–36.

Daniel, Myrlène. 1991. Ouvriers: Salaire minimum—Patrons: Avantages maximum? *Haiti Progrès*, 10–16 July.

Danner, Mark. 1993. The fall of the prophet. *New York Review of Books* 40, no. 20 (December): 44–53.

Danroc, Gilles, ed. 1990. *Haiti, quelle démocratie: Les élections générales de 1990*. Port-au-Prince: Solidarité Internationale.

Davies, Frank. 2004. Pressures, fear for life led to exit. *Miami Herald*, 1 March.

Deibert, Michael. 2002a. Protests sweep Haitian city for second day. Reuters, 21 November.

———. 2002b. Thousands protest against government in Haiti. Reuters, 17 November.

Delince, Kern. 1979. *Armée et politique en Haïti*. Paris: Éditions l'Harmattan.

———. 1993. *Les forces politiques en Haïti: Manuel d'histoire contemporaine*. Paris: Éditions KARTHALA; Plantation, Fla.: Pegasus Books.

Delva, Joseph Guyler. 2004. Haiti rebel leader vows to launch a guerrilla war. Reuters, 18 December.

———. 2005a. Haiti will hold elections on November 13. Reuters, 31 January.

———. 2005b. UN condemns "lynching" in Haiti. Reuters, 22 August.

———. 2005c. UN peacekeepers in Haiti will crack down on violence that threatens elections. Reuters, 9 June.

———. 2005d. US Ambassador to Haiti called the release from jail of a former death squad leader a scandal. Reuters, 12 August.

———. 2006a. Ally of Aristide released from prison to seek medical treatment in the United States. Reuters, 29 January.

———. 2006b. Former soldiers threatened violent protests over back pay. Reuters, 6 March.

———. 2006c. Gangs will give up their weapons if Rene Preval becomes president. Reuters, 10 February.

———. 2006d. Haiti's presidential election tainted. Reuters, 17 February.

Delva, Guyler, and Jim Loney. 2006. Rival candidates said voters had chosen René Préval. Reuters, 14 February.

Democracy Now. 2005. Amnesty International declares Father Jean-Juste a "prisoner of conscience." 28 July. http://www.democracynow.org/article.pl?sid=05/07/28/149242.

DeWind, Josh, and David Kinley. 1986. *Aiding migration: The impact of international development assistance on Haiti*. New York: Columbia University Immigration Research Program, Center for the Social Sciences.

Diederich, Bernard, and Al Burt. 1969. *Papa Doc: The truth about Haiti today*. New York: McGraw-Hill.

Dodds, Paisley. 2004a. Haitian government takes office. Associated Press, 17 March.

———. 2004b. Haiti's rebel fighters advancing on capital. Associated Press, 27 February.

———. 2004c. Pressure for President Aristide to step down. Associated Press, 26 February.

Doubout, Jean-Jacques, and Ulrick Joly. 1976. Notes sur le movement syndical en Haiti (extracts). In Cary Hector, Claude Moïse, and Émile Olivier, eds., *1946–1976: Trente ans de pouvoir noir en Haiti*. Vol. 1, *L'explosion de 1946: Bilan et perspectives*. Lasalle: Collectif Paroles.

Dupuy, Alex. 1989. *Haiti in the world economy: Class, race, and underdevelopment since 1700*. Boulder, Colo.: Westview Press.

———. 1997. *Haiti in the New World Order: The limits of the democratic revolution*. Boulder, Colo.: Westview Press/Perseus Books.

———. 2001. Globalization, the nation-state, and imperialism: A review essay. *Diaspora* 10, no. 1 (Spring): 93–116.

———. 2002. Haiti: Social crisis and population displacement. UNHCR/WRITENET Reports, no. 18/2001. http://www.unhcr.org/cgi-bin/texis/vtx/publ/opendoc.pdf?tbl=RSDCOI&id=3d8f11fe4&page=publ.

———. 2003. Who is afraid of democracy in Haiti? A critical reflection. *Haiti Papers*, no. 7 (June): 1–12.

———. 2005a. From Jean-Bertrand Aristide to Gérard Latortue: The unending crisis of democratization in Haiti. *Journal of Latin American Anthropology* 10, no. 1 (April): 186–205.

———. 2005b. Globalization, the World Bank, and the Haitian economy. In Franklin W. Knight and Teresita Martinez-Vergne, eds., *Contemporary Caribbean cultures and societies in a global context*. Chapel Hill: University of North Carolina Press.

Dussel, Enrique. 1992. Liberation theology and Marxism. *Rethinking Marxism* 5, no. 3 (Fall): 50–74.

Easterly, William. 2001. The lost decade: Developing countries' stagnation in spite of policy reform, 1980–1998. *Journal of Economic Growth* 6 (June): 135–57.

ECLAC (Economic Commission for Latin America and the Caribbean). 2005. *Combatting poverty and hunger: The millennium goals; A Latin American and Caribbean perspective*. New York: United Nations.

Economist, The. 2002. Where racketeers rule a rickety island becomes yet more unstable. 31 January.

———. 2004. Peacekeeping in Haiti: Operation Deep Pockets. 16 December.

Entente. 2005. Entente Politique pour la Démocratie et la Modernité, Port-au-Prince, 28 November. E-mail correspondence from MaxBlanchet@worldnet.att.net.

Evans, Peter. 1989. Predatory, developmental, and other apparatuses: A comparative political economy perspective on the Third World state. *Sociological Forum* 4, no. 4: 561–87.

———. 1995. *Embedded autonomy: States and industrial transformation*. Princeton, N.J.: Princeton University Press.

———. 1997. The eclipse of the state? Reflections on stateness in the era of globalization. *World Politics* 50 (October): 62–87.

Farmer, Paul. 1994. *The uses of Haiti*. Monroe, Maine: Common Courage Press.

Fatton, Robert. 2002. *Haiti's predatory republic: The unending transition to democracy*. Boulder, Colo.: Lynne Rienner.

Ferguson, James. 1987. *Papa Doc, Baby Doc: Haiti and the Duvaliers*. Oxford: Blackwell.

Ferguson, Niall. 2004. A world without power. *Foreign Policy* (July/August): 32–39.

FBIS (Foreign Broadcast Information Service). 1991a. Aristide comments on negotiations with IMF. FL1709202491 Port-au-Prince Radio Métropole in French 1600 GMT, 16 September.

———. 1991b. Aristide discourages revenge; urges unity, faith. FL10001024191 Port-au-Prince Radio Haiti-Inter in Creole 1700 GMT, 9 January.

———. 1991c. Aristide donates paycheck to citizens groups. FL1605012291 Port-au-Prince Radio Soleil Network in Creole 1100 GMT, 15 May.

———. 1991d. Aristide interview on economy, foreign relations. FL1903222091 Port-au-Prince Radio Métropole in French 1700 GMT, 18 March.

———. 1991e. Aristide meets with unemployed people, 18 June. FL2006151691 Port-au-Prince Radio Soleil Network in Creole 1100 GMT, 19 June.

———. 1991f. Aristide, private sector debate economic solutions. FL0304225091 Port-au-Prince Radio Métropole in French 1700 GMT, 2 April.

———. 1991g. Aristide, Quayle sign two aid agreements. FL1308003891 Port-au-Prince Radio Métropole in French 1600 GMT, 12 August.

———. 1991h. Authorities detail operations against zenglendos. FL210322091 Port-au-Prince Radio Soleil Network in Creole 1200 GMT, 20 March.

———. 1991i. Bazin comments on Aristide's first six months. FL0608215591 Port-au-Prince Radio Métropole in French 1600 GMT, 6 August.

———. 1991j. Bishop Romélus reacts to archbishop's statements. FL0401211591 Port-au-Prince Radio Métropole in French 1145 GMT, 4 January.

———. 1991k. Chamber votes Aristide six-month reform limit. FL0403210391 Port-au-Prince Radio Haiti-Inter in French 1200 GMT, 28 February.

———. 1991l. Demonstration reported in Grand Goave 4 May. FL0705001991 Port-au-Prince Radio Antilles Internationales in French 1145 GMT, 6 May.

———. 1991m. Further on results of 20 January elections. FL2901004591 Port-au-Prince Radio Soleil Network in Creole 1200 GMT, 28 January.

———. 1991n. Government implicated in Operation Storm Wind. FL1806011091 Port-au-Prince Radio Galaxie in French 1130 GMT, 17 June.

———. 1991o. Government officials react to market fire. FL1804190591 Port-au-Prince Tele-Haiti in French 1230 GMT, 18 April.

———. 1991p. Government uncovers plot; urges popular vigilance. FL2404203391 Port-au-Prince Radio Haiti-Inter in French 2100 GMT, 23 April.

———. 1991q. Hundreds demonstrate for higher minimum wage. FL1207011291 Port-au-Prince Radio Soleil Network in Creole 1100 GMT, 11 July.

———. 1991r. Macoutes arrested, weapons seized in Archaie. FL1904193591 Port-au-Prince Radio Antilles Internationales in French 1145 GMT, 19 April.

———. 1991s. Mesyeux announces Operation Storm Wind. FL0306232591 Port-au-Prince Radio Antilles Internationales in French 1145 GMT, 31 May.

———. 1991t. Military-peasant conflict reported in L'Estere. FL2106235391 Port-au-Prince Radio Soleil Network in Creole 1100 GMT, 20 June.

———. 1991u. Peasant Congress opens, land reforms demanded. FL0105012691 Port-au-Prince Radio Soleil Network in Creole 1100 GMT, 29 April.

———. 1991v. Police use tear gas to end demonstration, 13 August. FL1408193291 Port-au-Prince Radio Galaxie in French 1700 GMT, 14 August.

———. 1991w. Political leaders react to cabinet appointments. FL2102150891 Port-au-Prince Radio Haiti-Inter in Creole 2100 GMT, 20 February.

———. 1991x. Popular organizations propose economic plan. FL2505002191 Port-au-Prince Radio Métropole in French 1600 GMT, 23 May.

———. 1991y. President Aristide addresses youth rally. FL0508222591 Port-au-Prince Radio Métropole in French 1600 GMT, 5 August.

———. 1991z. President Aristide's inaugural address, 7 February. FL0702224591 Port-au-Prince Radio Nationale in Creole 1945 GMT, 7 February.

———. 1991aa. President-elect Aristide outlines tasks, goals. FL1401015591 Mexico City NOTIMEX in Spanish 1329 GMT, 13 January.

———. 1991bb. Prime minister, deputies trapped by violent mob. FL1408013791 Port-au-Prince Radio Métropole 2200 GMT, 13 August.

——. 1991cc. Private sector employers condemn wage increase. FL3008190791 Port-au-Prince Radio Métropole in French 1600 GMT, 29 August.

——. 1991dd. Rights honored; Aristide donates paycheck. FL1106002591 Port-au-Prince Radio Soleil Network in Creole 1300 GMT, 10 June.

——. 1991ee. Students protest IMF, "imperialist countries." FL2308200291 Port-au-Prince Radio Soleil Network in Creole 1100 GMT, 23 August.

——. 1991ff. Tense, quiet climate prevails. PA1408232391 Hamburg DPA in Spanish 2002 GMT, 14 August.

——. 1991gg. Thousands demonstrate against high cost of living. FL2404215091 Port-au-Prince Radio Soleil Network in Creole 1100 GMT, 24 April.

——. 1991hh. Trade unions protest poor living conditions. FL1609183191 Port-au-Prince Radio Métropole in French 1600 GMT, 13 September.

——. 1991ii. Unions discuss demands with President Aristide. FL2703202191 Port-au-Prince Radio Nationale in Creole 1400 GMT, 27 March.

——. 1991jj. Youth groups demonstrate support for Aristide. FL 2603212091 Port-au-Prince Radio Métropole in French 1700 GMT, 25 March.

——. 1991kk. "Senate approves René Préval as prime minister." FL1402124091. Bonaire Trans World Radio in English. 1130 GMT, 14 February.

——. 1991ll. "Senate president postpones censuring debate." FL1508120991. Bonaire Trans World Radio in English, 1130 GMT, 15 August.

——. 1991mm. "Chamber of deputies president Casseus resigns." PA1708044091. Paris, AFP in Spanish. 0358 GMT, 17 August.

Fils-Aimé, Marc-Arthur. 2006. Haiti: Préval et les perspectives populaires. *Alter-Presse*, 6 March.

Foster, Charles R., and Albert Valdman, eds. 1984. *Haiti—Today and Tomorrow*. Lanham, Md.: University Press of America.

French, Howard. 1990. A Duvalier ally and foe seeks election in Haiti, raising fears of violence. *New York Times*, 5 November.

——. 1991a. After 6 months of changes, Haiti is surprised by its leader's moderation. *New York Times*, 4 August.

——. 1991b. Ex-backers of ousted Haitian say he alienated his allies. *New York Times*, 22 October.

——. 1991c. Haitian victor's backer is harsh toward U.S. *New York Times*, 31 January.

——. 1991d. Haiti's army crushes revolt by Duvalier loyalist. *New York Times*, 8 January.

——. 1991e. Haiti's parliament shows leader its backbone. *New York Times*, 11 September.

Fuller, Anne. 2003. "Anti-Lavalas protests in Cité Soleil: what's going on?" *Haitian Times*, 19–25 November.

Gaillard, Micha. 1991. Gouvernement: Il faut redresser la barre! In Castor et al. 1991.

Gilles, Alain. 1991. Mouvement populaire et développement politique. In Hector and Jadotte 1991.

Girault, Christian, and Henri Godard. 1983. Port-au-Prince, dix ans de croissance, 1970–1980. *Collectif Paroles*, no. 24 (July–August): 5–13.

Godard, Henri. 1983. Port-au-Prince: L'innefficacité de la gestion urbaine et les problèmes fanciers. *Collectif Paroles*, no. 25 (September–October): 9–15.

Goshko, John M. 1991. Aristide seeks OAS delegation to confront Haiti junta leaders. *Washington Post*, 3 October.

Group of 184. 2002. Declaration of 183 institutions, groups, and organizations of 12 vital sectors of Haitian society (Port-au-Prince), 26 December. E-mail correspondence to Haiti mailing list MaxBlanchet@worldnet.att.net.

———. 2003. Déclaration de 184 organisations de la classe politique haitienne (Port-au-Prince), 16 January. E-mail correspondence to Haiti mailing listhaiti@lists.webster.edu.

———. 2006. Note de presse du Groupe des 184, Port-au-Prince, 17 February. E-mail correspondence from MaxBlanchet@worldnet.att.net.

Grunwald, Joseph, Leslie Delatour, and Karl Voltaire. 1984. Offshore assembly in Haiti. In Foster and Valdman 1984.

Gutiérrez, Gustavo. 1990. Expanding the view. In Marc H. Ellis and Otto Maduro, eds., *Expanding the view: Gustavo Gutiérrez and the future of liberation theology*. Maryknoll, N.Y.: Orbis.

Habermas, Jürgen. 2001. *The postcolonial constellation: Political essays*. Cambridge, Mass.: MIT Press.

Haiti. 1991. Ministère de la Planification de la Coopèration Externe et de la Fonction Publique and Ministère de l'Économie et des Finances. *Cadre de politique économique et programme d'investissement public*. Port-au-Prince: République d'Haiti.

———. 1994. Cabinet Particulier du Président de la République. *Témoignages sur les performances économiques du Gouvernement Aristide/Préval*. Port-au-Prince: République d'Haiti.

Haiti Beat. 1988. The anatomy of a coup. Vol. 3, no. 1.

Haiti/Conseil Electoral Provisoire (www.cep-ht.org). 2006a. Décret-loi electoral.

———. 2006b. *Elections 2006*. Port-au-Prince: République d'Haïti.

Haiti en Marche. 1988a. Haiti au lendemin du coup: Soulagement, déchoukaj, prudence. 21–27 September.

———. 1988b. Les divisions au sein de l'Armée permettent le retour en force des Duvaliéristes. 24–30 August.

———. 1988c. Les élections d'Avril. 9–15 November.

———. 1988d. Namphy abolit la constitution. 13–19 July.

———. 1988e. Qui est Prosper Avril? 21–27 September.

———. 1989a. Calendrier électoral. 27 September–3 October.

———. 1989b. Haiti: L'occupation économique. 13–19 September.

———. 1989c. Pillage du budget public. 29 November–5 December.

———. 1989d. Rebrassage des cartes politiques. 6–12 December.

———. 1989e. Situation des droits de l'homme. 20–26 September.

———. 1990a. Avril fut forcé de plier bagages. 14–20 March.

———. 1990b. Conseil d'État: Et maintenant? 15–22 August.

———. 1990c. Gouvernement de Consensus. 7–13 March.

———. 1990d. Le peuple est incontournable: Interview avec Aristide. 31 October–6 November.

———. 1990e. Le piège qui guette le Conseil d'État. 2–8 May.

———. 1990f. Mgr. Romélus appelle au boycott du carnaval. 21–27 February.

——. 1991a. Aristide–FNCD: Ça barde! 29 May–4 June.

——. 1991b. Armée: Abraham a-t-il été "démisionné"? 10–16 July.

——. 1991c. FNCD—Gouvernement: Le rapport des forces. 21–27 August.

——. 1991d. La politique économique du gouvernement: Rencontre avec le Ministre des Finances Marie-Michèle Rey. 14–20 August.

——. 1991e. L'atmosphère autour du procès. 31 July–6 August.

——. 1991f. Le gouvernement attaque: Mesures contre la vie chère et la fraude fiscale; La police sous le contrôle de la justice. 27 March–2 April.

——. 1991g. Les négociations entre le gouvernement et le FMI se poursuivent: Note de presse du Ministère des Finances. 18–24 September.

——. 1991h. Les riches ont peur de la démocratie. 8–14 May.

——. 1991i. "Procès du siècle" ou "procès baclé"? 31 July–6 August.

——. 1991j. Révocations en masse. 7–13 August.

——. 2001. Et si la vérité etait ailleurs! 5–11 August.

——. 2002a. Convergence serait aussi pour la reprise de l'assistance. 6–12 May.

——. 2002b. Corruption et criminalité menacent de tuer par étouffement le Pouvoir Aristide. 3–9 February.

——. 2002c. Grande agitation des acteurs politiques. 6–12 March.

——. 2002d. Le Président Aristide rencontre les protagonistes de Cité-Soleil. 6–12 March.

——. 2003. Au-dela de l'escalade menaçant pour la premiere fois d'aussi pres le pouvoir Aristide. 13 December.

——. 2005. Corruption sous le Pouvoir Aristide. 30 July.

——. 2006a. Aristide se trompe. 24 February.

——. 2006b. Lespwa ce n'est pas que Lavalas. 24 February.

——. 2006c. Préval demande d'arrêter les manifestations. 16 February.

Haiti Info. 2005. Rebels should have had role in struggle against armed gangs, Haiti's interim leader says. Associated Press, July 15.

Haiti Observateur. 1988. Ouvert au dialogue, le Général Namphy aspire à durer le plus longtemps possible au pouvoir. 15–22 July.

——. 1989a. Avril pour cinq ans? 15–22 November.

——. 1989b. Le Congrès du MIDH. 1–8 November.

——. 1989c. Le gouvernement Avril met en place une répression modulée. 29 November–6 December.

——. 1991a. Another coup d'état? 24–31 July.

——. 1991b. Le conflit Aristide—Armée demeure. 17–24 July.

——. 1991c. Le Premier Ministre Préval expose les grandes lignes de sa politique générale. 20–27 February.

——. 1991d. Mobilisation contre Aristide et la bourgeoisie. 11–18 September.

——. 1991e. President Aristide's September 27 speech. 9–16 October.

——. 1991f. Réalités économiques obligent: L'accord avec le FMI signé à la cloche de bois. 18–25 September.

——. 1991g. Vitriolic speech of Aristide. 2–9 October.

Haiti Press Network (www.haitipressnetwork.com). 2002. 7 février 2001–7 février 2002, une nouvelle année de gâchis politique. 7 February.

Haiti Progrès. 1991a. Les 100 jours d'Aristide: Une interview exclusive sur des questions brûlantes. 15–21 May.

——. 1991b. Qui veut piéger le gouvernement Aristide/Préval? 12–18 June.

——. 1991c. "Vent Tempête": Une provocation. 19–25 June.

——. 2002. With prime minister out, hot-seat has few takers. 20–26 February.

Haiti Support Group (www.haitisupport.gn.apc.org). 2002. Haiti: Three statements from the organized popular sector, translated from the French by Charles Arthur.

——. 2003. European Union funding for members of the Group of 184. Press release, 11 November. http://haitisupport.gn.apc.org/184%20EC.htm.

——. 2004. Interim government paves way for return of the military. 20 August.

——. 2005a. Military approach criticised. *Haiti Briefing*, no. 55 (July).

——. 2005b. The significance of killing of Ravix and Grenn Sonnen. 25 April.

Hartlyn, Jonathan. 1998. *The struggle for democratic politics in the Dominican Republic*. Chapel Hill: University of North Carolina Press.

Harvey, David. 2003. *The new imperialism*. Oxford: Oxford University Press.

Hector, Cary. 1972. Fascisme et sous-développement. *Nouvelle Optique*, no. 5 (January–March): 39–72.

Hector, Cary, and Hérard Jadotte, eds. 1991. *Haiti et l'après-Duvalier: Continuités et ruptures*. Port-au-Prince: Henri Deschamps; Montréal: Éditions du CIDIHCA.

Heinl, Robert Debs, and Nancy Gordon Heinl. 1978. *Written in blood: The story of the Haitian people, 1492–1971*. Boston: Houghton Mifflin.

Held, David. 1995. *Democracy and the global order*. Stanford, Calif.: Stanford University Press.

Helps, Horace. 2004. Caribbean leaders, Aristide, agree on Haiti steps. Reuters, 1 February.

Hérard, Jean-Robert. 1990. Pour questionner la candidature d'Aristide. *Haiti en Marche*, 24–30 October.

Hockstader, Lee. 1991a. Haitian army crushes coup by Duvalierist; 37 are killed. *Washington Post*, 8 January.

——. 1991b. Haiti's new president purges army. *Washington Post*, 8 February.

Honorat, Jean-Jacques. 1980–81. Haïti: La crise paysanne. *Collectif Paroles*, no. 9 (December–January): 13–16.

Hooper, Michael S. 1987. Model underdevelopment. *NACLA Report on the Americas* 21, no. 3 (May–June).

Howell, John. 2004. Forces behind the ouster. *New York Newsday*, 1 March.

Hudson, Saul. 2004. US questions for first time if Aristide can stay. Reuters, 26 February.

Human Rights Watch. 2001. Aristide's return to power in Haiti. http://www.hrw.org/campaigns/haiti/backgrounder.html.

Hunter, Aina. 2005a. Haitian police distribute machetes in Bel Air. *Village Voice*, 19 August.

——. 2005b. UN to investigate alleged massacre. *Village Voice*, 4 August.

Huntington, Samuel P. 1999. The lonely superpower. *Foreign Affairs* (March).

Hurbon, Laennec. 2001. La désymbolisation du pouvoir et ses effets meurtriers. *Chemins Critiques* 5, no. 1 (January).

ICG (International Crisis Group; www.crisisgroup.org). 2005a. Can Haiti hold elections in 2005? *Latin America/Caribbean Report*, no. 8 (3 August).

———. 2005b. Spoiling security in Haiti. *Latin America/Caribbean Report*, no. 13 (31 May).

Ignatieff, Michael. 2003. The American empire: The burden. *New York Times Magazine*, 5 January.

Ives, Kim. 1991. Flood of hope marks Haiti's 200th year. *Guardian*, 28 August.

Jackson, Robert H., and Carl G. Rosberg. 1982. *Personal rule in black Africa: Prince, autocrat, prophet, tyrant*. Berkeley: University of California Press.

Jacobs, Stevenson. 2006. Opponents could use disputed election result to weaken Préval. Associated Press, 18 February.

James, C. L. R. 1963. *The Black Jacobins: Toussaint L'Ouverture and the San Domingo Revolution*. New York: Random House.

Jean, Jean-Claude, and Marc Maesschalck. 1999. *Transition politique en Haïti: Radiographie du pouvoir Lavalas*. Paris: Éditions l'Harmattan.

Joachim, Marie Frantz. 2006. D'Aristide à Préval et au-delà . . . Vive l'utopie d'une Haiti nouvelle. *AlterPresse*, 18 February.

John, Mark. 2004. France urges Aristide to quit in Haiti talks. Reuters, 27 February.

Joseph, Leo. 1990. Business in shock as Haiti adjusts to new president. *Wall Street Journal*, 21 December.

Kaufman, Michael. 1985. *Jamaica under Michael Manley: Dilemmas of socialism and democracy*. London: Zed Books; Westport, Conn.: Lawrence Hill.

Klarreich, Kathie. 2006. The fight for Haiti. *Nation*, 13 March.

Kovac, Ana. 2006. Interview with Haitian president-elect René Préval: Haiti has voted for change. Radio Havana Cuba, 24 February.

Kramber, Michael. 2005. A troubled Haiti struggles to gain its political balance. *New York Times*, 2 January.

Kramer, Kirstin. 2004. Keeping the peace in Haiti. *Washington Report on the Hemisphere* 25, no. 6 (August). Washington, D.C.: Council for Hemispheric Affairs.

Krauss, Clifford. 1991. Military's role raises U.S. hopes for better ties. *New York Times*, 8 January.

Laguerre, Michel S. 1987. Electoral politics in Haiti: A public opinion poll. Working Papers Series. Berkeley: Institute for the Study of Social Change, University of California.

———. 2005. Homeland political crisis, the virtual diasporic public sphere, and diasporic politics. *Journal of Latin American Anthropology* 10, no. 1 (April): 206–25.

Layne, Christopher, and Benjamin Schwartz. 1993. American hegemony—without an enemy. *Foreign Policy*, no. 92 (Fall): 5–23.

Lemoine, Maurice. 2004. Retour sur la chute d'un president haitien. *Le Monde Diplomatique* (September).

Lewis, Gordon K. 1987. *Grenada: The Jewel Despoiled*. Baltimore: The Johns Hopkins University Press.

Lindsay, Reed. 2004. Violent tide vs. Aristide supporters. *Newsday*, 7 November.

Ljunggren, David. 2004. Canada says Aristide should consider resigning. Reuters, 26 February.

Loney, Jim, and Alistair Scrutton. 2004. Aristide quits Haiti, Bush orders Marines in. Reuters, 29 February.

Louverture, Jean-Jacques. 1987. "Terreur sur commande: Un long sillage de sang." *Libération Magazine*, no. 8 (December).

Löwy, Michael. 1993. Marxism and Christianity in Latin America. *Latin American Perspectives* 20, no. 4 (Fall): 28–42.

Lundahl, Mats. 1979. *Peasants and poverty: A study of Haiti*. New York: St. Martin's Press.

Maguire, Robert E. 1991. The peasantry and political change in Haiti. *Caribbean Affairs* 4, no. 2: 1–18.

——. 2002. Haiti's troubles continue. *Nueva Sociedad* (Caracas), January.

Manigat, Leslie. 1964. *Haiti of the sixties: Object of international concern*. Washington, D.C.: Washington Center for Foreign Policy Research.

Manigat, Sabine. 2005. Amnesty International rejoint-il le club des accusateurs? *Le Matin* (Port-au-Prince), 5–8 August.

Marquis, Christopher. 1993. Aristide ouster surprised CIA, officials say. *Miami Herald*, 15 December.

Marx, Karl, and Friedrich Engels. 1978. The communist manifesto. In Robert C. Tucker, ed., *The Marx-Engels Reader*, 2nd ed. New York: W. W. Norton.

Midy, Franklin. 1988. Qui êtes-vous, père Aristide? *Haïti en Marche*, 26 October–2 November.

——. 1991. Il faut que ça change: L'imaginaire en liberté. In Hector and Jadotte 1991.

Moïse, Claude. 1980. Jean-Claudisme: Le plein est fait. *Collectif Paroles*, no. 8 (September–November): 5–7.

——. 1990. *Constitutions et luttes de pouvoir en Haiti*. Vol. 2, *1915–1987*. Montreal: Éditions du CIDIHCA.

Moïse, Claude, and Émile Olivier. 1992. *Repenser Haïti: Grandeur et misères d'un mouvement démocratique*. Montreal: Éditions du CIDIHCA.

Montas, Michele. 2002. Is another assassination of Jean Dominique about to take place? *Radio Haiti Editorial*, Port-au-Prince, 3 March.

Montesquiou, Alfred de. 2005. Jailed Roman Catholic priest says he is waiting for backing of Aristide. Associated Press, 24 August.

Moral, Paul. 1961. *Le paysan haitien: Étude sur la vie rurale en Haiti*. Paris: G. P. Maisonneuve et Larose.

Mozingo, Joe. 2006a. Barricades go up in Haiti to protest vote tallies. *Miami Herald*, 13 February.

——. 2006b. Préval's victory eases week of tension. *Miami Herald*, 16 February.

Naim, Moises. 2000. Fads and fashion in economic reforms: Washington Consensus or Washington confusion? *Third World Quarterly* 21, no. 3: 505–28.

National Coalition for Haitian Rights (www.nchr.org). 2003. Yon Sèl Dwèt Pa Manjé Kalalou: Haiti on the eve of its bicentennial. *Policy Report*, September.

——. 2004. Chamblain's trial: In keeping with tradition, Haiti delivers swift injustice. 17 August.

——. 2005. NCHR-Haiti does not speak for the National Coalition for Haitian Rights (NCHR). 11 March.

National Labor Committee. 1994. Sweatshop development. In James Ridgeway, ed., *The Haiti Files: Decoding the Crisis*. Washington, D.C.: Essential Books/Azul Editions.

New York Times. 2004. Justice scorned in Haiti. 20 August.

Nicholls, David. 1979. *From Dessalines to Duvalier: Race, colour and national independence in Haiti*. New York: Cambridge University Press.

——. 1984. Past and present in Haitian politics. In Foster and Valdman 1984.

——. 1986. Haiti: The rise and fall of Duvalierism. *Third World Quarterly* 8, no. 4 (October): 1239–52.

Norton, Michael. 2002. Thousands of students in Haiti protest shooting of students. Associated Press, 21 November.

——. 2004. Anti-government rebels take control of at least nine towns. Associated Press, 9 February.

Nouvelle Optique. 1972. Haiti: Porto Rico 2? Notes sur la conjuncture économique. No. 8 (October–December): 1–15.

OAS (Organization of American States; www.oas.org). 2000. Note du Secrétaire Général transmettant le rapport final de la Mission d'Observation Éléctoral pour les Éléctions Législatives, Municipales et Locales en Haïti, Février–Juillet 2000. OEA/Ser.G, CP/doc. (3383/00), 13 December.

——. 2001. Inter-American Democratic Charter. Lima, 11 September.

——. 2002a. Fifth Report of the Mission of the Organization of American States to Haiti. OEA/Ser. G, CP/doc (3541/02), 8 January.

——. 2002b. Report of the Commission of Inquiry into the Events of January 17, 2001, in Haiti. OEA/Ser. G, CP/INF. 4702, 1 July.

——. 2002c. The situation in Haiti. OEA/Ser.G, CP/RES. 806 (1303/02) corr. 1, 16 January.

——. 2002d. Support for strengthening democracy in Haiti. OEA/Ser. G, CP/RES. 822 (1331/02), 4 September.

——. 2003a. Draft resolution: Support for strengthening democracy in Haiti. OEA/Ser. P, AG/CG, doc. 3/03 rev. 1, 8–10 June.

——. 2003b. La CIDH se dit préoccupée par les récents évènements en Haiti. CIDH 33-03, 9 December.

——. 2003c. La Mission Spéciale de l'OEA condamne énergiquement les actions violentes perpétrées à Port-au-Prince. OEA HA-08-03, 8 December.

——. 2004a. Situation in Haiti: Strengthening of democracy. AG/RES 2058, 34th Sess., 6–8 June.

——. 2004b. Support for public order and strengthening democracy in Haiti. OEA/Ser. G CP/doc. 3834/04, 19 February.

——. 2005. Inter-American Commission on Human Rights. Preliminary observations of the Inter-American Commission on Human Rights upon conclusion of its April 2005 visit to Haiti. 6 June. http://www.cidh.org/preliminary_observations_of_the_iachr_upon_conclusion_of_its_april_2005_visit_to_haiti.doc.

O'Neill, William. 1993. The roots of human rights violations in Haiti. *Georgetown Immigration Law Journal* 7, no. 1: 87–117.

Opération Lavalas. 1990a. *La chance à prendre*. Port-au-Prince: Opération Lavalas.
———. 1990b. *La chance qui passe*. Port-au-Prince: Opération Lavalas.
Oreste, Nader. 1992. Réponse à Manno Charlemagne. *Haiti en Marche*, 26 August–1 September.
Organisation Politique Lavalas. 1992. Pour convertir nos rêves en victoires.
Péan, Leslie J. R. 1985. Le secteur privé, le capital international et le pouvoir duvaliériste. *Nouvelle Optique*, no. 32 (May–December): 24–34.
Petras, James. 2000. Globalization: A critical perspective. In Ronald Chilcote, ed., *The political economy of imperialism: Critical appraisals*. Lanham, Md.: Rowman & Littlefield.
Pierre, Goston. 2006. A quel défi doit-il faire face? *AlterPresse*, 23 February.
Pierre-Charles, Gérard. 1967. *L'économie haitienne et sa voie de développement*. Paris: Éditions G. P. Maisonneuve et Larose.
———. 1973. *Radiographie d'une dictature: Haïti et Duvalier*. Montreal: Éditions Nouvelle Optique.
———. 1988. The democratic revolution in Haiti. *Latin American Perspectives* 15, no. 3 (Summer): 64–76.
———. 1991. Fondements sociologiques de la victoire électorale de Jean-Bertrand Aristide. In Castor et al. 1991; reprinted in Gérard Barthélemy and Christian Girault, eds., *La République haitienne: État des lieux et perspectives*. Paris: Éditions KARTHALA.
———. 1993. "Fondements sociologiques de la victoire électorale de Jean-Bertrand Aristide." In Gérard Barthélemy and Christian Girault, eds., *La République haitienne: État des lieux et perspectives*. Paris: Éditions KARTHALA.
Prince, Rod. 1985. *Haiti: Family Business*. London: Latin America Bureau.
Przeworski, Adam. 1985. *Capitalism and Social Democracy*. Cambridge: Cambridge University Press.
———. Democracy and the market: Political and economic reforms in Eastern Europe and Latin America. Cambridge: Cambridge University Press.
Quigley, Bill. 2005. Haiti human rights report, presented to the International Association of Democratic Lawyers. June. http://www.ijdh.org/pdf/QuigleyReport.pdf.
Radio Kiskeya. 2006a. Hugo Chàvez invite René Préval au Vénézuela at annonce sa visite en Haiti le 12 mars. 17 February.
———. 2006b. René Préval annonce au Brésil l'abolition prochaine de l'armée, mais souhaite le maintien des casques bleus en Haiti. 10 March.
———. 2006c. Texte intégral de la déclaration de politique générale du Premier Ministre Jacques Édouard Alexis. 6 June.
Radio Métropole (Port-au-Prince). 2003a. Aristide suggère à l'Opposition un partage du Pouvoir: Un retour au 6 mars '99? 1008 GMT, 16 January.
———. 2003b. Le pouvoir Lavalas sur le point d'exécuter son projet controversé d'amendement constitutionnel. 1247 GMT, 3 September.
———. 2003c. Scandales des cooperatives: David Chéry fait de nouvelles revelations. 1128 GMT, 16 September.
———. 2005. L'installation du nouveau cabinet ministerial reportée à ce jeudi 3 février. 2 February.
Reeves, Tom. 2003. Between a sharp tongue and a blind eye: The politics of criticism and propaganda. *NACLA Report on the Americas* (July/August).

Regan, Jane. 2002. Haiti protesters demand Aristide's exit. *Miami Herald*, 18 November.

—— 2003. Haiti: Burning slums signal gang rule. *IPS/GIN*, 1 October.

Regan, Jane, and Marika Lynch. 2003. Haitian legislative elections are planned for end of the year. *Miami Herald*, 14 August.

Regan, Jane, and Michael A. W. Ottey. 2003. Protests, violence paralyze Haitian cities. *Miami Herald*, 12 December.

René, Jean Alix. 2003. *La séduction populiste: Essai sur la crise systémique haïtienne, 1986–1991*. Port-au-Prince: Imprimerie Henri Deschamps.

Renois, Clarens. 2006. Haiti's Préval vows to tackle poverty. *Mail and Guardian Online*, 16 February. http://www.mg.co.za/articlePage.aspx?articleid=264420&area=/breaking_news/breaking_news__international_news.

Reuters. 2002. Head of Haiti investment scheme arrested. 6 September.

——. 2004. France proposes force for Haiti, blames Aristide. 25 February.

——. 2005. Haiti signs $41 million election aid. 11 January.

Rizvi, Haider. 2005. Group charges "massacre" in UN raid. *IPS*, 14 July.

RNDDH (Réseau National Haitien de Défense des Droits Humains). 2006. RNDDH à la Commission Internationale de Droits Humains: Présentation sur la situation générale des droits humains en Haiti. 3 March.

Robinson, William I. 1996. *Promoting polyarchy: Globalization, US intervention, and hegemony*. Cambridge: Cambridge University Press.

Roc, Gesner. 1968. *Haiti: Tournant après Duvalier?* Montreal: Editions Jean-Jacques Acaau.

Roemer, John E. 1994. *A future for socialism*. Cambridge, Mass.: Harvard University Press.

Roig-Franzia, Manuel. 2006. Preval declared victor in Haitian elections. *Washington Post*, 16 February.

Rotberg, Robert I. 1971. *Haiti: The politics of squalor*. Boston: Houghton Mifflin.

Rueschemeyer, Dietrich, and Peter Evans. 1985. The state and economic transformation: Toward an analysis of the conditions underlying effective intervention. In Peter Evans, Dietrich Rueschemeyer, and Theda Skocpol, eds., *Bringing the state back in*. Cambridge: Cambridge University Press.

Saint-Gérard, Yves. 1988. *Haiti: Sortir du cauchemar*. Paris: Éditions l'Harmattan.

San Martin, Nancy. 2005. US: No troops for Haiti. *Miami Herald*, 1 July.

Saunders, Chris. 2002. Head of Caribbean Community criticizes U.S. stance on Haiti. *South Florida Sentinel* (Fort Lauderdale), 8 February.

Schmidt, Hans. 1971. *The United States Occupation of Haiti, 1915–1934*. New Brunswick, N.J.: Rutgers University Press.

Secteur Privé des Affaires. 2006. Note de Presse, Radio Kiskeya, Port-au-Prince. 20 February.

Selsky, Andrew. 2006. Smashed ballot boxes found in Haiti. Associated Press, 15 February.

Semple, Kirk. 2004. Haitian cabinet installed as interim leader apologizes to people. *New York Times*, 18 March.

Sérant, Vario. 2003. SOS pour Haiti. *AlterPresse*, 12 December.

——. 2005. Haiti/Sécurité: Le hic ne serait que Port-au-Prince. *AlterPresse*, 12 July.

Singham, A. W. 1968. *The hero and the crowd in a colonial polity*. New Haven, Conn.: Yale University Press.

Slavin, J. P. 1991. Purge of army officers continues in Haiti. *Miami Herald*, 4 July.

Slevin, Peter, and Mike Allen. 2004. Former ally's shift in stance left Haiti leader no recourse. *Washington Post*, 1 March.

Sontag, Debbie. 1990. Populist priest captures hearts of Haitians. *Miami Herald*, 26 November.

Soukar, Michel. 1987. *Seize ans de lutte pour un pays normal*. Port-au-Prince: Éditions SCIHLA.

Stallings, Barbara. 1995. The new international context of development. In Barbara Stallings, ed., *Global change, regional response: The new international context of development*. New York: Cambridge University Press.

Stepick, Alex. 1984. The roots of Haitian migration. In Foster and Valdman 1984.

Storper, Michael, 1997. Territories, flows, and hierarchies in the global economy. In Kevin R. Cox, ed., *Spaces of globalization: Reasserting the power of the local*. New York: Guilford Press.

Sutton, Jane. 2004. Old foes join forces against Haiti president. Reuters, 17 February.

Tabb, William K. 2001. New Economy . . . Same Irrational Economy. *Monthly Review* 52, no. 11 (April): 16–27.

Talbot, Jim. 1987. State of Haiti's environment. *Caribbean Contact* 14, no. 1 (April): 8–9.

Tarr, Michael. 1991a. Haitian president gets respite in feud with parliament. *Miami Herald*, 27 September.

———. 1991b. Haiti wins regard for economic moves under Aristide. *Miami Herald*, 22 August.

Thomas, Clive Y. 1984. *The rise of the authoritarian state in peripheral societies*. New York: Monthly Review Press.

Thompson, Ginger. 2006a. Candidate of Haiti's poor leads in early tally with 61% of vote. *New York Times*, 9 February.

———. 2006b. A deal is reached to name a victory in Haiti's election. *New York Times*, 15 February.

Trouillot, Michel-Rolph. 1986. *Les racines historiques de l'état Duvalierien*. Port-au-Prince: Henri Deschamps.

———. 1990. *Haiti: State against nation*. New York: Monthly Review Press.

UNDP (United Nations Development Program). 1996. *Human development report, 1996*. New York: Oxford University Press.

———. 1998. *Human development report, 1998*. New York: Oxford University Press.

———. 1999. *Human development report, 1999*. New York: Oxford University Press.

———. 2000. *Human development report, 2000*. New York: Oxford University Press.

———. 2002. *Human development report, 2002*. New York: Oxford University Press.

United Nations. 2004. United Nations Stabilization Mission in Haiti. http://www.un.org/Depts/dpko/missions/minustah/mandate.html.

———. 2005a. Peacekeeping mission in Haiti says armed groups have gone underground. *UN News*, 22 August.

——. 2005b. Report of the secretary-general on the United Nations Stabilization Mission in Haiti. S/2005/313. 13 May.

——. 2005c. Report of the Security Council Mission to Haiti, 13 to 16 April 2005. S/2005/302. 6 May. http://daccessdds.un.org/doc/undoc/gen/n05/322/19/pdf/n0532219.pdf?openelement

United Press International. 2005. Aristide aide describes drug payments. 20 July.

U.S. Department of State. 2002. Haiti: Country reports on human rights practices, 2001. Washington, D.C.: GPO.

——. 2005. Haiti: Country reports on human rights practices, 2005. Washington, D.C.: GPO.

Vital, Raoul. 2003. Alter retrospective, Octobre 2003: Agitation, intolerance et repression. *AlterPresse*, 7 November.

Voltaire, Frantz. 1982. État et société. *Collectif Paroles*, nos. 19–20 (September–December).

Walker, James L. 1984. Foreign assistance and Haiti's economic development. In Foster and Valdman 1984.

Wallerstein, Immanuel. 1985. *The politics of the world-economy: The states, the movements and the civilizations*. New York: Cambridge University Press.

——. 1996. *Historical capitalism with capitalist civilization*. London: Verso.

——. 2003. *The decline of American power: The U.S. in a chaotic world*. New York: New Press.

Washington Post. 2005. UN peacekeeping more assertive, creating risk for civilians. 15 August.

Weber, Max. 1968. *From Max Weber: Essays in sociology*. Edited and translated by H. H. Gerth and C. Wright Mills. Oxford: Oxford University Press.

——. 1978. *Economy and society: An outline of interpretive sociology*. Edited by Gwenther Roth and Claus Wittich. 2 vols. Berkeley: University of California Press.

Weiner, Tim. 1993. CIA formed Haitian unit later tied to narcotics trade. *New York Times*, 14 November.

——. 2004. U.S. begins transfer of shaky Haiti to U.N. hands. *New York Times*, 2 June.

Weissenstein, Michael. 2005. Haiti police kill prominent rebel leader. *Guardian* (London), 10 April.

White, Robert. 1997. Haiti: Democrats vs. democracy. *International Policy Report*, November.

White House. 2000. Statement by the press secretary: The Letter President Clinton Wrote to President-elect Jean-Bertrand Aristide, Washington D.C. December 7/U.S. Newswire.

Wickham, Peter, 1998. Towards recapturing popular sovereignty in the Caribbean through integration. *Critical Issues in Caribbean Development* (Kingston), no. 6: 9–43.

Wilentz, Amy. 1989. *The Rainy Season: Haiti since Duvalier*. New York: Simon & Schuster.

——. 1990. Preface to Aristide 1990.

——. 1991. "The Oppositionists," *New Republic*, 28 October.

———. 2004. Haiti's occupation. *Nation*, 1 April.

Williams, Carol J. 2004. Protectorate touted to mend Haiti's crippled society. *Los Angeles Times,* 25 December.

———. 2006. 'Belgian Option' helped avert crisis in Haiti. *Los Angeles Times*, 19 February.

Williamson, John. 1990. What Washington means by policy reform. In John Williamson, ed., *Latin American adjustment: How much has happened?* Washington, D.C.: Institute for International Economics.

Wilson, Michael. 1991. Will aid reap bitter fruit? *Washington Times*, 18 February.

Wood, Ellen Meiksins. 1986. *The retreat from class: A new "true" socialism.* London: Verso.

———. 1995. *Democracy against capitalism.* Cambridge: Cambridge University Press.

World Bank, The. 1987. *Haiti: Public expenditure review.* Washington, D.C.: World Bank.

———. 1991. *World development report: The challenge of development.* New York: Oxford University Press.

———. 2001. *World development report, 2000/2001: Attacking poverty.* New York: Oxford University Press.

Wright, Jonathan. 2002. US resists Caribbean appeal for aid to Haiti. Reuters, 7 February.

Index

Abraham, Hérard, 104, 114, 180, 190
Adams, Alvin, 71, 99n4, 117
Adrien, Antoine, 71
Agreement ("A Political Agreement for
Democracy and Modernity"),
199–200, 205n7
Agricultural Credit Bureau, 47
agriculture, 48–49
Alexandre, Boniface, 172
Alexis, Jacques Edouard, 203
Allen, Mike, 175
*Alliance Nationale pour la Démocratie
et le Progrès* (ANDP, National
Alliance for Democracy and
Progress), 70, 107
Americas Watch, 131
Amnesty International, 181, 184, 185,
188
anarcho-populism, 96
Anglade, Georges, 134n3
Anthony, René-Jean "Grenn Sonnen,"
191
Apaid, Andre (Andy), 158–59
Aristide, Jean-Bertrand: assassination
attempts against, 82–83, 99n5, 117;
authoritarian tendency of, 90, 93–94,
136, 142, 145–46, 178–79; and
Catholic Church, 75, 77–78, 104,
132; and *chimès*, 144–45, 155–57,

172; and comparison of himself to
Jesus, 78, 85; on coup, 131–32; in
current situation, 202–3; on
democracy, 109; education of, 74;
election rigging by, 139–40; hybrid
politics of, 90, 102; and liberation
theology, 65, 78–79, 81, 85–86, 94;
and mass movement, 20–21, 76,
83–84, 89–90, 94, 107, 121–22; and
1990 elections, 73–74, 83–89;
paradoxes of, xiii–xv; and the poor,
74, 76, 82, 87, 105–6, 143;
popularity of, 88–89, 94, 163–64;
and presidency, reasons for seeking,
83–87; previous dictators versus,
146–47; prophetic character of,
75–76, 85–90, 93, 94, 170;
restoration of, to office, 135; security
protection for, 115–16, 155, 162,
172; speeches of, 105, 109–10,
124–25, 127, 131, 133, 142–43,
163–64; and violence, 78, 98, 105,
124–30, 143–45, 155, 166, 178. *See
also* opposition to Aristide (2000);
presidency, first-term; presidency,
second-term
"Aristide backlash," xi
Aristide Foundation for Democracy, 161
Aristide University, 161

227

About the Author

Alex Dupuy is professor of sociology at Wesleyan University in Middletown, Connecticut. He is an internationally recognized scholar and specialist on Haiti. He has lectured at universities and colleges across the United States and abroad and has given many interviews and commentaries on Haitian affairs on local, national, and international radio and television networks, including the *News Hour with Jim Lehrer*, WBAI, National Public Radio, Pacifica Radio, the BBC, the CBC, and the Australian Broadcasting Company. In addition to his more than thirty articles in professional journals and anthologies, he has written reports for the United Nations High Commissioner for Refugees and is the author of *Haiti in the World Economy: Class, Race, and Underdevelopment since 1700* (1987) and *Haiti in the New World Order: The Limits of the Democratic Revolution* (1997).